Dedication

To all readers of my previous books who have used the lessons to build a solid foundation of knowledge in 3ds Max, and then unselfishly used that knowledge to contribute to the various online forums to support other new users.

About the Author

Ted Boardman is a traveling Autodesk 3ds Max and Autodesk 3D Studio VIZ training consultant. He is one of a handful of Autodesk Authorized Master Trainers. His training sessions are custom classes designed to increase 3D modeling and animation productivity for a wide range of clients, from architects to aerospace engineers, and television and computer-gaming professionals.

An integral part of Ted's training process is the books he authors and coauthors about the production issues that people encounter when using 3ds Max. These books include 3ds Max Fundamentals and several books from the Inside 3D Studio Max series and the Inside 3D Studio VIZ 3 series, all from New Riders. Ted has also contributed to several other books about 3ds Max and to Discreet Advanced Modules. He writes a monthly column covering topics related to 3ds Max at CGarchitect.com (www.cgarchitect.com). He is also an award-winning speaker at the annual Autodesk University symposium, covering CAD and visualization topics.

Outside the 3D world, Ted traveled, lived, and worked in Europe for many years. He ran a small architectural design/build firm that specialized in hand-cut post-and-beam structures for nearly 18 years. Long-distance bicycle travel and 28,000 miles of blue-water yacht deliveries served as a diversion from work for many years. Photography, painting, and opera are other interests.

Ted lives in Portsmouth, New Hampshire.

3DS MAX® 8
FUNDAMENTALS

Ted Boardman

New Riders

Berkeley, California

3ds Max® 8 Fundamentals

Ted Boardman

New Riders

1249 Eighth Street
Berkeley, CA 94710
510/524-2178
800/283-9444
510/524-2221 (fax)

Find us on the World Wide Web at: www.newriders.com
To report errors, please send a note to errata@peachpit.com
New Riders is an imprint of Peachpit, a division of Pearson Education.

Copyright © 2006 by New Riders

ISBN: 0-321-41253-2

9 8 7 6 5 4 3 2 1

Printed in the United States of America

Editor
Jill Marts Lodwig

Production Editor
Simmy Cover

Copy Editor
Elissa Rabellino

Compositor
Craig Johnson

Indexer
Rebecca Plunkett

Cover Design
Aren Howell

Cover Production
Andreas Schueller

About the Technical Reviewer

 **Tim Wilbers** has been teaching at the University of Dayton in Ohio since 1983. He started working with digital imaging in 1986 and with 3D computer modeling and animation on a professional level in 1988. He began teaching digital imaging/photography in 1988 and offering courses in 3D for computer graphic artists in 1992. His courses are central to the Computer Imaging concentration in the university's BFA Visual Communication Design program. Tim is a Forum Assistant on the Autodesk 3ds Max user-discussion Web board, and is committed to making 3D computer modeling and animation accessible to students and professionals. He lives south of Dayton with his wife and son.

Acknowledgments

Producing a book, especially a technical book, is a team effort that requires a dedicated and diligent editorial and production staff. I'd like to acknowledge the team members who have made this book possible.

Jill Marts Lodwig and Elissa Rabellino have buffed and polished my writing into a form that is much more pleasing to read and, more important, understandable for you, the reader.

Tim Wilbers, my technical reviewer, has helped forge the exercises and descriptions so that they make sense and function properly as you progress step-by-step through the book.

The production team, led by Simmy Cover and including Craig Johnson and the production staff at Peachpit, has done an exemplary job with the layout and organization that makes the book pleasing to the eye and easy to follow.

Table of Contents

Introduction

Learning 3ds Max 8 is similar to learning how to speak a foreign language. On the first day of class, everything is confusing, and you may leave feeling a bit frustrated. You might even feel that you know less than when you came in. Then you spend the next few classes going over the fundamental building blocks—nouns, verbs, adjectives, and adverbs—and before long you find that you're able to assemble these elements into sentences and paragraphs that others can understand. Likewise, when learning 3ds Max, you may struggle a bit at first, but if you invest some time in gaining an understanding of the fundamentals, the rest falls easily into place.

The content and tutorials in this book assume that you're already familiar with the basic 3ds Max 8 interface and that you have spent enough time reading and studying the manuals, tutorials, and online reference tools that ship with the program to be able to concentrate on the lessons. As the book title implies, you will learn some fundamental workflows of 3ds Max 8. These are not basic topics designed for the first-time user. Instead, they are techniques that anyone can use to build a solid working knowledge base. Whether you're a novice or an experienced 3ds Max user, you will find techniques in this book that can help you speed your day-to-day workflow.

The Concepts

Chapter 1, "Workflow," explains the fundamental workflow of 3ds Max 8 and provides planning steps to help you get started. Chapter 2, "Fundamental Concepts," introduces ideas that are basic to the way 3ds Max 8 is designed. These ideas will help you to understand how the approaches to modeling, materials, and lighting presented in later chapters can help you to get the most from the software.

If you're like most 3ds Max 8 users, you're probably eager to dive into the more advanced features and start producing stunning results as soon as possible. However, if you take the time to develop a solid understanding of the fundamentals, the fancy footwork will come much more naturally as you dig deeper into the software.

A good strategy for tackling each chapter is to read through it first to see where it leads, return to the beginning to perform the exercises while keeping in mind the intended goals, and then finally skim through the text again to make sure that you have a good grasp of the important concepts covered before moving on to the next chapter.

The CD-ROM that accompanies this book contains project files for the beginning and end of each exercise so that you can jump into the book at any point and begin learning. However, I recommend that you start at the beginning of the book and work through the chapters and exercises sequentially.

The Techniques

Beginning with Chapter 3, the exercises in the book walk you through the techniques and workflow that are central to an understanding of how 3ds Max 8 functions, and the discussions show you how you might apply this fundamental knowledge to your projects. You'll learn about the following:

- The reference coordinate systems that let you manipulate objects in 3D space efficiently
- How to work in 2D and apply modifiers to create complex 3D scenes that can be edited quickly and easily
- Three-dimensional procedural modeling techniques that utilize the power of the modifier stack and lofting for flexibility and efficiency
- Camera angles and composition techniques that maximize the emotional impact on the viewer
- Efficient rendering techniques for still images and animations

- Creating and applying convincing materials to objects in the scene, with an emphasis on flexible editing
- Standard lighting techniques that yield the most control and efficiency; global-illumination lighting methods that calculate bounced light from surfaces
- Keyframe and controller/constraint animation techniques that utilize hierarchical linking and inverse kinematics methods
- Special-effects and dynamics collision calculations that will make your scenes and animations more interesting
- Scene-assembly techniques that enhance collaborative workflow and content sharing

The Exercises

Interior, exterior, and underwater scenes serve as the bases for the exercises in this book, which are designed to help you learn some of the techniques that are fundamental to a range of production scenarios, such as computer gaming or architecture.

The exercises walk you step-by-step through a process similar to what you might encounter during a real-life project. Processes and methods are designed to help you form work habits that will be relevant whether you are a gamer, background artist, stage or set designer, or engineer.

While performing the exercises, try to project how you might apply the methods and techniques covered in your own line of work. When I'm showing you how to create a building, for instance, you might be thinking about how to use the same process to create the rough form of an automobile.

Use the lessons you learn from each exercise to produce scenes of your own that incorporate the techniques and methods presented until you understand the process. Start with simple scenes that let you focus on understanding the concepts, and the fundamentals will quickly become part of your daily routine.

Hopefully, when you work on your own projects, you will not be thinking, "I learned this from Ted Boardman." Instead, the lessons learned here should become an automatic reaction to the challenges you face every day in your own production schedules.

The Project Files

The CD-ROM that accompanies this book includes all the files you need for the exercises. In addition to using the files for this purpose, you can also use them to analyze, for instance, how the objects were modeled by stepping through the Modifier stack, how the lights were adjusted in the Light Lister, how the materials were created with the Material/Map Navigator, and how animations were created in the Motion panel. But best of all, you can use the files to play with each scene until you produce your own approaches to improving them.

Because the CD-ROM files are color figures, as opposed to the black-and-white reproductions in the book, it will be much more helpful if you reference the CD-ROM files, particularly when you're working with materials and lighting and you need to see the details.

The exercises and work methods in the book are derived from situations that have developed in my Max classes and during my consulting work. I have tried to make the exercises as real as possible while staying true to my teaching strategy of helping you build a base of fundamental information.

Above all, good luck and have fun with 3ds Max 8!

CHAPTER 1

Workflow

In This Chapter

Creating 3D scenes is often a complex task, but it can be accomplished much more efficiently with a little foresight and planning.

In this chapter, you'll learn what to be aware of as you prepare to start a 3D project and then execute it.

Some of the topics covered in this section include:

- **The chain of command**—Clearly defining the responsibilities of team members.

- **Needs assessment**—Determining the scope of the project and the needs of the audience.

- **Storyboarding**—Creating a visual outline of the project.

- **Choosing a team**—Selecting the right talent and capabilities for a specific project.

- **Setting up a productive working environment**—Both equipment and training are critical to productivity.

- **Knowing when to stop**—Avoiding the temptation to tweak the project into financial loss.

- **Developing office standards**—Utilizing written procedures and standards can dramatically reduce the time it takes to complete projects.

- **Working in layers**—Layers, in this case, are compositing tools that let you manage sets of objects as a group.

- **Output capabilities**—Production plans should include a variety of output-type possibilities, so that you'll have multipurpose images for video, Web, or printing.

Key Term

- **Storyboard**—A *storyboard* is a graphical outline that displays the scope of the project.

Preparation and Planning

Good planning is essential to the success of any project. Everyone knows this instinctively, but putting good planning into practice usually involves more time and effort than most people are prepared to take on. However, skipping the planning step won't save you more time and effort in the long run; it will simply be an exercise in false economy.

When preparation and planning are not part of a project, teams typically hold off on executing the project and instead discuss it until the deadline looms. Then they suffer through long, continuous hours of high-pressure work to complete the project on time, only to find that they've generated a mediocre presentation. It's better to learn to channel that discussion time into a clear battle plan so that everyone knows the expectations and scope of the project beforehand.

Even the smallest projects with only one or two staff members benefit from a solid plan going into production. When there are more than a few collaborators, developing a solid script that each team member can refer to as the work progresses is paramount to ensure that everyone is working toward a common goal in an organized manner.

Once you've developed a good plan of attack, it's unrealistic to think it will never change. Typically, 3D projects are in a state of flux for a variety of reasons, including the client's expectations, technical problems, or budget constraints. However, the changes will be much less disruptive to the overall goals if those goals are spelled out in the beginning for everyone involved.

The Chain of Command

Establishing lines of communication between those who order the work, those who create the content, and the team members who present the work to the client is critical, with each team member having an understanding of the available talent and resources.

Communication between the client and production staff will constantly evolve and become more refined as the visualization process matures. However, educating the client about the general process involved in creating the visualizations can smooth these communications. For example, clients don't need to know exactly how scenes are created, but they should know what types of requests will take more time and what types can be executed quickly.

In addition, letting the client-management team members sit in on a half-day hands-on training session with the 3D software can give them more insight into some of the difficulties the production staff faces—they eventually understand that there is no magic "make art" button on the computer.

Finally, regular short meetings between the production staff and the in-house clients can keep each team up-to-date on processes that increase or hinder productivity on either side.

Needs Assessment

To ensure high productivity, it's important to determine the scope and quality of work required to satisfy the client's expectations within the confines of the allotted time and budget.

For instance, not every job that goes out the door requires photorealistic-quality images to communicate important messages. Feature films certainly need all the cutting-edge refinements that technology has to offer, but public service announcements that will be shown on regional television might not have the same budget considerations. It's important to determine beforehand where you can trim production costs with the least effect on quality.

Flexible stages of production can also help avoid costly changes that require starting again from scratch. If complex modeling and high details are developed too early in the design development, or if completed materials with high-resolution maps are applied to models, that may focus unnecessary attention on decisions that should be left for later. A better approach might be to rough out models much the same way a stone sculptor would, and then go back and add details as they become necessary. You could use low-resolution stand-in maps in the 3ds Max materials while developing the scenes to allow for faster test rendering, for instance, and then replace those with the high-quality maps near the end of the project.

Storyboarding

Storyboarding is the process of creating a graphic outline that illustrates the story and workflow and provides insight into potential production issues before any actual production begins.

Storyboards range from simple sketches to airbrushed or hand-painted panels, some of which could be classified as works of art in their own right (see **Figure 1.1** on the next page).

For rendered still images, such as those that an architectural-visualization artist might require, the storyboard panels could contain information about the camera angles and direction, as well as notes that describe specific colors or materials. Lighting scenarios with notes about the lighting quality might also prove helpful.

Animation storyboards could contain the same information, plus notes and sketches referring to the action in the scene. One storyboard panel per major action change in the animation motion is a good place to start.

You can even include additional information pertaining to timing codes and dialogue or sound effects in the margins of the panels.

FIGURE 1.1 *High-quality storyboard panels by Andrew Paquette.*

A storyboard for a small project can be created on a few sheets of paper, with several panels or sketches on each sheet. For more complex projects, however, individual panel sheets pinned to a large corkboard give a quick overview and are easy to change. Avoid the temptation to use sticky notepads, because you may come back from lunch to find that a change in temperature or a breeze has scattered your storyboard across the room, like so many fallen leaves in an autumn storm.

Keep in mind that the importance is not so much in the quality of the storyboards' artwork as in how clearly they explain the scope and scheduling of the project.

Execution

Another crucial component of high productivity is planning the use of available talent and tools. It's important to meet with team members and management to discuss some of the following topics before getting into actual production.

Choose a Team with Both Desire and Talent

Try to familiarize a broad range of personnel with the creation process and cultivate a pool of artists who have a strong desire to apply the extra effort required to become proficient at several tasks. This provides you some flexibility in managing the team. It is especially important for smaller teams in which you don't have the luxury of large numbers of specialists.

However, keep in mind that forcing staff members to become directly involved in processes they are not comfortable with, whether it's modeling, lighting, materials, or animation, leads to bad office politics and pulls good talent from areas where they could probably be more productive.

Set Up a Productive Working Environment

One of the most critical components of a productive work environment is up-to-date technology. Make sure you provide and maintain current and powerful computer systems. Hardware is a fixed-cost item that can be passed through the office, first as rendering stations; then, when they're not as current, they can be delegated as clerical machines for years to come. Do not, however, rely on new hardware as the sole method of increasing productivity until you have mastered the art of scene optimization, such as reducing the amount of geometry or tweaking shadow parameters. Using new hardware as a fix for poor production practices is a waste of resources and time.

In a production office, pay particular attention to seating, lighting, and input devices. For example, both a mouse and a tablet at each workstation can minimize stress and injury during long work sessions. And a clean, stable network system for network rendering can increase production (while requiring very little cost and maintenance).

Make sure that team members have an understanding of all the tools available to them before deciding on a production process. With a little practice, choosing the right tool for the right job becomes second nature, and you'll avoid many of the pitfalls that come with forcing a tool to do a job for which it is not appropriate.

Know When to Stop

Focus on the elements of 3D production that will have the most dramatic impact on your output, and leave the rest by the wayside. In other words, don't use technology for the sake of the technology alone. For example, radiosity rendering may not add enough to your story line to justify the extra time involved in setting up or rendering.

Another important management skill is "knowing when to stop." Once you reach a satisfactory level of production quality, as spelled out in the planning stages of the project, it is important to be able to stop and move on to the next task. Perfection is an unobtainable goal—it's always worth striving for, but not if it becomes a burden on production.

FIGURE 1.2 *The image on the left, by the author, is low quality and was made from scratch in about 4 hours. The image on the right, by Tangram3ds, is very high quality. It required about 21 hours to create the scene and match it to the photo.*

Integration and Output

Your clients may ask you to simultaneously create content for multiple uses. For instance, you might be creating a computer game, but you will need higher-quality scenes for the marketing trailers, and you may need even higher-quality still images. Don't forget that more than one software package can be used to generate this content. Just make sure you use the appropriate converters and workflow methods so that the output is usable by all team members who access the data.

Develop Office Standards

Object-naming conventions, material and map libraries, and 3D-object libraries are some of the areas in which establishing and maintaining standards can go a long way toward enhancing productivity.

Standards for object naming cannot be stressed enough. Good naming control can provide an enormous return in productivity for a very minor cost.

Material-naming standards and material-library organization can also help avoid duplication of effort. Make sure you develop central depositories for maps and basic materials that are organized by category so that all users have easy access to a fundamental starting point for creating custom materials for projects.

Rendering standards to which everyone has ready access ensure that the renderings from one team member will match the renderings of others on the team. Nothing is more frustrating than having occasional frames in an animation or perhaps a whole scene that is rendered using a different anti-aliasing setting or shadow parameter that no one else uses.

Work in Layers

Layers in this sense are elements such as background walls, mid-ground furniture, or foreground details that are based on the distance from the camera or viewer. Layers let you omit detail for faster rendering but include as much detail as necessary for communicating information to the client. For example, you can simulate geometry that will not change with prerendered images for the background objects, while modeling and manipulating the foreground objects.

Investigate compositing—the combining of 2D information in layers—using video editing programs such as Discreet Combustion or Adobe After Effects, or even Adobe Photoshop, for still images. Compositing may prove especially important in offices that use multiple software packages to generate content by allowing them to combine elements from many sources into a single, coherent output file type.

Layers also enable you to work discretely. For instance, using layers, you can manipulate special image elements to modify shadows, reflections, or object colors without having to re-render the entire 3D scene.

Learn Cinematic Animation Techniques

Learn traditional film and television movement techniques so that you can develop short-duration animations that you can edit into a cohesive presentation. These movement techniques will enable you to develop much smaller scenes with minimal camera movement—scenes that are easy to manage and that clients will find exciting and informative. Everyone wins!

Determine Output Capabilities in Advance

Predetermine file types and image resolutions that will enable you to reuse content in a wide array of output types (for instance, videotape and DVD, streaming media and Web sites, and large printed still images). Render all scenes to individual still image sequences and convert them to compressed animation files as necessary.

Summary

You no doubt can think of more processes that could be streamlined in a typical office to speed up content creation. However, if you can make use of just several of the suggestions in this chapter, it will be a good beginning. Later you can adapt your office practices to fit your needs.

Start with an officewide naming scheme and materials organization, and then focus on scene optimization (only modeling what you will see and making that as efficient as possible). All the while, focus on integrating a new spirit of communication between those who order the work and those who do the work, to minimize the necessity of changes later.

Finally, consider the ways in which the workflow is speeded by the compositing and layering of scene elements. It is not uncommon in film and video work to combine 30 or more layers that come from a variety of production sources into a single output image or animation. These methods will work equally well for productions in architecture, computer gaming, film and television, and engineering fields.

CHAPTER 2

Fundamental Concepts

In This Chapter

In this chapter, you'll learn some basic concepts that will help you to more fully understand the tools that are a part of 3ds Max 8 and the processes involved in using it.

A good strategy for tackling this chapter is to read through it quickly to get an overview of the processes, and then read it again more slowly, experimenting with your own simple scenes to test the concepts in their basic form. After a little practice, and by incorporating these concepts into your daily work routine, you will find that your productivity has been enhanced without your having to think about what you're doing.

This chapter covers the following topics:

- **Coordinate systems**—The various ways to describe the three axes (X, Y, and Z) in 3D space.

- **Layers**—A method of organizing objects into common groups and assigning properties to those objects.

- **Setup and startup files**—Files that store parameters you want to have active when creating new files.

- **Lofting**—A powerful modeling technique that requires some knowledge of the basic concepts of working efficiently.

Key Terms

- **Coordinate system**—*Coordinate systems* in 3ds Max 8 define the directions of the X, Y, and Z axes as they relate to the 3D workspace.

- **Layer**—*Layers* are organizational entities used to select or set properties of sets of objects on the active layer.

- **Lofting**—*Lofting* is the modeling technique that creates 3D objects by extruding one or more 2D cross-section shapes along a 2D path.

Coordinate Systems in 3ds Max 8

Users can easily identify the World reference coordinate system in 3ds Max 8 because it is defined by the default grid planes that display in the viewports when you start 3ds Max (**Figure 2.1**). Keep in mind, though, that while the Home grid that defines the World reference coordinate system is perhaps the most commonly used, it is really only the starting point for all the possibilities for maneuvering and manipulating objects in 3D space.

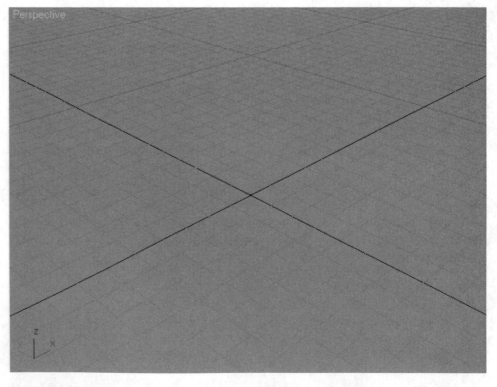

Figure 2.1 *The Perspective viewport, with the grid defining the World reference coordinate system.*

I emphasize coordinate systems because one issue 3ds Max I see as a fundamental hindrance to production for many users, both new and experienced, is a lack of understanding of the complete coordinate system in 3ds Max.

To use several important commands, such as the Align and Transform Type-In commands, 3ds Max 8 users must understand the various coordinate systems in the software. With both Array and Transform Type-In, for example, you must enter numeric data to align or array objects along the X, Y, or Z axis. However, the direction of X, Y, or Z depends on which coordinate system and viewport are active.

Getting the Lay of the Land

On the main toolbar in 3ds Max 8, to the right of the transform buttons, is a drop-down list that shows the currently active reference coordinate system; View is selected by default. Click View in the list field to see the different reference coordinate systems available (**Figure 2.2**).

FIGURE 2.2 *The drop-down list that displays the available reference coordinate systems for 3ds Max 8.*

Let's do a simple walkthrough of the various reference coordinate systems to illustrate some of their differences. You can either try the exercises on your computer or, better yet, just read along to get the idea, and then go to the computer and do the exercises afterward. In any case, at some point you should sit down and just play with very simple objects to get a feel for how the system works. At the end of this section, you can read a summary of the attributes of each system.

As with many 3ds Max 8 tools, don't try to learn this during a deadline crunch on a large project. With a little practice, the reference coordinate systems will become second nature, and your productivity will increase accordingly.

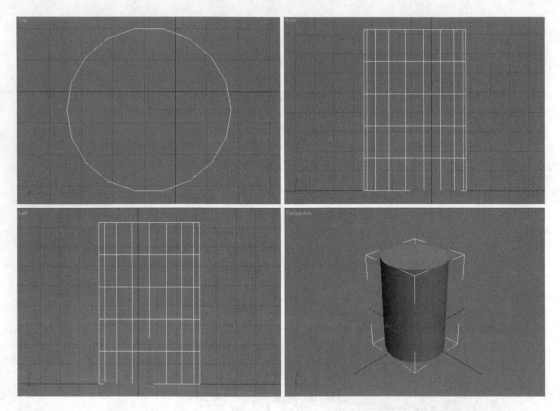

Figure 2.3 *All four viewports fill with a cylinder.*

Start with a new session of 3ds Max 8. The display should be set to four viewports: Top, Front, Left, and Perspective. In the Top viewport, create a cylinder in the middle of the display (**Figure 2.3**) and click the Zoom Extents All button, which is the upper right button in the lower right corner of the display (**Figure 2.4**).

Figure 2.4 *To fill all viewports with all objects in the scene, click the Zoom Extents All button.*

The following subsections provide descriptions and some exercises that highlight the individual reference coordinate systems that appear in Figure 2.2.

The View Reference Coordinate System

In the Top viewport, notice the following:

- The red and gray axis tripod at the bottom center of the cylinder shows positive X to the right, positive Y up, and positive Z out toward the viewer.

- The current active reference coordinate system is set to View in the main toolbar (**Figure 2.5**).

FIGURE 2.5 *The reference-coordinate-system drop-down list is located on the main toolbar.*

Right-click in the Front viewport to activate it without deselecting the cylinder. Notice that the axis tripod adjusts so that the positive axis is pointing in the same relative direction as it was pointing when the Top viewport was active. Right-click the Left viewport to see a similar change. When using the View reference coordinate system, the axis tripod adapts itself to the orthographic viewports so that positive X is always to the right, positive Y is always up, and positive Z is always out toward the viewer.

Now right-click in the Perspective viewport. Notice that the axis tripod corresponds to the World reference coordinate system by aligning with the Home grid. You can check it against the small tricolor tripod in the lower left corner of each viewport, which always indicates the World reference coordinate system. When the View reference coordinate is active, the World reference coordinate is the default system for all nonorthographic viewports—Perspective, User, Camera, and Light. (The orthographic viewports are viewed from the top, bottom, left, right, back, or front.)

The Screen Reference Coordinate System

Right-click in the Top viewport to activate it. Then on the main toolbar, choose Screen from the reference coordinate system drop-down list. Right-click in the other viewports and notice that the axis tripod behaves the same as it did in View mode.

The Screen reference coordinate system is exactly the same as the View reference coordinate system for orthographic viewports—the positive X axis is always pointing to the right, the Y axis is pointing up, and the Z axis is pointing out. However, for nonorthographic viewports, the positive Z axis points out of the screen toward the viewer. Use the Arc Rotate button, located on the lower right corner of the display, to change the view in the Perspective viewport, and watch the axis tripod rotate in the other viewports to keep the Z axis pointed at you in the nonorthographic viewport.

The Screen reference coordinate system lets you move objects in space based on your line of sight in nonorthographic viewports and is useful for doing things like moving flying logos across the scene.

The World Reference Coordinate System

Right-click in the Top viewport and switch to the World reference coordinate system. Right-click in the other viewports and you will see that the World reference coordinate system is always active for all viewport types.

The Parent Reference Coordinate System

The next reference coordinate system in the list is Parent, which requires an object to be hierarchically linked to another object in the parent/child relationship. In the Parent reference coordinate system, the child always uses the parent's Local coordinate system (discussed in the next section).

The Local Reference Coordinate System

Right-click in the Top viewport and choose Local in the reference-coordinate-system list. Right-click in the other viewports, and you'll find that the axis tripod performs the same as it did when you were using the World reference coordinate system. This is a coincidence, because you created the cylinder in the Top viewport, which has the same axis directions as the World reference coordinate system. To see that the Local reference coordinate system stays local to the object, you can right-click in the Perspective viewport, click the Select and Rotate transform button on the main toolbar, and rotate the cylinder roughly 45 degrees in both the X and Y axes by dragging the red or green circle of the Rotate gizmo in the viewport (**Figure 2.6**).

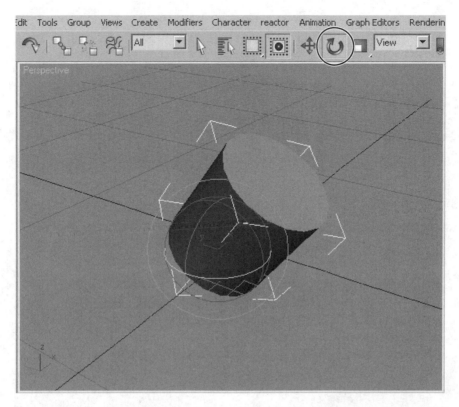

FIGURE 2.6 *Click the Select and Rotate button on the main toolbar and rotate the cylinder about 45 degrees along the X and Y axes.*

Notice that even though you had the reference coordinate system set to Local while in Select mode, it switched automatically to View when you clicked the Select and Rotate button. This is because the active reference coordinate system works independently for each transform, such as Move, Rotate, and Scale. The transform will use the reference coordinate system you set in the current session until you change it again. The axis tripod also changes the red and gray axis tripod to the Transform gizmo when the transform buttons are clicked.

> **tip**
>
> All the graphics that are printed in this book are also available in full color on the CD-ROM that accompanies this book. You will be able to see the details of each graphic much more clearly onscreen.

Right-click in the Top viewport, click the Select and Move transform button in the main toolbar, and set the reference coordinate system to Local. Right-click in the other viewports, and you'll see that the Move Transform gizmo orients itself with the object as it was created (**Figure 2.7**). Familiarize yourself with the Local reference coordinate system. It's an especially powerful production tool because it is most closely related to the object itself, regardless of the object's rotation.

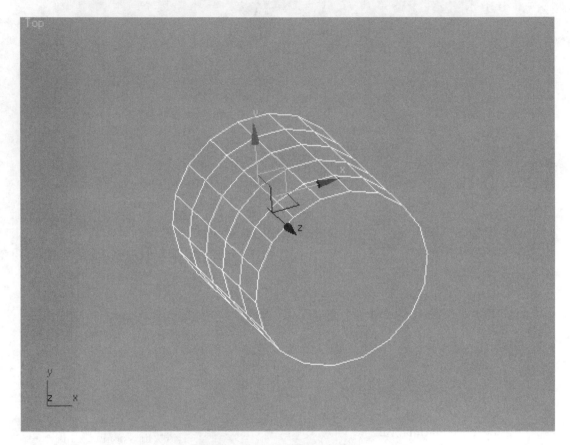

FIGURE 2.7 *In Local reference coordinate mode, the axis tripod and the Transform gizmo stay aligned with the object's creation axes.*

The Grid Reference Coordinate System

The Grid reference coordinate system requires you to create a new grid "helper" object as the active work plane. Right-click in the Top viewport to activate it.

On the Create panel, expand the Geometry rollout, click the Box button, and activate the AutoGrid feature by selecting the AutoGrid option. As you move your pointer over the cylinder, notice that a tricolor cursor tracks the face normal of the face under the pointer. Press and hold the Alt key, and pick with the mouse and drag to define the opposite corner of a box primitive on the end cap of the cylinder. Click the Select Object button on the main toolbar and select the new Grid object at the top of the cylinder (**Figure 2.8**).

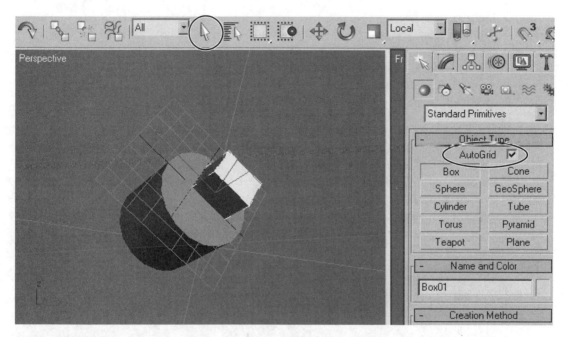

Figure 2.8 *You can create objects directly on any surface using the AutoGrid feature; press and hold the Alt key during the process to create a permanent grid object on that plane.*

Holding down Alt while creating an object in AutoGrid mode concurrently produces a new, active grid in the scene.

Click the Select and Move button, and switch to the Grid reference coordinate system. The X, Y, and Z axes of the grid will be used for the current transform.

With the new Grid object selected in the active viewport, right-click the grid and, in the pop-up menu, choose Activate HomeGrid to return to the default grid system. You can have as many of these grid helper objects as you want, but only one can be active at any time. You can reactivate the new grid at any time.

The Pick Reference Coordinate System

In the Pick reference coordinate system, you can assign the coordinate system of another object in the scene as the active system.

Right-click in the Top viewport to activate it, and create a small sphere to one side of the cylinder. Click the Select and Rotate transform button, change the reference coordinate system to Pick, and click the cylinder in the Top viewport. The Sphere is now using the cylinder's Local reference coordinate system axes directions, and Cylinder01's coordinate system will be added to the list of available reference coordinate systems.

Pivot Point Options

Another aid to production that goes hand in hand with the reference coordinate systems is the active Pivot Point type, which lets you switch to different types of pivot locations when rotating objects. Just to the right of the reference coordinate system drop-down list field is a fly-out menu with three choices of pivot point types. Choosing the bottom option, Use Transform Coordinate Center, for example, changes the rotation center to be at the base of the cylinder (**Figure 2.9**).

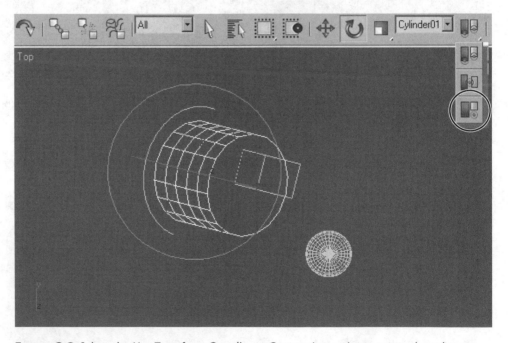

FIGURE 2.9 *Select the Use Transform Coordinate Center pivot point to rotate the sphere around the cylinder's Local Axis pivot point.*

Use Pivot Point Center

In the Top viewport, select all the objects in the scene. Choose the Use Pivot Point Center pivot point option (the top option on the fly-out menu). Notice that as you rotate the selection set, each object is transformed based on its current active reference coordinate system around its own individual pivot point rather than the center of the selection set. This is particularly useful when you are in Rotate mode and you need to rotate many objects at once on their own individual pivot points. The Local reference coordinate system always uses this pivot point option.

Use Selection Center

Choose the Use Selection Center pivot point, (the middle option on the fly-out menu) and you'll discover that the entire selection set of objects uses a single pivot point in the geometric center of the bounding box of the selected objects. This keeps the objects in the same relative positions to each other. Like Use Pivot Point Center, the Use Selection Center pivot point is most useful when rotating.

Use Transform Coordinate Center

The Use Transform Coordinate Center pivot point uses the Absolute World coordinate point (coordinate location 0,0,0), unless the Pick reference coordinate system is active. If it is active, the selected object then uses the pick object's pivot point as its own.

Coordinate Systems Summary

The following list summarizes the attributes of the various reference coordinate systems:

- **View**—The axis tripod adapts itself to each orthographic viewport so that the positive X axis is pointing to the right, the positive Y axis is pointing up, and the positive Z axis is pointing perpendicularly out of the display. Nonorthographic viewports resort to using the World reference coordinate system.
- **Screen**—The same as View in orthographic viewports. In nonorthographic viewports, the positive Z axis always points at the viewer.
- **World**—The coordinate system always corresponds to the Absolute World coordinates, as measured from the 0,0,0 point in World space.
- **Parent**—The child object uses the parent's Local coordinate system in a hierarchically linked parent-child relationship.
- **Local**—The coordinates always remain with the object as it was created, regardless of the object's rotation angle.
- **Grid**—Uses the active grid system's coordinate system.
- **Pick**—Uses the Local coordinate system of a picked object in the scene.

For the Align, Array, and Mirror commands in 3ds Max, always check the active reference coordinate system to see which X, Y, and Z axis is being used by the command. The mode is noted in the Align Selection or Array dialog (**Figure 2.10**).

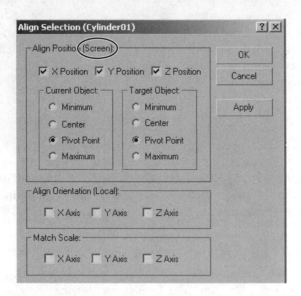

FIGURE 2.10 *The active reference coordinate system is shown in parentheses next to Align Position in the Align Selection dialog.*

Layers

Knowing how to work in layers using 3ds Max 8 is an important skill in a production environment. Although layers have been available in previous versions of 3ds Max, version 8 provides improvements in workflow that make layers more user-friendly and functional.

Layers are organizational elements containing objects you've placed on them. You can use layers as selection tools to quickly choose specific objects so that you can transform them or to change the visibility of the layer's objects in the viewports or the renderer. You can also use layers to set object properties, such as setting the radiosity lighting properties for all objects currently on a layer.

I don't want to rewrite here all the layer information contained in the 3ds Max 8 user reference manual, but I do want to make sure you're aware of the concepts behind this production tool. I also want to point out that two 3ds Max 8 elements affect how layers are managed: the Layer Manager and the Object Properties dialog.

The Layer Manager

Figure 2.11 shows the Layer toolbar and Layer Manager. In this example, the scene contains four layers—three with teapots and the default layer, with nothing on it.

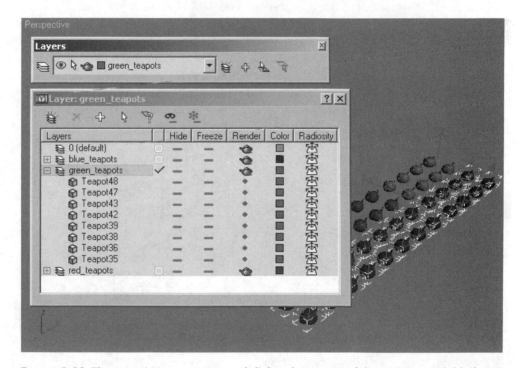

FIGURE 2.11 *The Layer Manager menu and dialog show some of the options available for creating and manipulating layers.*

The Layer Manager menu and dialog enable you to create and manipulate layers and toggle on and off Layer object properties, such as render ability, visibility, and radiosity settings.

To further investigate layers and their functionality, use the 3ds Max 8 Help files. Work with a simple file similar to this teapot example so that you learn the fundamentals of how the concept can be applied to your production workflow.

The Object Properties Dialog

When you first begin using the layers in 3ds Max 8, it's easy to be confused by the fact that, by default, the objects you create in Max have their properties determined by the object settings, not by any layer settings. This means that no amount of layer manipulation will have any bearing on the properties of the objects—color or visibility, for example—on that layer until you enable the By Layer option for the objects' properties.

Figure 2.12 shows the Object Properties dialog with the General tab and Advanced Lighting tab selected. On the General tab, the Display Properties and Rendering Control sections of the selected objects have been set to the By Layer control, whereas the Motion Blur section on the General tab and the Geometric Object Properties section on the Advanced Lighting tab are still set to the default By Object control.

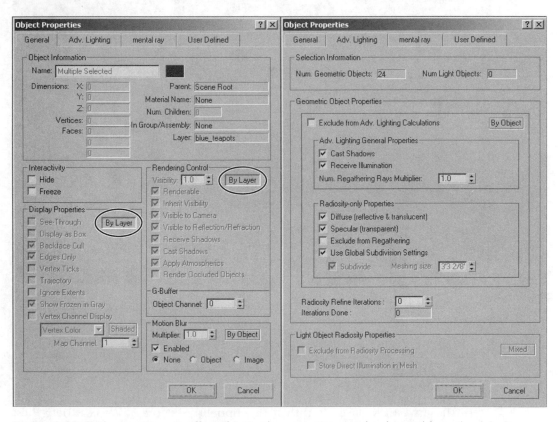

FIGURE 2.12 *For layer settings to affect objects, the properties must be changed from the default By Object control to the By Layer control. Individual object properties may be changed in the Layer Manager with the properties set to either Object or Layer.*

Again, search the 3ds Max 8 Help files for "using layers to organize a scene" to get a more complete overview and more details on layers.

Settings and Startup Configuration

You can use several files in 3ds Max 8 to enhance productivity, such as 3dsmax.ini, maxstart.max, plugin.ini, and MaxStartUI.cui. These files can store such settings as how units are expressed (metric or U.S. standard units, for example) and which menu and viewport layouts will be available when you open a new scene or reset the current one.

Of these files, maxstart.max is the most important time-saving tool. The maxstart.max file lets you save the state of the workspace so that it displays using the same settings each time you start a new file or reset the scene. Unlike the other setup files that have preset default values, however, it does not exist until you create it.

Although it would be possible to save a maxstart.max file that contains objects or lighting to load with each new file or reset action, you usually want to change only the viewport configurations to your preferences, as each new scene typically would have different objects and lighting.

The maxstart.max file will be saved by default in the /3dsmax8/scenes subdirectory (at least it should be), but you can save it anywhere on your hard drive and use the Configure Paths dialog to point to the location.

Basic Lofting Concepts

In my view, lofting is the most powerful modeling tool in 3ds Max, but one that is underutilized because it often exhibits "strange" behavior when you're using it. In reality, the behavior is not all that exotic. Because lofting is unlike any creation method you use in other software, it requires that you understand a few simple concepts before it will make sense to you.

The term *lofting* comes from old shipbuilding practices in which the patterns for the ribs of a ship were laid out in the upstairs loft of the shipbuilder's shop. Long, thin metal bands, or *splines*, were set on edge and bent to the curvature of the hull at given points along the keel. To hold the splines in place so that the lines could be traced on the patterns, the ship designer placed heavy steel or lead *ducks* at the tangency points. The ribs (loft shapes) were then attached along the keel (loft path), and the planking was attached to form the hull (mesh object).

But I Don't Speak the Language!

To fully understand 3ds Max lofting, you need to be familiar with the following terms:

- **Shape**—A 2D object in 3ds Max. It may occupy 3D space as a helix shape does, but it does not have any surface information. A shape has a name and a color, and it must contain at least one sub-object-level spline. If it has more than one spline, it is a compound shape. For example, the donut primitive is a compound shape made of two splines (that is, concentric circles).

- **Spline**—A sub-object-level component of a shape.

- **Loft path**—The shape that defines the extrusion length of the loft object.

- **Loft shape**—The shape that defines the cross sections of the loft object. A loft object can have only one closed or open spline as a path, but it can have an unlimited number of open or closed shapes as cross sections. Each shape or path can have an unlimited number of vertices, and different shapes can have different numbers of vertices. However, each shape on a path must have the same number of splines. For example, you cannot loft a circle and a donut primitive on the same loft path.

- **Local reference coordinate system**—3ds Max 8 has several different reference coordinate systems, as you learned earlier in this chapter; however, the Local system is the most important one in lofting. The Local system is the coordinate system of the shape as it is created. When you create a shape in any given viewport, the rule is that the local positive X axis is pointing to the right, the local positive Y axis is pointing up, and the local positive Z axis is pointing out toward the viewer. This Local reference coordinate system stays relative to the shape as the shape is rotated.

- **Pivot point**—The pivot point of a shape is usually positioned at the geometric center of the shape's bounding box. It can be repositioned through the Hierarchy panel. The pivot point defines the apex of the X, Y, and Z axes of a shape.

- **First vertex**—Each spline has a first vertex, indicated by a white box when in Vertex sub-object mode (**Figure 2.13**). Open splines can have either end vertex as a first vertex, and closed splines can have any vertex as a first vertex.

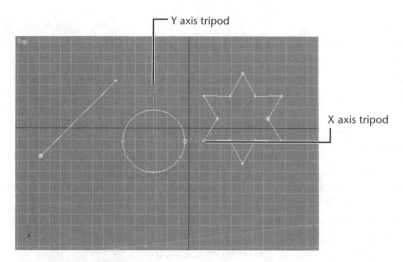

Y axis tripod

X axis tripod

FIGURE 2.13 *A viewport showing white boxes, indicating the first vertex of various shapes, and the red X and Y axes tripod at the pivot point of the circle.*

The pivot point and first vertex are very important in the lofting process, and a lack of understanding of them is probably the prime reason for frustration while lofting.

The pivot point of the shape attaches to the first vertex of the path.

The orientation of the shape on the path is a bit more complex. I'll talk you through it and show an example here, and then discuss it in more detail in Chapter 5. The local Z axis of the shape aligns itself "down" the path; the local Y axis of the shape aligns with the local Z axis of the path (**Figure 2.14**).

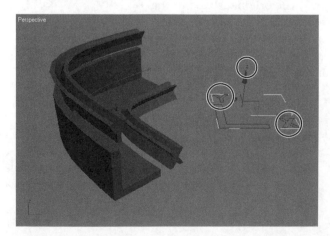

FIGURE 2.14 *The curved path and L shape have been created in the Top viewport. The loft object shows the orientation of the shape on the path. You also can see the local axis directions of the 2D shapes, indicated by the Move Transform gizmo arrows.*

Lofting Options

The lofting process itself is simple enough, but a couple of options are worth mentioning. You can access lofting from the Compound Objects drop-down list (Create panel > Geometry > Compound Objects). You must have a valid 2D shape selected or the Loft button will be dimmed in the Object Type rollout.

In the Creation Method rollout are two buttons: Get Path and Get Shape (**Figure 2.15**). The usual workflow is to have the path selected and to use the Get Shape button. However, you could select the shape and use Get Path. The determining factor is that whichever object is selected remains in place, and the other shape or path reorients and moves to the selected shape. Generally, I prefer to select the path and use Get Shape.

Beneath the Get Path and Get Shape buttons are some other options: Move, Copy, and Instance. The Instance radio button is selected by default. This means that a clone of the shape jumps to the path, not the original shape itself. The advantage of this option is that you can modify the original 2D shape, and the lofted 3D mesh will change accordingly.

The Move option moves the original shape to the path, and Copy places a clone of the shape with no connection to the original (making either choice much less editable). I have never found the need to use either Move or Copy.

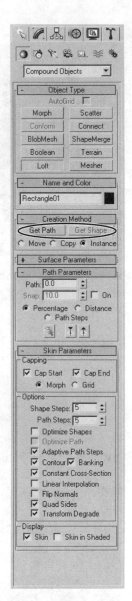

FIGURE 2.15 *The Loft panel with Name and Color, Creation Method, Path Parameters, and Skin Parameters rollouts expanded.*

In **Figure 2.16**, most of the petals, stems, pistil, and vase are lofted from 2D shapes, allowing for quick and easy editing.

As mentioned earlier, the fundamental process is simple enough, but you must understand more options to make an efficient lofting modeling choice.

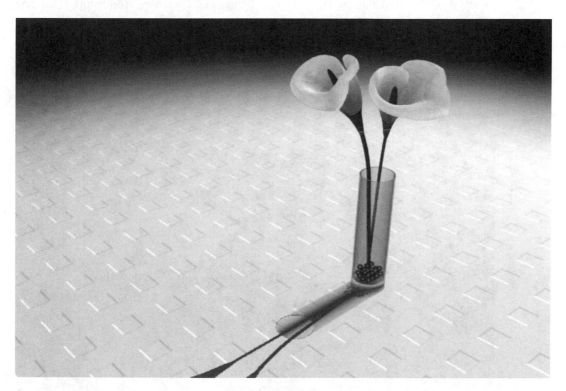

Figure 2.16 *This simple lily scene was created primarily with lofting. Lofting allows for quick editing at the 2D shape level to make major changes to 3D objects.*

The Importance of the First Vertex

3ds Max 8 builds the lofted mesh objects by first connecting the first vertex on each shape along the path and then building a mesh surface using the shape steps and path steps. Therefore, the relative position of the shape's first vertex determines the twisting of the object along the path of a lofted object created from more than one unique shape.

To remove (or apply more) twisting, you must modify the loft object itself at the sub-object level to rotate either of the shapes on the loft path—not the original shape mind you, but the instance clone of the shape that has attached itself to the loft path. **Figure 2.17** shows a circle and a rectangle lofted along a straight-line path, illustrating the twisting that can occur.

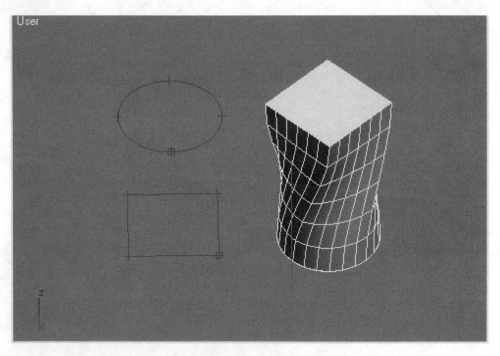

FIGURE 2.17 *Circle and rectangle shapes lofted along a straight line produce a twisted object because of the relative positions of the first vertex of each shape.*

Modifying the lofted object at the Shape sub-object level and rotating the circle on the loft path by 45 degrees (in this case, around its local axis) removes the twisting (**Figure 2.18**).

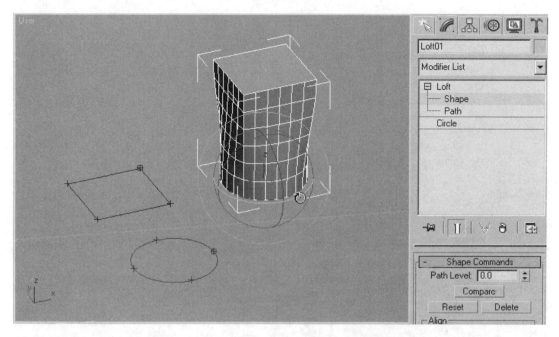

FIGURE 2.18 *By rotating the circle shape at the base of the loft object around its local Z axis, you can easily remove or enhance the twist.*

Lofting Efficiency

If you want 3ds Max 8 to be a cost-effective tool in your office, you must keep models as simple as possible. (Modeling overhead is the primary hindrance to production that I encounter in my training sessions.) Each vertex and face in a model uses valuable computer overhead, and you can very quickly overwhelm even the most powerful systems and render them ineffective in a production scenario.

Lofting offers controls for adjusting the mesh density of models while retaining the necessary details. First you have two new terms to learn:

- **Shape steps**—Intermediate points between vertices of the shape that define curvature in the connecting shape segment.

- **Path steps**—Intermediate points between vertices of the path that define curvature in the connecting shape segment.

When a shape is lofted along a path, segments are created in the loft mesh for each vertex and path step or shape step. These segments can clearly be seen in the preceding loft example, which has the Edged Faces option enabled in the viewport. Right-clicking the selected Loft object and going to the Object Properties dialog shows that the object has 332 faces. On the Modify panel, Skin Parameters rollout, there are two numeric fields: Shape Steps and Path Steps. Each is set to 5 by default in 3ds Max 8.

Setting the path steps to 0 reduces the information that shows the curvature between the path's vertices. The object shows less definition in the transition from circular base to rectangular top (**Figure 2.19**).

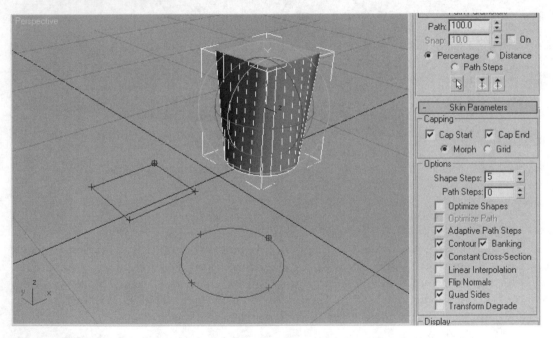

FIGURE 2.19 *Reducing the path steps from 5 to 0 reduces the definition of the transition from circular to rectangular along the length of the object. It also reduces the number of faces from 332 to 92, with a corresponding loss of visual detail.*

Increasing the path steps to 3 might give an acceptable level of detail, depending on the distance from the camera or the background, and it raises the overall face count to a moderate 236. You must be the judge of how much detail is enough, but you have the option to change it at any time to optimize the object for any occasion.

Reducing the shape steps of this loft object to 0 ruins the integrity of the object because the base is changed to a rectangular shape. A circle has four vertices, so removing any intermediate steps that define the curvature makes it rectangular (**Figure 2.20**).

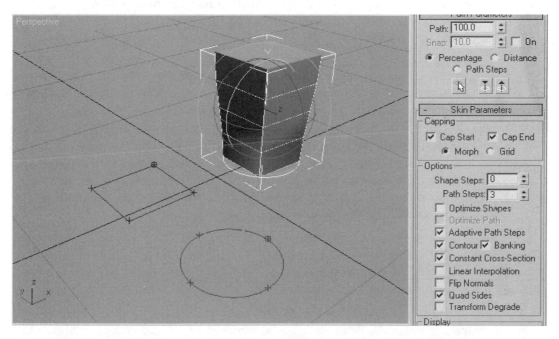

FIGURE 2.20 *Setting the shape steps to 0 ruins the integrity of the intended mesh by removing all curvature from the circular shape.*

Increasing the shape steps to 3 might result in an acceptable mesh object with a total face count of 156, less than half of the original 332 faces.

The important fact is that you can easily adjust the density of your lofted objects at any time to achieve an optimum balance between the object's detail and efficiency, which is so critical to production.

Summary

This chapter presented several important concepts:

- **The reference coordinate systems in 3ds Max 8**—These include View, Screen, and Local. Without a fundamental understanding of them, particularly of Local, you'll have a difficult time navigating through 3D space, transforming objects in scenes, and taking full advantage of the alignment tools available in the program.

- **Layers**—A management tool that lets you manipulate objects as a group to transform them as one entity, or to change properties such as object visibility or radiosity rendering parameters.

- **Lofting**—A relatively straightforward modeling technique that requires a fundamental understanding of underlying concepts before you can use it efficiently. These concepts include the orientation of shapes and paths, the first vertex, and path and shape steps. While you hopefully had a chance to experiment with lofting in this chapter, the information presented here sets the stage for the in-depth lofting practice you'll do in Chapter 5.

The axes of the World reference coordinate in 3ds Max 8 follow common mathematical practice. If you were graphing on paper, X would be the horizontal axis and Y the vertical axis. Three-dimensional space is defined by the Z axis, which projects off the paper toward you.

Just performing a set of orchestrated steps or exercises is not conducive to learning a complex program like 3ds Max 8. It's far more important to use the exercises in this book only as a guide for investigating the processes being presented. Then concentrate on really learning the underlying concepts by practicing your own versions of the processes afterward.

CHAPTER 3

Fine-Tuning Productivity Via the 3ds Max Interface

In This Chapter

By now you've been using 3ds Max 8 long enough to become familiar with the general layout of the user interface. With a little practice, using it will become second nature as you perform your daily tasks. However, a few of version 8's interface features aren't readily apparent to new users, but are critical if you want to be able to quickly navigate in 3D space. The goal of this chapter isn't to show you the nuts and bolts of the interface, but rather to introduce you to a few of these fundamental features that will enhance your productivity.

For instance, transforming objects by moving, rotating and aligning them in 3D space most likely occupies a significant portion of your day-to-day work using 3ds Max 8, so it's very important to master the tools that will make this a seamless process. In this chapter, we'll practice using the Align tool and Transform gizmos, in combination with some tips on choosing the best reference coordinate system, to fine-tune your productivity.

This chapter also shows you a few of the programmed shortcuts that are indispensable for routine operations. Rather than simply mention the shortcut buttons and what happens when you click them, the shortcut operations are integrated into the exercises themselves to give you an opportunity to learn how to use them in the context of a realistic production workflow.

Key Term

- **Gizmo**—While the term *gizmo* can be found throughout 3ds Max 8's documentation, in this chapter gizmo refers to the control apparatus that lets you transform objects in specific axes.

Using the Align Tool and Transform Gizmos

In the previous chapter, you learned how important the reference coordinate systems are for using 3ds Max 8 productively. In this chapter, you'll extend some of that knowledge to quickly and efficiently align objects with one another. Without a fundamental understanding of how the reference coordinate systems function in relation to the Align tool and Transform gizmos, the transformation of objects in a scene is often a random process of eyeballing objects as you move and rotate them into position. For instance, many users who are new to 3ds Max try using the Align tool but quickly abandon it because they don't understand the corresponding reference coordinate system.

note

Almost all of the commands in 3ds Max 8 can be accessed using keyboard shortcuts. Take the time to become familiar with them. To view the many preassigned shortcuts and customizable commands, click the Customize button on the main toolbar, choose Custom User Interface, and then click the Keyboard tab.

Transform gizmos appear in the viewports when you are using the Select and Move or the Select and Rotate tools. These gizmos let you accurately constrain the transformation of a shape along specific axes, such as X, Y, or Z. You can also constrain transformations to just two of the three axes. For example, you can freely move or rotate an object in both the X and Y coordinates at the same time.

The Transform gizmos are displayed as red, green, and blue indicators that turn yellow to indicate the active axis as the pointer passes over them. Incidentally, the choice of red, green, and blue isn't coincidental in 3ds Max 8: the formula RGB = XYZ is evident throughout the software as a visual reference for clearly identifying the three axes.

Aligning Objects Quickly and Accurately

In the first exercise, you'll use a simple 3ds Max 8 scene containing several 2D shapes that form the basis of a building, a pier, and some pilings. (In another exercise later in this book, you'll import this same scene into another scene.) The 2D shape in the scene that represents the pier has already been positioned so that it will match up with the landscape you'll use in Chapter 6. Your task in this exercise is to transform and align the other shapes into positions that will be useful later when you construct 3D objects in Chapter 4.

> **note**
>
> The Scale Transform gizmo is another type of Transform gizmo you can use. However, because you must take extra care in scaling objects in 3ds Max 8, we'll cover that tool in more detail in Chapter 5.

Exercise 3.1: Transforming and aligning shapes

1. Open the **Pier01.max** file on the CD-ROM, and save it to your project folder with the name *Pier02.max*.

2. Right-click in the Top viewport to activate it (the active viewport is indicated by a yellow border). Press the G key, a keyboard shortcut that toggles the grid on and off in any viewport.

   This scene contains a line, circle, and several rectangles that will eventually become a pier with a building at one end. The large rectangle representing the pier has been positioned and rotated to fit in a landscape scene in later chapters.

> **note**
>
> It is always best to activate a new viewport by right-clicking in it. While it is possible to activate the viewport with a left click, you may be in Select and Move mode or Select and Rotate mode and accidentally transform an object.

3. To rotate and align the building rectangle with the pier rectangle, first make sure the Select Object button is highlighted in the main toolbar and then, with the left mouse button, pick on the edge of the rectangle called shack01.

   The rectangle turns white, and the red and gray axis tripod representing the rectangle's pivot point displays (see **Figure 3.1** on the next page).

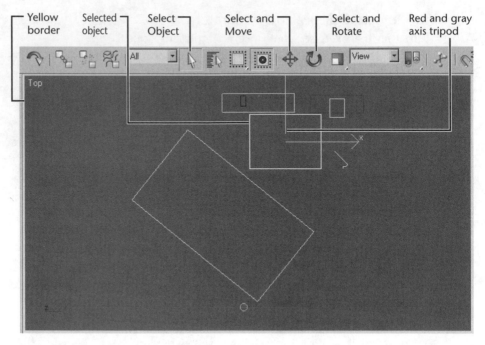

Yellow border | Selected object | Select Object | Select and Move | Select and Rotate | Red and gray axis tripod

Top

FIGURE 3.1 *A selected object in the viewport turns white and displays an axis tripod at the pivot point.*

In this exercise, you'll be rotating shack01 so that it is aligned with the large rectangle called pier_shape. However, this is difficult to do at the moment because you don't know the angle of the large rectangle. Notice in the main toolbar that the View reference coordinate system is active, which means that no matter which shape you select in the Top viewport, the axis tripod will always indicate the positive X axis to the right, the positive Y axis up, and the positive Z axis toward you, the viewer. This is no help in determining the rotation amount, so we need to change the active reference coordinate system.

tip

If you pause the cursor over an object in the viewport, the object's name displays in a Tooltip, making it easier to select objects in the scene.

You can also press the H keyboard shortcut to select objects by name.

4. On the main toolbar, to the right of the trans-
    form buttons, click View in the list field, and
    then choose Local (**Figure 3.2**).

    Because Shack01 is rotated at an unknown angle
    to the World reference coordinates, and because
    Local coordinates always remain oriented with
    the object, using the Local reference coordinate
    system makes it easier to perform transforms
    and alignments.

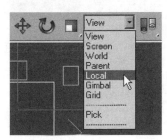

FIGURE 3.2 *Switch from View to the
Local reference coordinate system on
the main toolbar.*

5. Click the shack01 rectangle and then the pier_shape rectangle. Notice the axis
    tripod for each shape has retained its orientation to the original shape. This is
    useful information when you are aligning the shapes because you will align
    them from Local axis to Local axis.

6. In the Top viewport, select shack01. On the main toolbar, click the Align
    button. Move the pointer over the edge of the pier_shape rectangle, and click
    when you see the pointer change to a cross with two rectangles and a line.

    The Align Selection [pier_shape] dialog appears.

7. Uncheck all the boxes in the Align Position [Local] area. In the Align Orientation [Local] area, check the X Axis box (**Figure 3.3**). Click OK.

    The selected rectangle (shack01) will rotate so that its X-axis is aligned with that of the large rectangle (pier_shape).

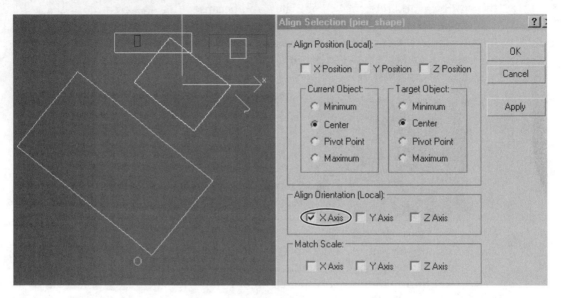

Figure 3.3 *The Align Orientation [Local] option, a feature of the Align tool, lets you rotate objects by aligning their Local axes.*

8. On the main toolbar, click the Select and Move button (Figure 3.1). Notice that a Transform gizmo is displayed at the pivot point of shack01, instead of the red and gray axis tripod.

9. In the Top viewport, click and hold on the X-axis arrow shaft to move the shape to the left. This restricts all movement to the X axis alone. Now click and hold on the Y-axis arrow shaft to move the shape up and down the viewport along the Y axis only. Finally, click and hold on the red and green lines forming a rectangle at the apex of the tripod (a yellow rectangle appears), to move the shape freely in the X axis and Y axis.

    Notice on the main toolbar that the reference coordinate system has reset itself to View. The reference coordinate systems are "sticky" to the transform buttons—View is the default system for the Select and Move tool.

10. On the main toolbar, reset the reference coordinate system to Local so that the Transform gizmo will rotate accordingly. You can now move the shape along its own axes.

At this point, trying to align the two shapes so that their upper corners match would be pure guesswork. You need the shapes to be aligned perfectly, and the Align tool will get you there.

11. With shack01 selected, click the Align button on the main toolbar, and click pier_shape in the Top viewport.

   The Align Selection [pier_shape] dialog appears again, indicating that the Align Position is based on the Local axes of the shapes.

12. In the Align Position [Local] area, check the X Position, Y Position, and Z Position boxes. The two shapes align according to the geometric centers of their bounding boxes (**Figure 3.4**). Click the Apply button to clear the axis-position check boxes.

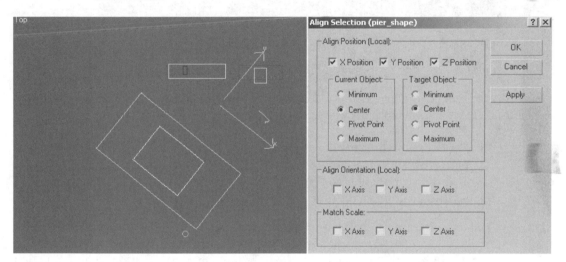

FIGURE 3.4 *The Align tool aligns the bounding boxes of objects according to the current reference-coordinate-system settings and the current active viewport.*

13. Now check the X Position box, and choose the Minimum radio buttons in the Current Object and Target Object columns. These selections align the two edges of the bounding box in their extreme negative Local X-axis dimension. Click the Apply button.

14. Check the Y Position box and choose the Maximum radio buttons in the Current Object and Target Object columns. These selections precisely align the upper left corners of the two shapes (see **Figure 3.5** on the next page). Click OK.

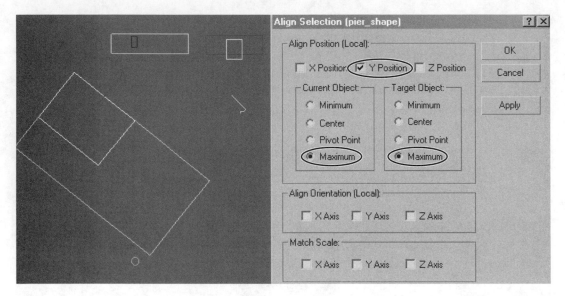

Figure 3.5 *You can use the Apply button, which is part of the Align tool, to align the bounding boxes of objects until they are positioned the way you want them.*

15. On the main toolbar, click the Select Object button and select the circle called pier_piling01 in the Top viewport (Figure 3.1). Notice that its Local axes have already been oriented to the Local axes of the large rectangle.

16. Save the file; it should already be called Pier02.max.

This simple exercise makes it evident that if you want to use the Align tool effectively, you must have a solid grounding in the reference coordinate systems. The Local system is perhaps the most useful, because in most situations it lets you align objects with other objects, regardless of their orientation in space.

Increasing Your Productivity: More Gizmo Practice

In the next exercise, you'll gain extra practice with the Transform gizmos and reference coordinate systems so that you get a sense of how they can increase your productivity once you master them. You'll also learn a few keyboard shortcuts that will help make your daily work go faster.

You'll use the Pier02.max file you created in the previous exercise to practice transforming a shape called roof_profile. This exercise is just for practice—you won't be saving the results to use in other exercises later in the book.

Exercise 3.2: Using Transform gizmos and keyboard shortcuts to enhance productivity

1. Open the **Pier02.max** file on the CD-ROM or from the last exercise. Make sure that the Top viewport is active and the Select Object button on the main toolbar is highlighted. Press the H key.

   This keyboard shortcut diplays the Select Objects dialog (**Figure 3.6**).

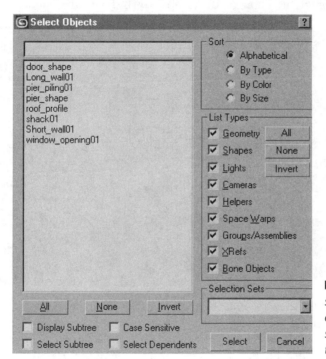

FIGURE 3.6 *The H keyboard shortcut lets you select objects in the scene by selecting the name of the object.*

2. Double click roof_profile in the list to select it.

   Let's assume for the purposes of this exercise that you can't see the roof_profile object in the viewport because the viewport is crowded with many other objects.

note

It is critical that you name all objects in your scene logically as you create them. Productivity is slowed considerably when users have to figure out what, for example, Line01 or Box10 is when it no longer resembles the original primitive object.

3. Access the Isolate Selection tool by pressing
    Alt + Q.

    All objects except the currently selected objects
    (roof_profile, in our case) are hidden, and 3ds
    Max 8 zooms to fill the screen with the selected
    objects (**Figure 3.7**). An Isolated Selection
    warning also appears, which includes an option to exit Isolation mode by
    clicking the bright yellow field. For now, we'll stay in this mode.

tip

The Isolate Selection tool can
also be accessed from the
Tools drop-down menu.

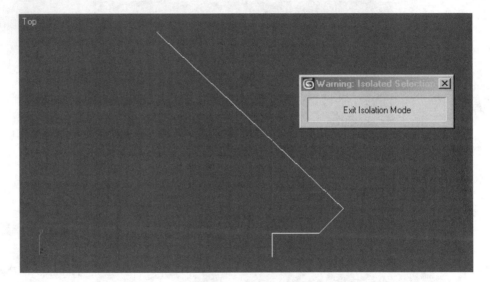

FIGURE 3.7 *The Isolate Selection tool, accessed here using the keyboard shortcut
Alt + Q, lets you clear the viewports of all but the selected objects.*

4. On the main toolbar, click the Select and Rotate button (Figure 3.1).

    The current reference coordinate system automatically changes to View
    because that is the default setting for the Select and Rotate tool, which is
    appropriate for this exercise.

5. As you pass the pointer over the Transform
    gizmo, the currently restricted rotation axis is
    highlighted in yellow. Drag the mouse on any
    of these axes to rotate the shape. Position the
    pointer in the space between the axes, and,
    when the sphere turns gray, drag to rotate the
    shape freely in two axes (**Figure 3.8**).

note

There are times when you
need to transform objects,
but the Transform gizmo gets
in the way. Pressing the X key
will toggle Transform gizmos
on and off.

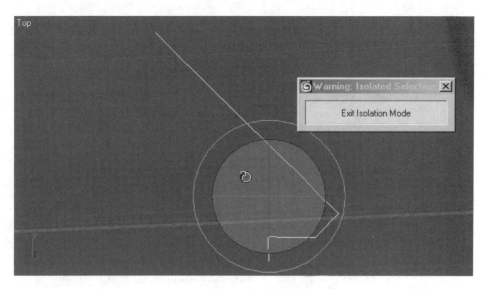

FIGURE 3.8 *Using the Transform gizmo, you can rotate objects by restricting movement to a specific axis or rotate them freely in two axes.*

6. To better see what you are doing in the current viewport, position the pointer at the intersection of the four viewports, and when you see the four-way arrow cursor appear, drag to the lower right to enlarge the Top viewport. Then press Alt + W to toggle the active viewport to full screen. Press Alt + W again to toggle the screen back to the four-viewport layout. Right-click at the intersection of the four viewports, and then click the Reset Layout button to return to four equally distributed viewports (see **Figure 3.9** on the next page).

note

The outer ring on the Rotate Transform gizmo restricts rotation around the viewer's line of sight. So when an orthographic viewport and the View reference coordinate system are active, the rotation restriction is the same as using the Z-axis Transform gizmo. However, in a non-orthographic viewport, such as Perspective or User, rotating around the line of site is quite different.

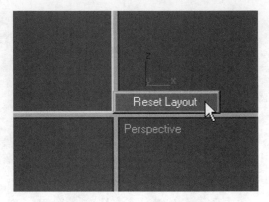

FIGURE 3.9 *Resize the viewports by dragging at their intersections, or maximize or minimize the active viewport using the Alt + W keyboard shortcut.*

7. On the main toolbar, click the Select and Move button. In the Top viewport, click and hold the Transform gizmo to move the shape in any direction, but don't release the mouse button. As the shape approaches the edge of the viewport, press the I key to pan transparently while still in the Select and Move mode. Press the left bracket ([) and right bracket (]) keys to zoom in and out respectively.

8. Click Exit Isolation Mode in the Isolated Selection warning to unhide all other objects in the scene.

9. Exit or Reset 3ds Max 8 without saving the file.

This exercise highlights just a few of the keyboard shortcuts you should get in the habit of using to work more efficiently in 3ds Max 8.

tip

You can also maximize or minimize the active viewport by toggling the Min/Max button at the lower right of the display.

Summary

Making the techniques covered in this chapter a part of your daily routine is critical if you want to efficiently control the transformation of objects using 3ds Max. Without some awareness of how to use the Align tool and Transform gizmos within the context of the reference coordinate systems, as well as the preassigned keyboard shortcuts that are available to you, you will waste precious time trying to maneuver objects into position.

This chapter is just an introduction to these very important concepts—you must take it upon yourself to delve deeper into them and actually use them if you want to truly maximize your productivity.

CHAPTER 4

Basic Modeling

In This Chapter

In this chapter, you'll continue working with the scene you created in Chapter 3 to learn some basic modeling techniques. First, you'll set up a prototype scene that enables you to start each work session with your preferred settings, mathematical units, grid spacing, and viewport layout. Then you'll practice using 2D shapes to build 3D walls, pilings, a pier, and a roof.

Using 2D shapes to create complex 3D objects is a very important skill if you want to be able to maximize your efficiency and flexibility when working in 3ds Max. As you create the objects for your building, you'll learn how to use the modifier stack in 3ds Max to apply discrete modifiers to objects in the scene, and then navigate up and down the stack to make changes at almost any level without affecting the other modifiers or the original object's parameters. You'll also learn how to work at the sub-object level to access the building blocks of the various primitive objects, in this case 2D shapes. Developing this workflow of flexible editing is known as procedural modeling and is a key component of efficient production.

Next you'll clone these objects, or copy them so that they reference the original object. This allows you to quickly and effortlessly make global changes to your objects. In some cases, depending on the type of clone you use, you can also dramatically conserve memory space.

Finally, you'll assemble the walls and roof to make a building. You'll do this by aligning and orienting the walls vertically using the Align to View feature of the Align tool, and then positioning them correctly using the Align tool itself.

Key Terms

- **Modifier**—A *modifier* is a discrete operator applied to a 2D shape or 3D object for editing purposes. You may use as many modifiers as you want and then navigate a modifier stack to make changes at any level.

- **Modifier stack**—The *modifier stack* is a linear history of the modifiers you have applied. The original object is at the bottom of the modifier stack, and each new modifier is applied to the top of the stack.

- **Compound shapes**—*Compound shapes* are shapes consisting of more than one spline and are used to efficiently create objects with holes through them.

- **Cloning**—Objects can be *cloned* in 3ds Max 8 in a variety of ways. An object can be copied so that it is an exact replica of the original, in which case it is referred to as a copy. It can be cloned to be an instance, which is an exact copy with a two-way connection to the original so that when either the copy or original changes, the corresponding original or copy changes too. Or it can be cloned as a reference, which means it is an exact copy and has a one-way connection to the original. If the original changes, the clone changes, but if the clone changes, the original is not affected.

- **Sub-object editing**—Two-dimensional shapes (and 3D objects) contain sublevel elements that may be edited; for example, a shape contains vertices, segments, and spline sub-object levels.

Setting Up a Scene

Whenever you open 3ds Max 8 or clear an existing 3ds Max scene, most likely you will have viewport configurations and settings you've used previously that you want to revert to or save for reuse later. In the first exercise in this chapter, you will practice switching the display units in 3ds Max 8 from the default decimal units to U.S. Standard feet and inches. The display units determine the visual and data-entry format for all numeric values in 3ds Max 8. You will also change the spacing and size of the World grid. Then you'll save these settings to configure a prototype file that you can use whenever you need to revert to those same settings.

It's also possible to save objects, lights, and cameras in a prototype file after you've created them, but generally this isn't a good idea. Because there should be only

> **caution**
>
> You may already have a prototype startup file called *maxstart.max* in the /3ds max 8/ Scenes folder of your computer. It most likely was created by someone else in your company so that all 3ds Max 8 users would begin new scenes using company standards. For the purposes of this book, you should rename this file so that you don't discard the company standards. Then you can name it maxstart.max again when you are finished with the exercises in the book.

one prototype file, it's best to adjust and save only the settings and viewport configurations so that you can maintain a more universal prototype file within your office.

Exercise 4.1: Setting the prototype file

1. Start or reset 3ds Max 8. Notice that the display initially shows grid lines in each of the four viewports, and the status line reports that the grid spacing is set to 10.0 units (**Figure 4.1**).

    Let's suppose you want the grid to be visible only in the Perspective viewport, the units to display in feet and inches, and the grid spacing to be 1 foot.

    It is best to set the display units before adjusting the grid size, so we'll tackle that first.

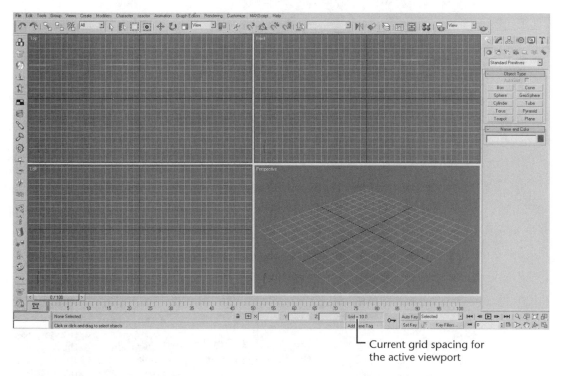

Current grid spacing for
the active viewport

FIGURE 4.1 *The default startup display in 3ds Max 8. It uses generic decimal units and a 10-unit grid spacing with grids displaying in each viewport.*

2. On the main toolbar, click Customize and choose Units Setup from the drop-down menu. In the Units Setup dialog that appears, choose the US Standard radio button. From the list, choose Feet w/Fractional Inches (**Figure 4.2**). Click OK.

   The grid spacing in the status line should now read 0'10".

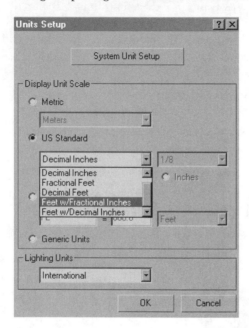

FIGURE 4.2 *The display units determine the visual and data-entry format for all numeric values in feet with fractional inches.*

3. On the main toolbar, click Customize and choose Grid and Snap Settings. In the Grid and Snap Settings dialog that appears, click the Home Grid tab. In the Grid Spacing field, enter 0'1". In the Major Lines Every Nth Grid Line field, enter 12; and, in the Perspective View Grid Extent field, enter 480. Press Enter to make sure the data is properly evaluated.

   Notice however, that the status line is reporting the grid size to be 1'0" (**Figure 4.3**). You'll learn in the next step why the grid size is not showing the 0'1" that you just set.

note

The Units Setup dialog also contains a button for System Units Setup, which displays the settings that are used in the program's internal mathematical calculation. These settings are not the same as the display units. If you're not getting the correct results in Step 2 of this exercise, set the System Units to the default 1 unit = 1 inch setting for the exercises in this book.

If you happen to be working with the metric system, however, then both the system units and the display units should be set to metric values in a production setting.

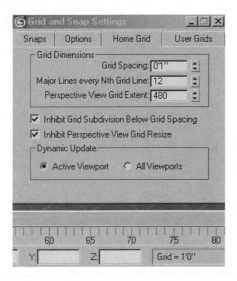

FIGURE 4.3 *Changing the Grid Spacing value sets the smallest grid size possible, but the actual grid spacing onscreen depends on the zoom level.*

4. Right-click in the Top viewport to activate it, and use the Zoom command or the mouse wheel to zoom in on the grid. At some point, the grid will shift to become smaller, and you will notice that the grid spacing in the status line has changed to 0'1", or 1/12 of what it originally was. Zoom out in the viewport, and the grid will shift back to 1'0". Zoom out to 12'0", then out to 144'0", and so on. The grid shifts by a factor of 12 as indicated by the Major Lines Every Nth Grid Line setting. Close the Grid and Snap Settings dialog, and click the Zoom Extends All button to return to the default zoom levels in all viewports.

5. For the purposes of this exercise, let's turn off the grid in the orthographic viewports so that there is less visual clutter. To do this, press the G key to toggle the grid off in the Top viewport, and then right-click in the Front viewport and turn the grid off there by pressing the G key again. Repeat this process to toggle the grid off in the Left viewport. However, you want to leave the grid visible in the Perspective viewport.

note

The Major Lines Every Nth Grid Line setting has two functions. First, it acts as the size-scaling factor of the viewport grid as you zoom in and out. Second, it displays every nth grid line a darker shade of gray—in this case, every 12th grid line. The black grid lines always indicate the 0, 0, 0 World coordinate origin.

note

The Perspective View Grid Extent value sets the physical size of the grid in the Perspective viewport in inches. However, you do not enter the inch sign, because inches is the only option.

6. Right-click in the Top viewport to activate it. This is the viewport that 3ds Max users generally begin working in, so you want it to be active each time you start a new scene.

7. From the File pull-down menu, choose Save As. In the Save File As dialog that appears, enter maxstart in the File Name field. Click Save.

    Make sure your filenames are one word. The filename is automatically appended with the .max file ending. Saving the file in the /scenes folder is fine, although it may be saved in any of the folders in the current path configuration.

8. From the File pull-down menu, choose Reset. In the 3ds Max dialog that appears, click the Yes button next to the "Do you really want to reset?" query.

    The display will load with the original settings and then quickly read the maxstart.max file and apply the settings you have saved.

You've now set the display units appropriately for the remaining exercises in this book and have configured a prototype file that causes 3ds Max 8 to start up with a consistent display each time. You may, of course, change the settings and overwrite the maxstart.max file at any time. You may also change the configuration settings for the current work session at any time without affecting the maxstart.max file.

Working with 2D Shapes

Why would you want to buy a relatively expensive 3D graphics program and work in 2D?

There are a couple of good reasons why working in 2D makes sense in 3ds Max 8:

- **Efficiency**—Creating and editing 2D shapes can be an efficient method of creating a basis that can be turned into more complex 3D objects.

- **Flexibility**—Modifying 2D shapes to edit complex 3D objects can increase productivity.

While the list of the advantages may not be long, attaining efficiency and flexibility are what this book is all about.

This chapter introduces you to some of the key aspects of creating and modifying 2D shapes, but it's up to you to investigate the many editing options and modifier combinations that can make working with 2D shapes such a powerful process. Make sure you start slowly using simple scenes and then build on complexity as you learn the fundamentals, rather than starting with the most complex project you can imagine.

The next exercise demonstrates just some of the power of working with 2D shapes. You'll begin by opening a scene containing 2D shapes. Later in this chapter, you'll turn these shapes into a pier with a building. But for now, you'll create a relatively complex hip roof, or a roof with sloping planes on all four sides, using only two 2D shapes. The roof will have a fascia board, a soffit, a trim board, and the roof surface itself. Finally, you'll adjust the height of the roof.

This exercise also introduces you to the process of applying modifiers and using the modifier stack to edit geometry by navigating through the history of the creation process to make changes to the base geometry at the modifier level. This technique is known as *procedural modeling*.

Exercise 4.2: Applying modifiers to shapes

1. Open the **Pier02.max** file from the CD-ROM or from the last exercise you performed in Chapter 3. This file contains the 2D shapes you worked with earlier. Save it to your project folder with the name *Pier03.max*.

2. In the Top viewport, select the rectangular shape called shack01. Don't forget—you can use the H keyboard shortcut to select a shape by name.

   We will add a roof to this shape.

3. On the Modifier panel, in the Object-Space Modifier list, double-click Bevel Profile (**Figure 4.4**).

FIGURE 4.4 *Applying a Bevel Profile modifier to a 2D shape will turn it into a flat 3D surface.*

The shape becomes a flat 3D surface, and the Bevel Profile modifier appears above the rectangle in the modifier stack.

4. On the Modify panel, in the Parameters rollout, click the Pick Profile button. In the Top viewport, pick the 2D shape called roof_profile (**Figure 4.5**). (You can also use the H keyboard shortcut to pick the shape by name.)

note

The Bevel Profile modifier can be applied only to 2D shapes. Once it has been applied, the shape turns into a 3D object.

roof_profile shape

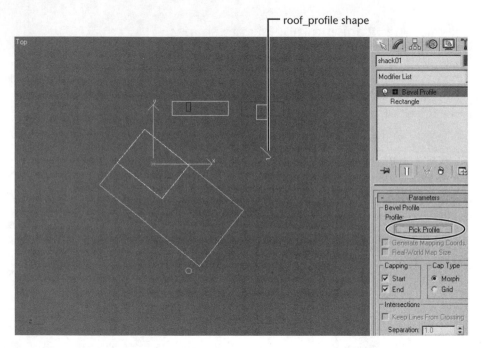

FIGURE 4.5 *The Bevel Profile modifier requires you to select another 2D shape (roof_profile in this exercise) that defines the extrusion profile of the base shape.*

The rectangle turns into a 3D roof with a flat top (**Figure 4.6**).

note

All the graphics that are printed in this book are also available in full color on the CD-ROM that accompanies this book. You will be able to see the details of each graphic much more clearly onscreen.

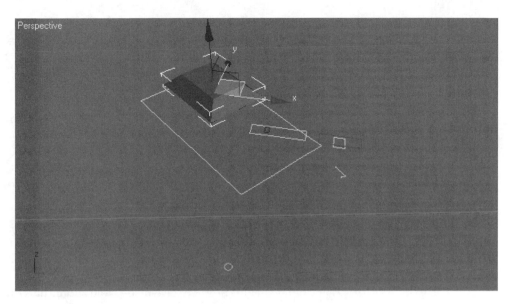

Perspective

FIGURE 4.6 *The Bevel Profile modifier extrudes the base shape in its positive local Z-axis to create a 3D object.*

5. Look in the modifier stack and note that the object started as a rectangle and has one modifier applied (**Figure 4.7**). Save the file; it should already be called Pier03.max.

FIGURE 4.7 *The modifier stack shows a history of your work and is evaluated from the bottom up.*

Using two 2D shapes and a modifier, you have created a relatively complex 3D object, the roof of the building in your scene. However, it should be a hip roof, which is not flat on the top but comes to a peak. We'll adjust the roof at the end of this chapter.

This simple exercise should convey two important points:

- Simple 2D shapes can be used as the basis for 3D objects.
- A modifier stack records the history of your editing, enabling you to make changes without affecting anything before or after a particular point in that history.

Working with 2D Compound Shapes

You've learned how to work with simple shapes to create a roof from a rectangle and a line. While you can accomplish a lot of your work using simple shapes, the real power of working with 2D shapes comes in knowing how to work with compound shapes, or shapes containing multiple splines.

Two-dimensional shapes are assemblages of sub-object-level components, such as vertices, segments, and splines. A vertex is a point in space, through which the shape passes. A segment is the visible line that connects any two vertices. And a spline is a sub-object level grouping of vertices and segments. All shapes are composed of at least one spline. Compound shapes, however, are made from more than one spline. If he compound shape contains closed splines that are islands within closed splines, the resulting 3D objects will appear as solid surfaces with holes through them.

In the next exercise, you'll use some compound shapes to create walls that have the window openings for the building you've been working on since Chapter 3. Along the way, you'll learn about sub-object-level editing, which lets you manipulate and edit vertices, segments, and splines.

Exercise 4.3: Creating and editing compound shapes

1. Open the **Pier03.max** file from the CD-ROM or from the last exercise. Save it to your project folder with the name *Pier04.max*. In the Top viewport, select and zoom in on the object called Long_wall01.

2. On the Modify panel, notice that Long_wall01 is a rectangle that is 10'0" in length and 40'0" in width (**Figure 4.8**).

   The Modify panel doesn't provide a way to work at the sub-object level on a primitive shape such as a rectangle, so you must first convert the object to an Editable Spline. We'll do that in the next step.

3. Right-click in the Top viewport, and choose Convert To from the bottom of the Quad menu. From the Convert To submenu, choose Convert to Editable Spline (**Figure 4.9**).

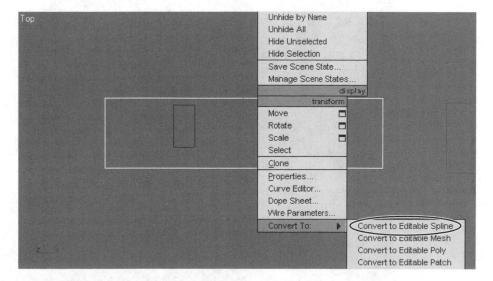

FIGURE 4.8 *You can see the parameters of a selected object on the Modify panel.*

FIGURE 4.9 *You can convert a primitive shape to an Editable Spline by selecting the spline and right-clicking in the current viewport.*

You now have access to sub-object-level editing options on the Modify panel. This will allow you to use the Attach button to add a window opening shape to this shape, thus creating a compound shape that will become a wall with a window opening when turned into a 3D object.

4. On the Modify panel, in the Geometry rollout, click the Attach button. In the Top viewport, move the pointer over the edge of the smaller rectangle called window_opening01, and pick this rectangle once the Attach cursor appears (**Figure 4.10**). Click the Attach button again to exit the Attach mode.

Long_wall01 is now a compound shape made of two splines: the original wall rectangle and the window opening rectangle. The name of the new compound shape is the same as the original shape you selected before using the Attach button. Creating 3D walls with window openings using this method is far more efficient and flexible than the alternative, 3D Boolean operations.

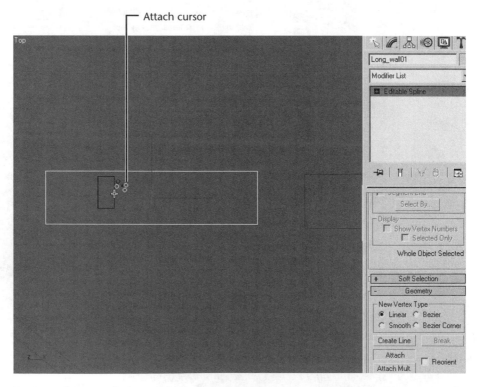

FIGURE 4.10 *Two-dimensional shapes can be attached to one another when you see the Attach cursor. The Attach operation creates compound shapes that result in solids with a hole in them once the shapes are turned into 3D objects.*

5. On the Modify panel, from the Modifier List drop-down menu, choose the Extrude modifier. In the Parameters rollout, enter 0'6" in the Amount field. Press Enter. Zoom in on the wall object in the Perspective shaded viewport, and you will see that it is a solid wall with a window opening (**Figure 4.11**).

The ability to turn compound shapes into 3D objects with holes through them is an important concept in 3ds Max 8. This exercise illustrates a simple example of the process. The technique uses very few computer resources and can be easily edited.

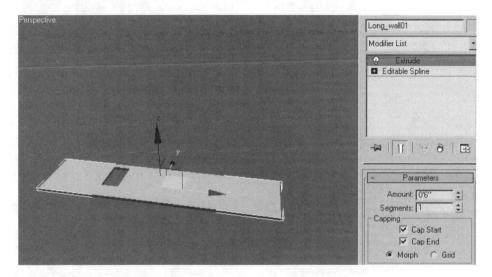

FIGURE 4.11 *The Extrude modifier turns the compound shape into a 3D wall that is 6 inches thick and has a window opening.*

6. Now let's assume that the client has asked for another window opening in the wall. With the Long_wall01 object selected in the Top viewport, go to the Modify panel and click the plus (+) button to the left of Editable Spline to expand the list of sub-object components. Highlight the Spline sub-object level and pick the small rectangle in the Top viewport that represents the window opening (see **Figure 4.12** on the next page).

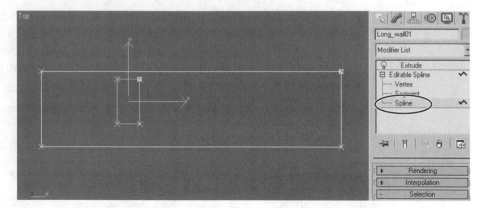

FIGURE 4.12 *The rectangular spline turns red when selected at sub-object level. (View the screenshot, which is included on the CD-ROM, on your computer to see it in color.)*

7. On the main toolbar, click the Select and Move button. To create a clone of the selected spline, press and hold the Shift key, and then drag the Transform gizmo's X-axis arrow shaft about halfway between the original spline and the right edge of the wall. Release the left mouse button and the Shift key (**Figure 4.13**).

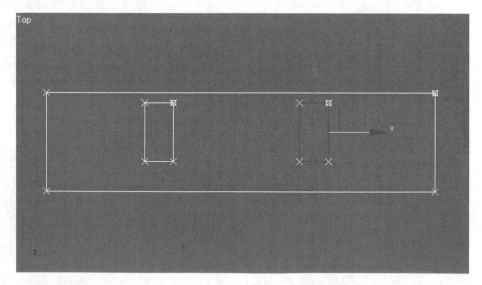

FIGURE 4.13 *Transforming a sub-object selection, in this case a Spline, while holding down the Shift key creates a clone that will become a new window opening in the extruded 3D object.*

8. On the Modify panel, in the modifier stack, click Editable Spline to exit sub-object mode. Highlight the Extrude modifier in the modifier stack to return to that level. Notice the 3D wall now has two window openings.

9. Save the file; it should already be called Pier04.max.

When combined, compound shapes, sub-object editing, and cloning make up a powerful toolset that lets you create buildings, windows and doors, grating, perforated panels, and many other objects.

Use your imagination to create your own objects using this technique. Practice using simpler objects first, and then work your way up to more complexity as you become comfortable with the creation and editing process. Compound shapes are a very efficient and flexible component of building 3D objects.

More Sub-Object-Level Editing

Many options exist for editing at each sub-object level. In the next exercise, you'll learn about another of these options: working at the vertex sub-object level.

Editing objects at the sub-object level provides access to the "building blocks" of shapes, such as vertex, segment, and spline, so that you can manipulate these individual components or selection sets of components using a host of new tools. For example, a vertex can be broken into multiple vertices to open a closed shape, or multiple vertices can be welded into a single vertex to close the shape or spline.

In Exercise 4.4, you'll create another wall for the building, one that has a large door opening with no threshold. To create it, you'll attach two shapes that overlap. However, if you extruded this new compound shape you'd end up with two overlapping 3D boxes, instead of a wall with a door opening. You must first edit the compound shape into a continuous, closed simple shape.

To edit the compound shape, you'll use the Trim and Extend feature at the Spline sub-object level to trim away parts of the shape to make a clean door opening. However, this operation creates a different but very common problem in 3ds Max 8: Open polygons do not create end caps on the extruded 3D object and will appear as thin ribbons and not solid objects.

Luckily, the fix is easy: vertex welding, which welds two or more vertices into a single vertex.

> **note**
>
> Two-dimensional or 3D files imported from CAD software will often have open vertices created from single vertices in the CAD program. This is caused by mathematical rounding errors that occur because of the internal precision of the two types of software.

Exercise 4.4: Trimming and welding 2D shapes

1. Open the **Pier04.max** file from the CD-ROM or the previous exercise. Save it to your project folder with the name *Pier05.max*. In the Top viewport, select the rectangle called Short_wall01 and zoom in on it.

    This rectangle has already been converted to an Editable Spline.

2. On the Modify panel, in the Geometry rollout, click the Attach button. In the Top viewport, move the pointer over the rectangle called door_shape01. Click the Attach button to disable it.

    The small rectangle turns white once it is attached to the selected large rectangle. The resulting compound shape is necessary for the trim operation we'll use to clean up overlapping areas of the door.

3. On the Modify panel, in the Stack view, expand Editable Spline and highlight the Spline sub-object level. In the Geometry rollout, click the Trim button. In the Top viewport, pick the bottom horizontal line of the large rectangle between the vertical sides of the small rectangle. Then pick the bottom horizontal line of the small rectangle to trim it (**Figure 4.14**).

    The trim operation will create two vertices in the same location that appear to be a single vertex. Two vertices that are not connected by a segment result in an open polygonal shape that has no end caps when turned into a 3D object.

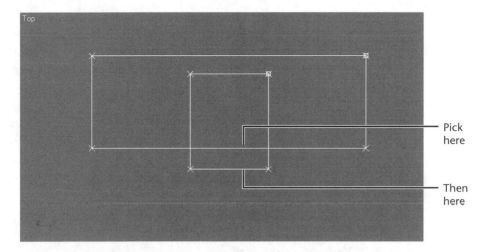

Pick
here

Then
here

FIGURE 4.14 *The trim operation at the Spline sub-object level trims portions of segments back to the next intersecting segment to create a continuous shape with no overlapping.*

4.   On the Modify panel, from the Modifier List choose Extrude modifier. Zoom in on the wall in the Perspective viewport and notice that it looks as if it's only a band or ribbon along the sides with no end caps to make it a solid 3D object (**Figure 4.15**). This is because open shapes don't extrude in a predictable way.

You'll use vertex welding to close this open shape caused by the trim operation.

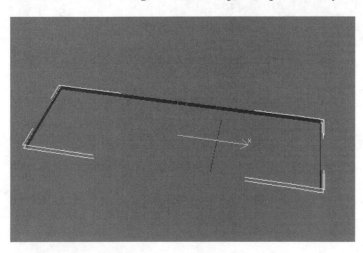

FIGURE 4.15
Open shapes don't extrude as a solid object that can be used as a wall; they appear to be only thin ribbons.

5. In Stack view, make sure that Editable Spline below the Extrude modifier is expanded, and highlight the Vertex sub-object level. On the main toolbar, click the Select Object button, and, in the Top viewport, drag a selection window around the vertices at the bottom of the door opening (see **Figure 4.16**).

    At the vertex sub-object level, you must use a window selection to make sure that you have all vertices in an area selected, and then you'll apply a Weld Threshold value that describes a sphere around each selected vertex. If the vertices' threshold spheres overlap, then the vertices will be welded into a single vertex, thus closing the shape and allowing it to extrude correctly. The Selection rollout on the Modifier panel says "4 Vertices Selected" to indicate that you have more than the two visible vertices selected.

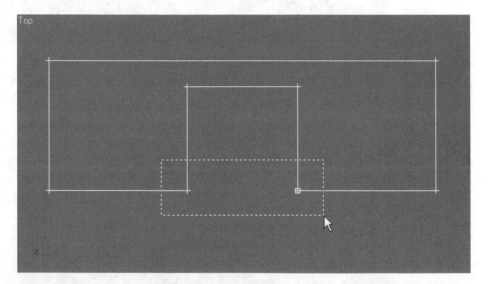

FIGURE 4.16 *Window mode lets you select all vertices within the dotted selection box.*

6. On the Modify panel, in the Geometry rollout, enter 0'1" in the Weld field to describe a weld threshold of 1 inch in diameter around each vertex. Click the Weld button. Drag a selection window around the vertices again, and notice that there are now only two vertices selected because each pair has been welded into a single vertex (**Figure 4.17**).

7. In Stack view, highlight Editable Spline to exit the Vertex sub-object-level mode, and then click the Extrude modifier to return to the top level.

caution

Setting the Weld Threshold value too high could collapse geometry and destroy detail. Make sure you select your vertices carefully and use a threshold value that is appropriate for the selection set.

The wall should now appear as a solid with an opening that has no door threshold.

8. Save the file. It should already be called Pier05.max.

    You now have walls that are ready to be moved into place for your building. Compound shapes should be an important part of vyour modeling technique in the future.

This exercise touched on just a few of the many options available at the sub-object editing level. Vertex welding is an extremely important concept, and understanding it is necessary for working effectively with 2D shapes. You should experiment with simple scenes of your own to try some of the 2D shape editing options. Use the online user reference files found in the Help pull-down menu.

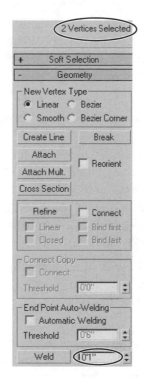

FIGURE 4.17
Enter 0'1" in the Weld field and click on the Weld button. Notice "2 Vertices Selected" is displayed at the top of the Geometry rollout.

Cloning Objects and Using More Modifiers

In the previous exercise, you learned how to clone splines within shapes. As you may have noticed, there were no options presented when cloning at the sub-object level; the clone is an independent copy of the spline with no connection to the original spline. However, in this section you'll learn to clone 3D objects in a way that presents you with several options. These options can help increase your productivity by using fewer computer resources and allowing global editing.

The process for cloning 2D and 3D objects is the same: you hold down the Shift key while transforming objects. What's different, however, is that as you are transforming the objects, you are presented with a Clone Options dialog, where you can choose the type of clone you want to create. The following are the different types of clones:

- **Copy**—A Copy clone is an exact replica of the original object, with no connection to the original. The clone also occupies the same amount of memory space as the original.

- **Instance**—An Instance clone shares a two-way connection with the original object or any other Instance clone. Modify any of the Instances and they will all be modified in the same way.

- **Reference**—A Reference clone is a one-way connection from the original object to the Reference clone. Modify the original object and all Reference clones will be modified; modify the Reference clone and only it will be modified.

Each clone type connects to the original object in a different way, so the type you choose depends on the degree of flexibility you'll require when editing objects.

In the next exercise, you will clone a circle in the scene that represents the base of pilings for your pier. All pilings must be the same, so you will make Instance clones, turn them into 3D objects, and make adjustments to things such as the radius or height of the piling that take advantage of Instance cloning in that if you change one, all the pilings change.

note

If you're using an Instance or Reference clone but you want to modify it independently of the other objects, you can break the clone's link to the original object by selecting the Make Unique option on the Modify panel. The clone then becomes a copy of the original, with no connection to it, allowing you to modify at will.

Exercise 4.5: Cloning objects for efficiency and flexibility

1. Open the **Pier05.max** file from the CD-ROM or from the last exercise. Save it to your project folder with the name *Pier06.max*.

2. In the Top viewport, select the circle near the bottom of the pier rectangle called pier_piling01. The piling needs to be in the same relative distance from the end of the pier, but just inside the pier rectangle itself.

3. On the main toolbar, click the Select and Move button and notice that the Transform gizmo is aligned with the World reference coordinate system. This reference coordinate system is not in alignment with the pier rectangle, so it's not an appropriate coordinate system to use.

4. On the main toolbar, click the reference-coordinate-system drop-down menu to the right of the transform buttons and choose Local. The Transform gizmo X axis and Y axis are now aligned with the sides of the large rectangle. Use the Transform gizmo to move the circle inside the rectangle along the Y axis (**Figure 4.18**).

Using the appropriate reference coordinate systems greatly enhances day-to-day production.

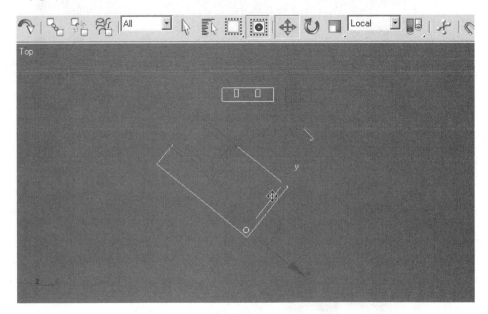

FIGURE 4.18 *The Local reference coordinate system of the pilings matches the Local reference coordinate system of the pier. Notice how the axes arrows align with the pier rectangle.*

5. Press and hold the Shift key, and in the Top viewport, move the circle along its X axis until the Transform Type-In X-axis field reads approximately 15 feet (**Figure 4.19**).

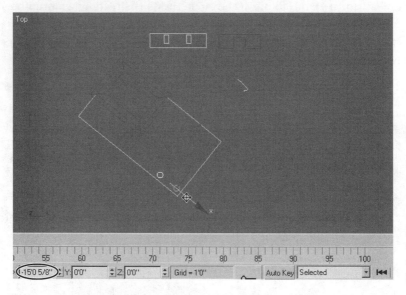

FIGURE 4.19
You can see the transformation values in the Transform Type-in fields as you transform objects. Accuracy is not important for this exercise.

6. In the Clone Options dialog, choose the Instance radio button in the Object area, and enter **5** in the Number of Copies field (**Figure 4.20**). Click OK.

You now have six pilings running parallel to the edge of the large rectangle.

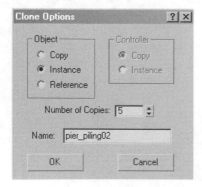

FIGURE 4.20 *This operation will make five clones that are all interconnected to each other and to the original object. The new objects are named sequentially.*

7. In the Top viewport, select the original circle and the first two clones. Press and hold down the Shift key, and transform the circles in their Y axis to the other side of the pier. In the Clone Options dialog, make sure that the Instance radio button is selected and the Number of Copies field is set to 1. Click OK.

8. In the Top viewport, select any one of the nine circles. On the Modify panel, enter 1'9" in the Radius field and press Enter.

    All Instance clones and the original shape change accordingly.

9. In the Modifier List, choose the Bevel modifier. In the Bevel Values rollout, Level 1, enter 60'0" in the Height field. Select the Level 2 option to activate it, and enter 0'3" in the Height field and -0'3" in the Outline field (**Figure 4.21**).

    This creates a slight level at the top of each piling, which will catch more light. The Instance clones are modified when the parameters or modifiers of any one of them are changed.

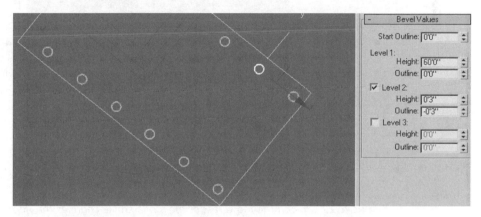

FIGURE 4.21 *Notice that all the instanced pilings, not just the one you are editing, have changed.*

10. In the Top viewport, select the shape called pier_shape, and, on the Modify panel, from the Modifier List, choose Extrude. In the Parameters rollout, enter -3'0" and press Enter.

    This extrudes the pier in the negative Z axis so that the top surface is at the same elevation as the original shape. Extruding along the positive Z-axis would have resulted in the pier projecting into the building.

    tip

    Cloned Instance and Reference objects appear in bold text in Stack view to indicate that other objects are dependent on them.

11. In the Top viewport, select the shape named roof_profile. On the Modify panel, in Stack view, expand Line and highlight the Vertex sub-object level. Select the top end vertex of the shape. It will turn red. Use the Select and Move transform to move the vertex up and to the left at about a 45-degree angle until the roof peak comes to a point (see **Figure 4.22** on the next page). Exit sub-object mode when you have edited the roof.

Editing a shape associated with the roof's Bevel Profile modifier also illustrates an example of an Instance relationship.

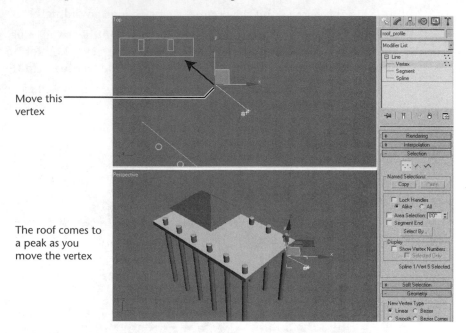

Move this vertex

The roof comes to a peak as you move the vertex

Figure 4.22 *Moving the top vertex of the roof's profile changes the slope and peak condition of the 3D roof.*

12. Click the Zoom Extends All button to fill all viewports with all objects in the scene.

13. Save the file; it should already be called Pier06.max.

This exercise produced a scene with several 3D objects, all created from 2D shapes, that are easily edited at the base level or at the modifier level.

Using Align Tools to Assemble the Building

Now that you have the 3D objects you need for this scene, you can clone the walls and assemble the parts to create a more recognizable building. Your task is to work as quickly and accurately as possible; you will learn how to use a new alignment tool in 3ds Max 8, called *Align to View*, and you'll use object cloning to increase your productivity.

Next you'll align the walls to the Front viewport to orient them vertically, and then you will use the Align tool to position them correctly. Several applications of the Align options will be necessary to position the wall correctly at the back of the pier.

You'll also learn about *Transform Type-in*, which allows accurate placement of objects when you know the dimensions or distances they must move.

Exercise 4.6: Aligning objects to the active viewport

1. Open the **Pier06.max** file from the CD-ROM or from the last exercise. Save the file in your project folder with the name *Pier07.max*.

2. Right-click in the Front viewport to activate it. Press the H key to display the Select Objects dialog. Highlight the Long_wall01 and Short_wall01 objects in the list, and click the Select button.

3. On the main toolbar, click and hold on the Align button, and from the pop-up menu choose the Align to View button at the bottom (**Figure 4.23**). In the Align to View dialog that appears, the Align Z radio button is selected (see **Figure 4.24** on the next page). Click OK.

   The Z axis of the walls will be aligned so that the axis is pointing out at you from the viewport, which flips the wall up so that it is in a vertical orientation to the pier. Next you'll align the walls so that they are correctly positioned on the pier at the back upper corner.

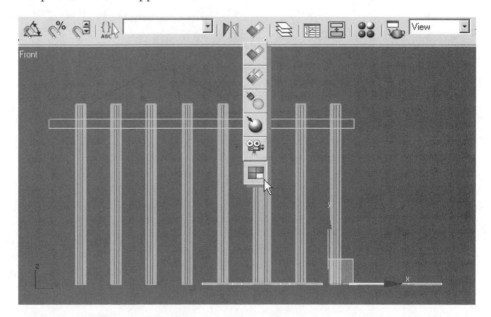

FIGURE 4.23 *The Align to View button is part of the Align tool. It lets you align the selected objects to the currently active viewport.*

FIGURE 4.24 *The Align to View dialog lets you align any axis of the selected objects to the view.*

4. Right-click in the Top viewport to activate it, and select the object called Long_wall01. On the main toolbar, set the reference coordinate system to Local.

You'll align the wall to the back upper corner of the pier. Because the pier and walls are not oriented to the World coordinate system, you must use the Local reference coordinate system.

5. The previously used Align tool, in this case Align to View, is now the button visible on the main toolbar, and you need to access the Align tool. On the main toolbar, click and hold on the Align to View button and choose the Align tool from the pop-up menu. The Align Selection (pier_shape) dialog appears. Pick on the edge of the pier. In the dialog, in the Align Position (Local) area, make sure that only the Y Position box is checked, and choose the Minimum radio button in the Current Object column and the Maximum radio button in the Target Object column. In the Align Orientation (Local) area, check the X Axis box (**Figure 4.25**). Click the Apply button to set this alignment and clear all check boxes.

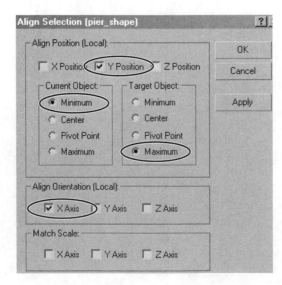

FIGURE 4.25 *You can align both the orientation and the position of the wall in one operation for this example.*

6. In the Align Selection (pier_shape) dialog, select the Z Position option and choose the Minimum radio button in both columns. This aligns the wall with the back corner of the pier (**Figure 4.26**). Click OK.

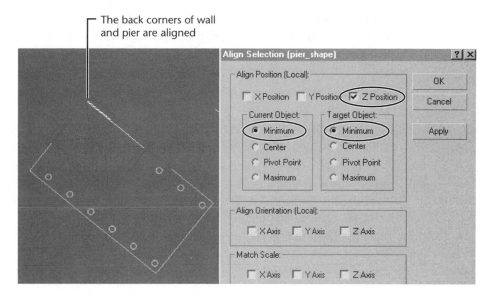

FIGURE 4.26 *The wall is sitting on the pier and aligned accurately to the back corner.*

7. In the Top viewport, select the object called Short_wall01. On the main tool-bar, click the Align button and press the H key. In the Pick Object dialog that appears, double-click Long_wall01 (**Figure 4.27**).

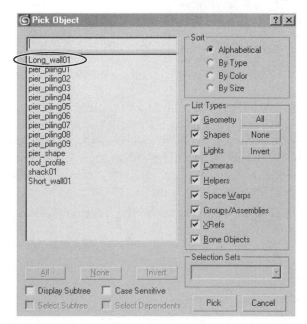

FIGURE 4.27 *The Pick Object dialog looks just like the Select Object dialog, but you use it in the middle of a command.*

Double clicking an object in the Pick Object dialog doesn't select the object; instead, it *picks* the object—in this case, Long_wall01—that the Align tool will apply changes to. Using the Align tool and the Pick Object dialog is very handy when there are many objects in the scene.

8. Select all three axes in the Align Position (Local) area and the X axis in the Align Orientation (Local) area. Click OK.

   This aligns the walls so that they are centered with one another. However, the short wall still needs to be rotated so that it's perpendicular to the long wall.

9. On the main toolbar, click the Select and Rotate button. Notice that the reference coordinate system has automatically switched to View mode. Toggle the Absolute Mode Transform Type-in button in the status line to Offset Mode and enter 90 in the Z-axis field (**Figure 4.28**). Press Enter.

   The wall rotates 90 degrees from its current position.

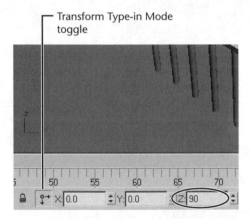

FIGURE **4.28** *It is important to toggle to Offset Transform Type-in mode to rotate the object based on its current location, and not the World Absolute rotation.*

10. On the main toolbar, click the Select and Move button. Click the Align button, press the H key, and double-click Long_wall01. In the Align Selection dialog that appears, select the X Position dialog and choose the Maximum radio buttons in both columns. Uncheck any Align Orientation (Local) check boxes from previous operations. Click Apply. Check the Z Position box and choose the Minimum radio buttons in both columns. Click OK.

    The walls are aligned so that the corners overlap (**Figure 4.29**).

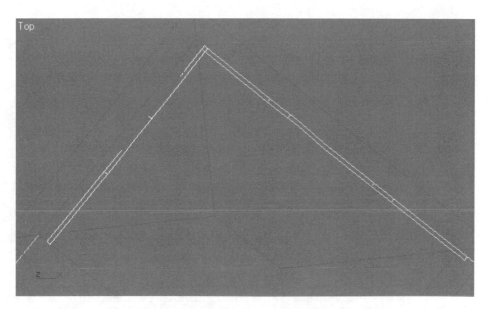

FIGURE 4.29 *Use the Align tool so that the corners overlap when viewed from the Top viewport.*

11. Now clone each wall as an instance and align them into position in the Top viewport so that all four corners overlap (**Figure 4.30**). If you make a mistake, use the Undo tool and begin again; with a little practice, aligning will become second nature.

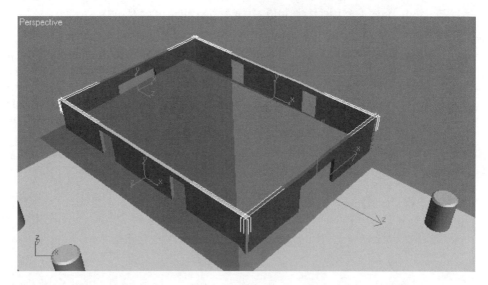

FIGURE 4.30 *Create instance clones of the walls and align them in position.*

12. On the main toolbar, click the Select and Move button, and set the reference coordinate system to View. In the Perspective viewport, select the roof object called shack01, and use the Align tool to position it on top of the walls by picking one of the walls as the target object (**Figure 4.31**).

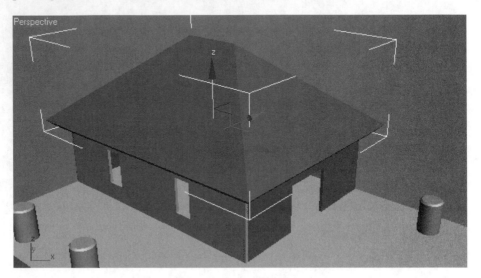

FIGURE 4.31 *The roof object can be aligned to sit on top of any one of the walls, because they are all the same height.*

13. Save the file; it should already be called Pier07.max.

The Align tool is one of the most useful production features of 3ds Max. This exercise may seem a bit confusing on your first try, but aligning generally is not a difficult task. The key is to practice over and over again on simple scenes with simple objects to get the hang of the reference coordinate systems and their relation to objects and viewports. You want to practice until you intuitively know which axes to use.

Summary

This chapter introduced some major procedural modeling techniques for easy editing and a smooth workflow. Working with simple and compound 2D shapes, using the Modifier Stack, editing at the sub-object level, and cloning are important skills when working with 3ds Max. In addition, efficiently using the Align tools in conjunction with the reference coordinate systems is perhaps one of the most productive methods you'll employ on a daily basis.

In the next chapter, you'll work with an underwater scene to learn to create a rope with a modeling technique called lofting, and you'll learn to apply modifiers to 3D objects to create irregular surfaces for the water and the ocean bottom. You also create lobster claws using a modeling technique called *box modeling*.

CHAPTER 5

3D Modeling

In This Chapter

In the last chapter, you worked with simple and compound 2D shapes and learned the basics of applying modifiers to objects. This chapter introduces you to some methods for creating 3D Primitive objects, to which you will apply some new modifiers, such as Noise, Lattice, and Symmetry. It also introduces you to *lofting* and *box modeling*, two modeling techniques that feature different levels of control and workflow for creating efficient models that are easy to edit.

The exercises in this chapter involve two scenes: an underwater scene with a lobster boat and lobster trap, and a scene containing half a lobster. In the first scene, you will apply modifiers to distort the ocean bottom and the water surface, turn a basic box into a wire mesh trap, and use lofting to create a rope to attach the trap to the boat. In the scene containing the partial lobster, you'll use the powerful Symmetry modifier to transform the lobster into a whole one.

The following are some of the modifiers and techniques you'll practice using in this chapter:

- **Noise modifier**—Applies random position changes to object vertices to make the surface appear rough.

- **Normal modifier**—One of several methods of flipping face normals to make object faces visible or invisible.

- **Wave modifier**—Applies a more regular wave pattern to objects.

- **Lattice modifier**—Uses the visible edges of 3D objects to generate an open mesh frame.

- **Symmetry modifier**—In one easy operation, this modifier lets you mirror an object and weld the two halves into a seamless mesh.

- **Sub-object editing**—By applying modifiers to selection sets at only the sub-object level, you gain more control.

- **Lofting**—A powerful modeling technique that enables extremely flexible editing and efficiency by extruding cross-section shapes along a 2D path. Lofting requires at least two 2D shapes.

- **Box modeling**—Also known as *polygon modeling*, this modeling method lets you create objects by manipulating at the sub-object level to precisely control each individual element of the object.

Key Terms

- **Face normal**—An imaginary vector perpendicular to each face. If a *face normal* points away from the viewer, the face will be invisible; if the face normal points toward the viewer, the face will be visible.

- **Lofting**—A modeling technique that is used to create 3D objects by extruding one or more 2D cross-section shapes along a 2D path. The term is derived from old shipbuilding techniques, in which the patterns for the ribs of a ship were laid out in the upstairs loft of a shipbuilder's shop using metal splines.

- **Hierarchical link**—A link between two objects that passes transformations from the parent object to the child object so that you only have to move or rotate the parent object to have all the children transform in the same manner.

Applying Modifiers to 3D Primitive Objects

In previous chapters, you've applied modifiers to 2D shapes to create 3D objects. In this section, you'll learn how to apply modifiers to 3D primitive objects, which can range from boxes, cylinders, or teapots to more complex extended primitives, such as capsule-shaped objects or oil-tank-shaped objects.

You'll use the Noise, Normal, Wave, Lattice, and Mesh Select modifiers to generate random or controlled distortions that represent an undulating ocean bottom and a wavy ocean surface, and change a closed box surface into an open mesh representing a wire lobster trap.

Applying a Noise Modifier

In the first exercise, you'll use a 3ds Max 8 file that contains several 3D objects: two Plane primitive objects, which represent the ocean bottom and the water surface; a lobster boat created using box modeling; and a Box primitive object, which represents a lobster trap.

You'll apply a Noise modifier to the Plane primitive representing the ocean bottom to randomly disturb the positions of the vertices in this primitive mesh object. The key to making the Noise modifier function properly is to have enough vertices in the object you are trying to modify to have sufficient distortion, but not so many that it impacts performance unnecessarily. You always want to be mindful of creating geometry that is complex enough to obtain the visual quality you require, but not so complex that you're wasting computer resources on detail that won't add to the information you are trying to convey to the client.

Exercise 5.1: Creating an undulating ocean bottom

1. Open the **Underwater01.max** file from the CD-ROM and save it to your project folder with the name *Underwater02.max*. In the Perspective viewport, notice that the boat seems to be floating in midair. In the Front viewport, notice the horizontal edge that runs through the bottom of the boat.

    This is the Plane primitive that represents the ocean surface. It has no thickness and is invisible when viewed from below because its face normals point away from the viewer.

2. In the Perspective viewport, select the ocean bottom object called Seabed01. It, too, is a Plane primitive, but it has face normals pointing up toward the viewer, so they are visible. On the Modify panel, from the Modifier List choose the Noise modifier. In the Parameters rollout, Strength area, enter 10'0" in the Z field.

The seabed distorts somewhat, as you can see in the Front viewport, but it is not an undulating surface (**Figure 5.1**). This is because there are not enough vertices in the Plane primitive to distort it convincingly. Modifiers need sufficient geometry to distort a surface properly. However, excess geometry is inefficient and should be avoided.

You'll have to modify the Plane primitive by adding segments to increase the density of the mesh enough to allow it to distort convincingly.

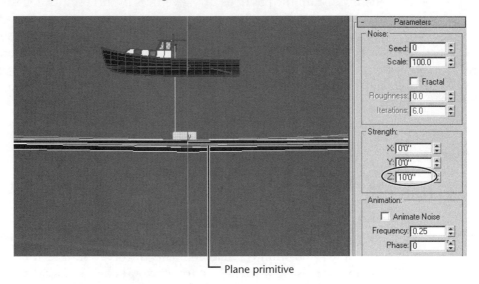

— Plane primitive

FIGURE 5.1 *The plane has too few vertices to undulate convincingly, so you need to increase the number of segments in the Plane primitive.*

3. On the Modify panel, in Stack view, highlight Plane at the bottom of the stack. In the Parameters rollout, enter 40 in both the Length Segs and Width Segs fields (**Figure 5.2**). Highlight the Noise modifier at the top of the Stack view.

    Increasing the number of segments in the Plane primitive also increases the number of faces from 32 to 3200. The seabed clearly shows more distortion, but the surface is still a little rough and faceted. However, it is sufficient for the purposes of this scene and shouldn't excessively tax computer resources.

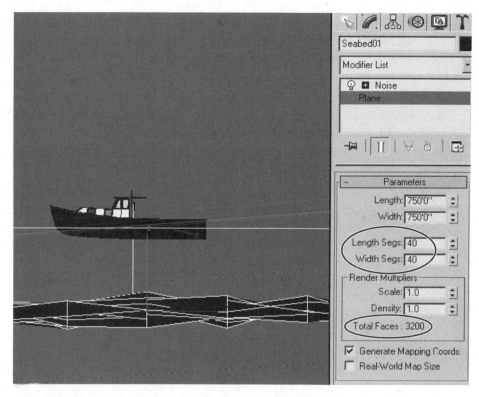

FIGURE 5.2 *Increasing the number of segments in the Plane results in more distortion and an increase in the number of faces from 32 to 3200.*

4. To create a slightly smoother surface, on the Modify panel, in the Parameters rollout, change the Z Strength value to 5'0".

   Lowering the Z Strength reduces the maximum distortion that can be applied to the mesh, resulting in less noticeable faceting because of the number of faces.

5. Save the file; it should already be called Underwater02.max.

In addition to using the Noise modifier to randomly disturb the vertices in a mesh object, you've also learned how to increase the geometry of 3D objects to give modifiers enough information to function correctly. Just remember: do not add more geometry than is necessary for the visual quality you need, or you'll end up with render times that are longer than necessary.

Applying Normal and Wave Modifiers

The Plane primitive that represents the water surface in the scene we're working with is invisible because, in the Perspective viewport, its face normals point away from the viewer.

In the next exercise, you will apply two modifiers to the Plane: a Normal modifier to flip the face normals so that they are pointing out toward the viewer, and a Wave modifier to distort the surface so that it appears to be wavy.

Working with Face Normals

The concept of face normals and their affect on your work can sometimes be a bit frustrating for 3ds Max users. Parts of objects appear to be missing, objects cannot be selected in the viewports, and objects imported from CAD software appear to have holes in the surface. However, learning how to manipulate face normals so that they are visible is an extremely important part of using 3ds Max efficiently. With a little practice, you'll quickly learn how to recognize issues with face normals and correct them.

When modifiers are applied to objects they orient themselves based on what the programmers assume is logical. This default orientation may or may not meet your particular needs, so you must often use sub-object mode to reorient the modifier. You'll do this in the next exercise to make the waves on the water surface go in a particular direction.

tip

It is important to note that face normals can also be used as alignment tools and as a method of controlling lighting and materials, although this is a bit beyond the exercises in this book. You can find more information by searching "face normals" in the 3ds Max Help files online.

Exercise 5.2: Creating a wavy ocean surface

1. Open the **Underwater02.max** file from the CD-ROM or from the last exercise. Save it to your project folder with the name *Underwater03.max*.

2. Right-click in the Perspective viewport to activate it. Because selecting objects with flipped face normals in viewports can be very difficult, use the H key to display the Select Objects dialog, and double-click Water01 in the list to select it.

3. On the Modify panel, from the Modifier List choose Normal.

   The Normal modifier in 3ds Max 8 has the Flip Normals option selected by default, so the face normals are automatically flipped either away from or toward the viewer, depending on which direction they were facing to begin with. In our case, the face normals were pointing away from the viewer, so they will be automatically flipped in the opposite direction.

The water surface becomes visible in the Perspective viewport and hides the upper part of the boat. However, it looks black because of the angle of incidence of the default lighting in the scene. All the light that you see in the viewport is coming from above and does not strike that surface.

4. To make the geometry easier to see in the shaded viewport, right-click on the Perspective Viewport label and choose Edged Faces.

Both the shaded surfaces and wireframe of all objects in the viewport are visible now and it's easier to visualize your mesh, even though the lighting is not ideal (**Figure 5.3**). You'll now increase the number of segments in the Plane that represents the water, so that the Wave modifier has enough geometry to distort the surface convincingly. This is the same process that you used on the ocean bottom in the previous exercise.

You'll have to learn to determine through experience when a mesh has enough density to be visually acceptable. Always start with the lowest density you can get away with for efficiency, and then increase the density until its visually acceptable to you.

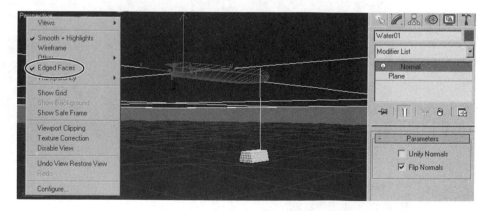

FIGURE 5.3 *The Normal modifier flips face normals to make them visible or invisible to the viewer, and selecting Edged Faces can make geometry clearer in shaded viewports.*

5. On the Modify panel, in Stack view, highlight Plane. In the Parameters rollout, enter 1 in the Length Segs field and 400 in the Width Segs field (**Figure 5.4**). Click the Normal modifier in Stack view to return to the top of the stack.

Because the waves in this scene will run perpendicular to the length of the boat, it is unnecessary to increase the number of segments that are running parallel to the boat. By increasing only the width segments and not the length segments, we avoid having to significantly increase the total number of faces, which in turn reduces unnecessary complexity in the object.

Now we can distort the surface of the water using the Wave modifier.

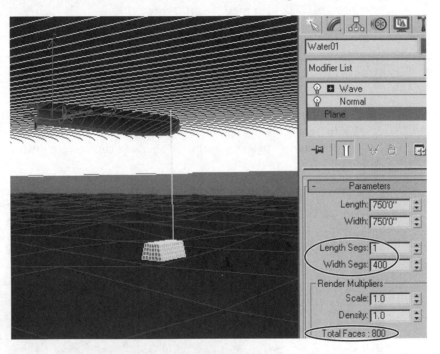

FIGURE 5.4 *By selectively increasing the density of mesh objects, you can strike a balance of visual quality and efficiency.*

6. On the Modify panel, from the Modifier List choose Wave. Enter 0'6" in both the Amplitude 1 and Amplitude 2 fields, and 20'0" in the Wave Length field (**Figure 5.5**).

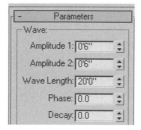

FIGURE 5.5 *Change the parameters of the Wave modifier to distort the mesh.*

Some 3D primitives, such as Plane, have Render Multipliers settings that let you set the scale of the object or the density (the number of faces) at render time. This helps keep the display efficient while you are working in the viewports, but also lets the renderer use a higher density mesh for better visual quality.

However, you cannot see the effect of these scale adjustments in the viewport. So you need to make sure you are judicious with Render Multipliers, because you may set them much higher than you need to for testing. And because you can't see them in the viewport, you may forget to reduce the number before rendering, which can result in significantly increased render times.

You won't immediately see the effect of these changes in the Perspective viewport because the direction of the Wave modifier is running perpendicularly to the segments in the water surface. You need to change the direction of the modifier's gizmo so that wave direction is parallel to the segments and can distort them.

7. Expand Wave in Stack view, and highlight Gizmo. To rotate the gizmo of the Wave modifier, on the main toolbar click the Select and Rotate button. On the Status bar, make sure that Offset Mode Transform Type-in is toggled on and enter 90 in the Z-axis field. Press Enter.

    The wave direction is now parallel to the segments in the water surface, and there is enough geometry to show the effect in this direction (**Figure 5.6**). The waves are now visible on the surface.

8. To exit gizmo mode at the sub-object level, highlight Wave in Stack view.

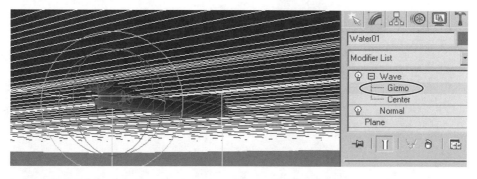

FIGURE 5.6 *You can change the direction of the Wave modifier by rotating the gizmo at the sub-object level.*

9. Save the file; it should already be called Underwater03.max.

Even when you're performing seemingly simple operations, there can be many variables to adjust before you get the expected results. For example, applying modifiers often has no effect at first, usually because either the mesh is too simple or the modifier is not oriented correctly. In this exercise, you had to first flip the face normals and rotate the gizmo of the Wave modifier before you could actually create waves on the surface, even though the numeric parameters for the Wave modifier were correct.

Applying a Lattice Modifier

A Lattice modifier is used to create space frame objects. A *space frame object* in 3ds Max 8 is a 3D object that appears to be made of wire mesh. Examples include simulated expansion joints in a building facade, a greenhouse frame, wire shelving, a chain-link fence, and a wire cage.

When you apply a Lattice modifier to a 3D object to create a space frame object, the modifier uses the visible edges of the object to generate struts, and it uses the vertices to generate joints. You can always enable or disable the struts and joints to simulate different types of space frames.

In the next exercise, you'll use the Lattice modifier to turn a solid Box primitive object into an open cage lobster trap that looks as if it were made of wires. The alternative to using the Lattice modifier would be to build each wire of the cage individually and assemble them into a box-shaped object.

Because the lobster trap will be viewed only from a distance, it's important to optimize the mesh for the least number of faces while still maintaining the look of a cage made of wire.

Exercise 5.3: Creating a wire cage lobster trap

1. Open the **Underwater03.max** file from the CD-ROM or from the previous exercise and save it to your project folder with the name *Underwater04.max*.

2. In the Perspective viewport, select the object called Lobster_trap01. (If the trap is difficult to see, don't forget that you can press the H key to open the Select Objects dialog and select the object by name.)

3. Press Alt + Q to isolate the selected object. To fill all viewports with the selected object, on the lower right corner of the display, click the Zoom Extents All button. Right-click the Perspective viewport label, and make sure that Edged Faces is enabled so that you can see the wireframe and shaded object (**Figure 5.7**).

Next you'll apply the Lattice modifier to the solid box to convert all the visible white edges seen on the box in the viewport to Lattice struts that will look like wires.

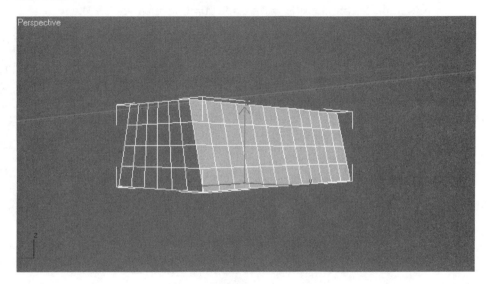

FIGURE 5.7 *Isolating the selection in the viewports and enabling Edged Faces will make it easier to see the effect of the Lattice modifier.*

4. On the Modify panel, from the Modifier List choose Lattice. Because the default lattice sizes are too large, the resulting object looks more like a stack of egg crates than a lobster trap. We need to adjust these settings.

5. In the Parameters rollout, Geometry area, choose the Struts Only from Edges radio button.

This disables the joints created by each vertex—they are not necessary in this case because they are adding extra geometry that will slow rendering, and they are not visible from the viewing distances used in this example.

6. In the Struts area, enter 0.25″ in the Radius field and press Enter. Now all the visible edges of the mesh are 1/4-inch radius wires. To clean up the viewport so you can more easily see the result of the Lattice modifier, right-click the Perspective label and disable Edged Faces (**Figure 5.8**).

Now we need to modify the struts so that the lobster trap looks as if it's made of rounded wire.

Although you entered 0.25″ in the Radius field, 3ds Max 8 will always display the number as a fraction to the nearest eighth of an inch, as specified in the Units Setup dialog.

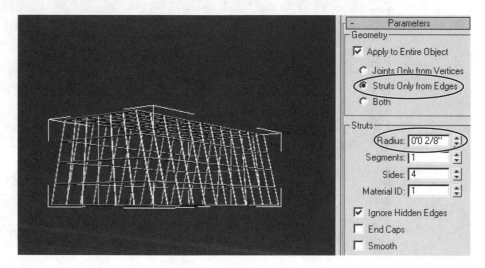

FIGURE 5.8 *Choosing the Struts Only from Edges option ensures that the lattice struts will be applied only to the visible edges of the mesh object, thereby reducing the overall amount of geometry and increasing rendering efficiency. The joints are too small to be visible from the viewing distances in this scene.*

7. In the Front viewport, zoom in closely on the lower right corner of the lobster trap, click the Front viewport label, and disable Edged Faces. In the Parameters rollout, in the Struts area, enter 6 in the Sides field to make the wires appear to be round, rather than square. Select the Smooth option, so that when the wires are rendered they will not appear faceted.

Smoothing is a process that takes place in the viewports and in the rendering to make low density mesh appear much smoother than the actual model, thereby adding to the efficiency of rendering (**Figure 5.9**).

8. Click the big yellow Exit Isolation Mode button to unhide all other objects in the scene.

FIGURE 5.9 *When you adjust the number of sides and smooth the struts, the Lattice modifier can simulate round wire.*

9. Save the file; it should already be called Underwater04.max.

No doubt the Lattice modifier is a powerful tool, but if you apply it at will, you end up creating unnecessarily complex mesh objects with too many faces. Make sure to use joints only when they make sense, and use smoothing options to simulate round struts with a minimum number of sides.

Applying the Mesh Select Modifier

In the last chapter, you learned how to edit 2D splines by modifying vertices, segments, or splines at the sub-object level. Three-dimensional geometry also has sub-object levels, which include the Vertex, Edge, Face, Polygon, and Element.

One way to access sub-object-level editing for 3D objects is to use the Mesh Select modifier. The Mesh Select modifier is a simple and efficient but powerful tool that can dramatically increase your productivity. Using it you can generate sub-object selection sets and then apply modifiers to them. The Mesh Select modifier then passes the modified selection set up the stack to the next modifier, using minimum computer resources.

An alternative to using the Mesh Select modifier is to use the Edit Mesh modifier for each change you want to make. However, because the Edit Mesh modifier has to create a completely new copy of the object in the computer's memory with each change, multiple Edit Mesh modifiers can become very inefficient.

In the next exercise, you'll use the Mesh Select modifier to bend a cylinder so that it hooks at the top third of the cylinder. The hooked cylinder is a davit that will support the pulley and rope on the boat. The davit isn't that significant an object in our scene—but the workflow you'll use to create it is significant. You're learning how to modify a selection without affecting the rest of the 3D object. Once you understand how to do this, you can practice applying the same methods to modeling problems that arise in your everyday projects.

Exercise 5.4: Creating a davit to support a pulley and rope

1. Open the **Underwater04.max** file from the CD-ROM or from the previous exercise. Save it to your project folder with the name *Underwater05.max*.

2. In the Left viewport, select the vertical cylinder on the left side of the boat called Davit01, or press the H key to select it from the list. Press Alt + Q to isolate Davit01, and use the Zoom Extents All button on the main toolbar to fill all viewports with the cylinder.

3. On the Modify panel, from the Modifier List, choose Bend. In the Parameters rollout, in the Bend area, enter 180.0 in the Angle field and -90.0 in the Direction field.

    The cylinder bends from its pivot point into a large arc with a 180-degree angle (**Figure 5.10**). To get the cylinder to bend only at the top, you can use a Mesh Select modifier, located below the Bend modifier. We'll do that next.

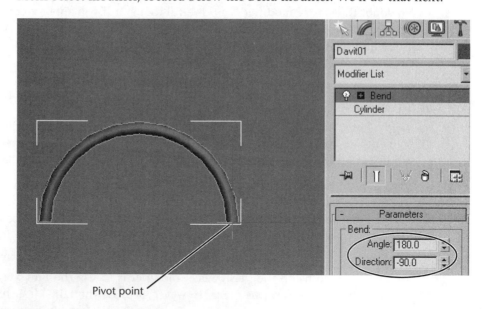

Pivot point

FIGURE 5.10 *The Bend modifier uses the object's pivot point as the bend center.*

4. On the Modify panel, in Stack view, highlight Cylinder at the bottom of the stack. In the Modifier List, choose Mesh Select, the first modifier in the list.

    The Mesh Select modifier is always applied above the currently selected level in the stack. Because Cylinder is selected, it is placed between Cylinder and the Bend modifier (**Figure 5.11**). The Bend modifier will now operate on whatever sub-object-level selection is passed up to it, so only the selection set is bent and not the whole cylinder.

FIGURE 5.11 *You can put new modifiers above any other modifier in the stack by highlighting a modifier in the stack before going to the Modifier List.*

Now you need to create the sub-object selection set that will be passed to the Bend Modifier.

5. Expand the Mesh Select modifier in the stack and highlight the Vertex sub-object level. On the main toolbar, click the Select button and drag a selection window around the upper half of the cylinder.

    The selected vertices turn red (**Figure 5.12**). Make sure you *do not* exit sub-object mode. By not exiting sub-object mode in the Mesh Select modifier, you cause only the selected vertices to be passed up the modifier stack.

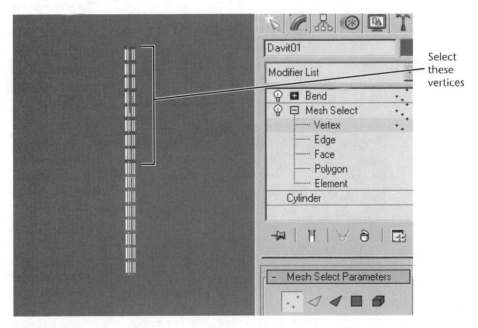

FIGURE 5.12 *The Mesh Select modifier lets you select vertices to pass up the stack to the bend modifier just above it.*

6. On the Modify panel, in Stack view, highlight the Bend modifier at the top of the stack.

The cylinder becomes a mess, but you'll soon fix that (**Figure 5.13**). The Bend modifier is now acting on the selected vertices and still bending from the original pivot point.

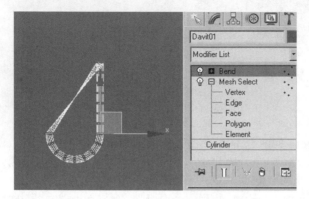

FIGURE 5.13 *If you do not exit sub-object mode in the Mesh Select modifier, only the selected vertices will be passed up the modifier stack.*

7. In Stack view, expand the Bend modifier and highlight Center. On the main toolbar, click the Select and Move button, and, in the Left viewport, move the Center tick up in the Y-axis to the beginning of the selected vertices (**Figure 5.14**). In Stack view, highlight Bend at the top of the stack to exit the Center sub-object-level mode.

tip

Stack view displays the sub-object-level selection as symbols on the right side of the stack. In our case, small dots represent vertices, indicating that this is the sub-object selection being passed up the stack.

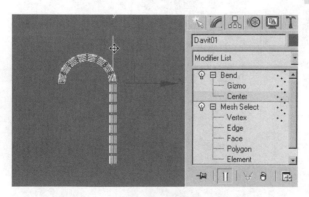

FIGURE 5.14 *Many objects in 3ds Max 8 have sub-object levels that let you fine-tune the object's parameters.*

8. To apply another Mesh Select modifier without accessing the sub-object level, from the Modifier List, choose Mesh Select.

This effectively exits sub-object level editing, giving control back to the whole object. It also simplifies the display in the viewports.

9. Click the big yellow Exit Isolation Mode button to unhide all other objects in the scene.

    The davit now appears to be supporting the pulley (**Figure 5.15**).

FIGURE 5.15 *By applying modifiers to sub-object selection sets, you gain much more control of your modeling.*

10. Save the file; it should already be called Underwater05.max.

You now know how to apply modifiers at intermediate points in an existing stack.

It's important to understand that modifiers do not necessarily have to be applied to the whole 3D object. They become much more versatile when you know how to efficiently select at a sub-object level so that the modifier only operates on that selection set.

Using Lofting to Create 3D Objects

In this section, you will gain more experience transforming 2D objects into 3D objects using lofting. Lofting in 3ds Max 8 requires a minimum of two 2D shapes: a path that will determine the length and direction of extrusion, and a shape, which will determine the cross-section of the 3D object. Chapter 2 discussed the process involved in lofting 2D shapes into 3D objects in some detail; you may want to review that section of Chapter 2 before embarking on the exercises in this section.

There is always more than one way in 3ds Max 8 to create an object, and it's up to you, the 3D artist, to choose the method that will provide the most efficiency and flexibility as you create and edit your scene. This ability to think ahead and predict potential changes and production issues is what will help make your 3D visualization career rewarding and successful.

For example, say you wanted to turn a 2D shape into a 3D object representing a rope. The easiest method would be to set the necessary parameters for the diameter of the rope on the Modify panel, in the Rendering rollout. However, if there's lots of rope in the scene, this method may not be very efficient because it's somewhat difficult with renderable splines to control the number of faces.

Lofting, on the other hand, has path steps and shape steps that let you control the density of the mesh around its girth and along its length to optimize the object and change those settings if necessary

Lofting is a modeling technique that lets a material pattern follow the curvature of the lofted object while controlling the number of length-and-width repeats of the pattern, and then automatically updates the pattern to follow the object when the curvature is changed. So if you wanted to create a rope, you could apply a material that represents the twisted strand pattern of typical rope so that it would always look realistic, no matter how you bent the rope.

The next exercise uses the same scene we've been working with in previous exercises. You'll use lofting to create—you guessed it—a rope that pulls the lobster trap into the boat. This is a very simple example of lofting, one in which you will learn important lessons about planning ahead.

Exercise 5.5: Creating a 3D mesh object representing a rope

1. Reset 3ds Max 8 and open the **Underwater05.max** file from the CD-ROM or from the last exercise and save it to your project folder with the name *Underwater06.max*.

2. In the Left viewport, select the shape called Trap_line01 that runs from the boat to the lobster trap. It is simply a hook-shaped line that will be the center-line of your rope. Press Alt + Q to isolate the selection (**Figure 5.16**). Right-click in the Left viewport to activate it, and press Alt + W to maximize it.

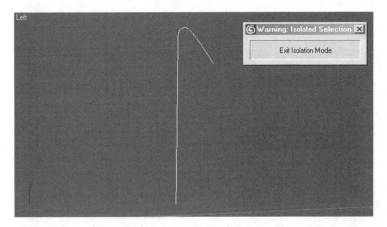

FIGURE 5.16 *Select the object you'll use as the loft path.*

3. On the Create panel, Shapes category, Object Type rollout, click Circle and drag a circle of any size in the viewport. On the Modify panel, change the name of the circle to *rope_shape01* and, in the Parameters rollout, enter 0'2" in the Radius field. Press Enter (**Figure 5.17**).

note

In the real world, a rope with a radius of 2 inches would be large enough to tow a cruise ship. Sometimes you must exaggerate objects to make them visible from distances. 3ds Max 8 allows you to edit objects at any time, so you could have the rope appear smaller as the viewer comes closer.

FIGURE 5.17 *Create a circle that will become the cross-section of the rope object in the scene.*

4. In the Left viewport, select Trap_line01 again. On the Create panel, in the Geometry category, click Standard Primitives and choose Compound Objects from the drop-down list (**Figure 5.18**). In the Object Type rollout, click the Loft button.

FIGURE 5.18 *You have to first go into the Compound Objects group to find the loft tool.*

5. In the Creation Method rollout, click the Get Shape button (**Figure 5.19**), and pick the circle in the Left viewport.

FIGURE 5.19 *Use the Get Shape button to select the circle as a cross-section for the rope.*

Notice the Instance radio button is selected by default. As a result, the original circle did not jump to the loft path; an instance clone was placed there instead. The instance clone lets you change the radius of the original circle to affect the loft object—a powerful function in lofting.

6. Press the 7 key to toggle the face count of the selected object in the upper left of the active viewport.

Notice the newly lofted object has 1196 faces, which is far more than necessary to create a convincing-looking rope (**Figure 5.20**).

FIGURE 5.20 *Modeling efficiency is paramount in 3ds Max 8. The face count of the selected object can be monitored in the viewports.*

7. On the Modify panel, rename the lofted object *Rope01*. In the Skin Parameters rollout, in the Options area, set Shape Steps to 3 and Path Steps to 0. This reduces the face count to 156 but doesn't leave any of the detail around the bend of the path. Increase the Path Steps to 2, and the lofted object will look acceptable and still have only 412 faces (**Figure 5.21**).

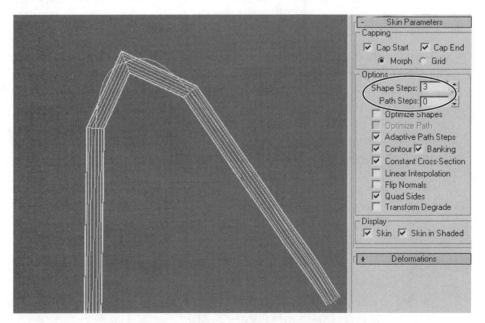

FIGURE 5.21 *Adjust the loft parameters for an efficient and acceptable looking mesh.*

8. Press Alt + W to minimize the active viewport, and click the big yellow Exit Isolation Mode button to unhide all other objects in the scene. Click the Zoom Extents All Selected button (it's a flyout under the Zoom Extents All button accessed by clicking and holding on the button) to fill all viewports with the rope.

9. Save the file. It should already be called Underwater06.max.

Lofted objects have more control over the density of the faces in the mesh than most other forms of modeling. This makes it a reasonable choice for 3D objects that will vary in detail, depending on the viewing distance in the scene.

Controlling Lofted Objects Using the Linked XForm Modifier

In the next exercise, we'll work with the same scene we've been using. You'll attach the end of the rope you just created to the lobster trap so that when the lobster trap is moved, the rope follows. You'll use the Linked XForm modifier to attach the end vertex of the rope to the trap.

The Linked XForm modifier is applied to sub-object-level selections and then linked to other objects to allow the object(s) to control the transformation of the sub-object selection. Using this modifier provides an opportunity to learn more about *hierarchical linking*, the parent-child relationship that gives you more control in transforming objects. Wherever the parent goes, which in our case is the lobster trap, the child, or the end vertex of the rope, follows.

Using hierarchical linking via the Linked XForm modifier is a very useful method of controlling lofted objects. For example, you can use it to simulate cables, belts, and hoses in all sorts of animated mechanical systems. You'll learn more about hierarchical linking in Chapter 16.

Exercise 5.6: Attaching the rope to the lobster trap

1. Open the **Underwater06.max** file from the CD-ROM or from the previous exercise. Save it to your project folder with the name *Underwater07.max*.

2. In the Front viewport, zoom in closely to the end of the rope at the lobster trap. Select the rope's loft path called Trap_line01.

This path determines the length and direction of the rope, not of the loft object itself.

3. On the Modify panel, in Stack view, highlight Vertex and select the vertex at the end of the rope (**Figure 5.22**).

You cannot use hierarchical linking to directly link the vertex to the lobster trap, because in general only 3-D objects can be linked to other 3-D objects. The Linked XForm modifier will help us get around that limitation.

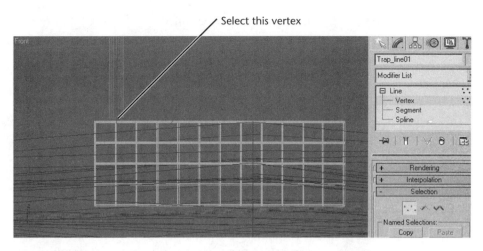

FIGURE 5.22 *The end vertex of the loft path controls the length and endpoint of the rope.*

4. On the Modifier panel, in the Modifier List, choose Linked XForm. In the Parameters rollout, click the Pick Control Object button, and select the lobster trap in the Front viewport. Make sure that Lobster_trap01 is displayed in the Control Object area of the Parameters rollout (**Figure 5.23**). You don't want to accidentally link the vertex to the ocean bottom.

The Linked XForm modifier will pass transformation information from the lobster trap (parent) to the end vertex (child) of the rope.

5. In the Modifier List, choose the Spline Select modifier. In Stack view, select Spline Select at the top of the stack to make sure you exit sub-object mode.

Spline Select is grayed out, indicating that control has been returned to the shape level so that you don't accidentally transform on the sub-object level.

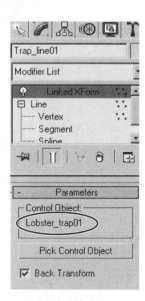

FIGURE 5.23 *You must designate the lobster trap in the scene as the control object for the modifier.*

6. Save the file. It should already be called Underwater07.max.

7. In the Front viewport, select the lobster trap, and on the main toolbar, click the Select and Move button. Move the lobster trap around to verify that the rope stays attached correctly. Right-click to cancel the move operation before releasing the left mouse button, or click the Undo button on the main toolbar to cancel the operation.

note

When you exit sub-object mode while the Spline Select modifier is highlighted, you may still see the vertex icon (three dots) indicating that you are in sub-object mode. This is a display issue. As long as the modifier name is grayed out, you have exited sub-object mode safely.

Hierarchical linking via the Linked XForm modifier is an easy but powerful method that works particularly well for controlling lofted objects. The control object passes its transformations through the Linked XForm modifier to the sub-object selection on the loft path. You might use it for any number of mechanical movements, such as attaching a fan belt to a tension-adjustment pulley or attaching the end of a hydraulic hose to a moving piston. Learn this concept, use your imagination, and enjoy the power of 3ds Max 8.

Box Modeling

Box modeling, sometimes known as polygon modeling, is about as far from lofting as you can get in 3ds Max 8. You generally start with a simple box, although any primitive or complex object could be a starting point. You then convert the object to an Editable Poly or apply an Edit Poly modifier to gain access to a completely new set of sub-object-level editing tools. Finally, you subdivide and transform at the sub-object level until you have created your 3D object.

Box modeling is similar to working with clay in the real world, where you push, pull, and stretch until you have what you want. You have explicit control over where each vertex, edge, and polygon is located, so the method lends itself to creating low-polygon models that are especially important in the computer-game industry.

note

Polygon objects are different from mesh objects in 3ds Max 8 in that they contain few or no triangles. They were originally developed for the computer-game industry to function within the game engine when exported but have grown into a tool set and workflow from which everyone can benefit.

The downside of box modeling is that it is a very linear process. As your model progresses, it is very difficult to drop back in history and make any significant changes. If you mess up a model, you often have to start all over again.

In this section, you'll use box modeling to create the claw of a lobster for your underwater scene and learn about an option that lets you smooth the rough edges. Similar to sculpturing with clay, box modeling is seldom an accurate method of modeling, but it is a process of working until the object looks the way you want.

In the first exercise, you'll open a file containing a stylized lobster—or, more accurately, one half of a stylized lobster—and by converting it to an Editable Poly, you will manipulate the box representing the claw into something that looks more like a stylized claw.

In the second exercise, you'll use a Symmetry modifier to turn the half-lobster into a whole one.

Exercise 5.7: Creating a stylized lobster

1. Open the **Lobster01.max** file from the CD-ROM. Save it to your project folder with the name *Lobster02.max*.

2. In the Perspective viewport, select the object called Claw02, a segmented box on the far right. Use the Zoom Extents All Selected navigation tool to fill all viewports with the box. Right-click the Perspective Viewport label and choose Edged Faces from the drop-down list. Working with Edged Faces mode in a shaded viewport lets you more easily select the sub-object level for editing. Press Alt + Q to isolate the selection.

    You now need to change the shape of the claw so that it's not a box but a more organic form.

3. On the Modify panel, in Stack view, expand Editable Poly and highlight the Vertex sub-object mode. In the Top viewport, drag a selection window around the visible vertices at the top of the box to select all of the 16 vertices that make up the end of the box. On the main toolbar, click the Select and Scale button. Click and hold the Use Pivot Point Center button and then click the Use Selection Center flyout button. In the Top viewport, click and drag on the Scale transform X-axis and scale the vertices together toward a common center (see **Figure 5.24** on the next page). Vertex selection sets must be scaled with the Use Selection Center button to function properly.

    You've now started to shape the box by tapering it into a form more suited to a stylized lobster.

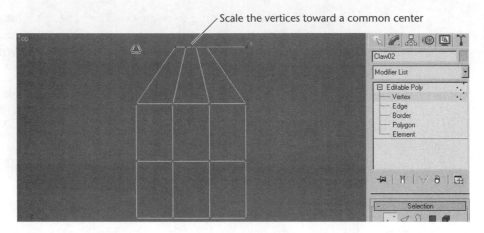

FIGURE 5.24 *Scale the vertices at the end to begin to taper the box.*

4. Continue scaling sets of vertices in the orthographic viewports until the box looks similar to that shown in **Figure 5.25**. Work slowly and carefully at first until you get a feel for selecting the correct vertices and scaling them in the direction you want.

    It's often useful to work in one viewport and then move to the next to better visualize the edits. This modeling technique requires patience and practice until you get used to it.

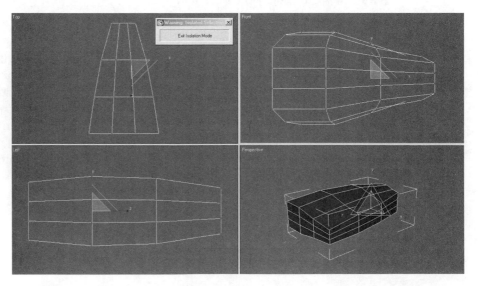

FIGURE 5.25 *Using only the Scale tool at the vertex sub-object level, mold the box into the beginnings of a lobster claw.*

5. In the Perspective viewport, hold down the
    Alt button and use the middle mouse wheel to
    arc rotate around to the other side of the box.
    Click the Select Object button on the main
    toolbar. On the Modify panel, in Stack view,
    highlight the Polygon sub-object mode, and, in
    the Perspective viewport, use the Control key to
    select the three polygons (**Figure 5.26**).

When you're experimenting
with box modeling, it is wise
to use the Edit, Hold, and
Fetch tools to bookmark your
modeling progress so that
you can return to a particular
point when you need to.

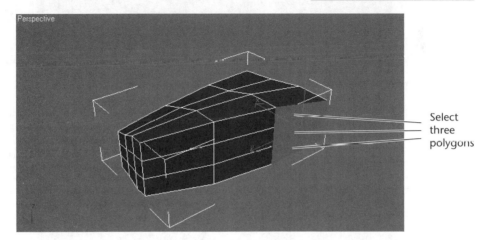

Select
three
polygons

FIGURE 5.26 *The polygons will turn red when selected, as they do when editing mesh objects.*

6. On the Modify panel, in the Edit Polygons rollout, click the Settings but-
    ton to the right of the Bevel button. In the Bevel Polygons dialog, enter
    1/2" in the Height field, -1/8" in the Outline Amount field, and press Enter
    (see **Figure 5.27** on the next page). Editable Poly lets you make changes to
    parameters and see the result before committing to the edit. Click the Apply
    button to bevel the currently selected faces with the same settings. Click OK
    to finalize the bevel operation.

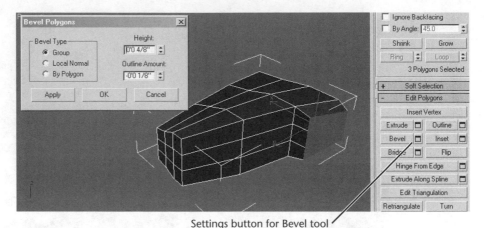

Settings button for Bevel tool

FIGURE 5.27 *The Edit Polygons tools let you access a Settings dialog to preview the changes before committing to them.*

7. In the Perspective viewport, select the three smaller polygons on the newly beveled portion and click the Settings button for Extrude. In the Extrude Polygons dialog, enter 1" in the Extrusion Height field to extrude the polygons straight out from their current position (**Figure 5.28**). Click OK.

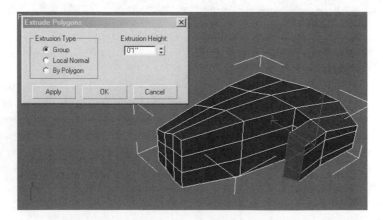

FIGURE 5.28 *The Extrude tool also has a Settings dialog.*

8. Use the Bevel Polygons dialog, accessed by clicking the Settings button, to assign a height of 2" and an outline amount of -1/8". Click OK. Click the Select and Move button on the main toolbar, and, in the Top viewport, move the polygon slightly to the right to form a "thumb" for the lobster's smaller claw (**Figure 5.29**).

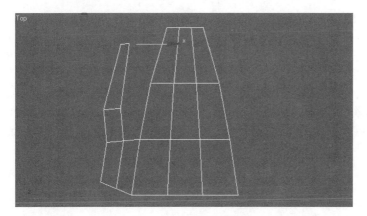

FIGURE 5.29 *A lobster claw has a smaller part that acts as a thumb.*

9. Highlight Editable Poly in Stack view to exit the sub-object-level mode. In the Subdivision Surface rollout, check the Use NURMS Subdivision box (**Figure 5.30**). Uncheck the Isoline Display box to see all the new geometry in the Editable Poly.

    The NURMS Subdivision adds geometry to round all edges and make a much more organic object from your box model.

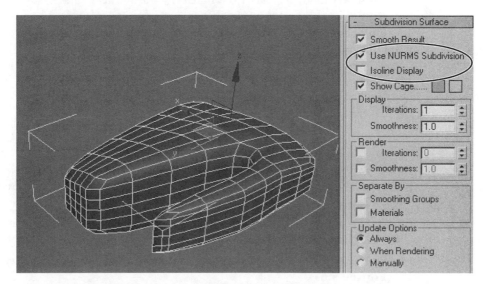

FIGURE 5.30 *Editable Poly objects can be made into more organic forms using the NURMS Subdivision option.*

10. Click the big yellow Exit Isolation Mode button to unhide all other objects in the scene. Click the Zoom Extents All navigation button to fill the viewports with all objects in the scene. Save the file; it should already be called Lobster02.max.

In this exercise, you started with a segmented box, pushed and pulled a few vertices and polygons, and then switched on the subdivision option. The result is a stylized representation of a lobster claw that can easily be edited at any time by returning to sub-object-level mode and making the appropriate adjustments.

Applying the Symmetry Modifier

Many objects are symmetrical enough that you can save a lot of time by creating only half of the object and then mirroring it to create a whole. However, if you simply create a mirror image manually and then try to attach the two halves together, you'll run into problems trying to close the seams where the two halves meet.

Instead, you'll want to use a special modifier called the Symmetry modifier. It automates most of the steps involved in mirroring an image for you: it creates a mirror image of your geometry, trims the excess overlapping portion, and welds the seam for a contiguous surface.

The Symmetry modifier is useful for creating mechanical objects, such as boats, cars, and airplanes, or anything else that is symmetrical. A word of caution, however: the Symmetry modifier doesn't work very well for creating human faces. In the real world, human faces are not the least bit symmetrical, so they look strange when they are symmetrical.

In this last exercise, you'll use the Symmetry modifier to create a whole lobster from a half in our scene.

Exercise 5.8: Creating a whole lobster from a half

1. Open the Lobster02.max file from the CD-ROM or from the last exercise. Save it to your project folder with the name *Lobster03.max*.

2. On the main toolbar, click the Select Object button. In the Top viewport, drag a selection window around all objects in the viewport.

Look at the top of the Modify panel to verify that 11 objects are selected (**Figure 5.31**).

FIGURE 5.31 *When you select multiple objects in the scene, you can see how many objects are selected at the top of the Modify panel or in the status bar at the bottom of the display.*

3. On the Modify panel, in the Modifier List, click the Symmetry modifier. Most of the lobster will disappear in the Top viewport, and you will see only the claws and part of the tail, along with an orange gizmo with two arrows. This represents the mirror axis (**Figure 5.32**).

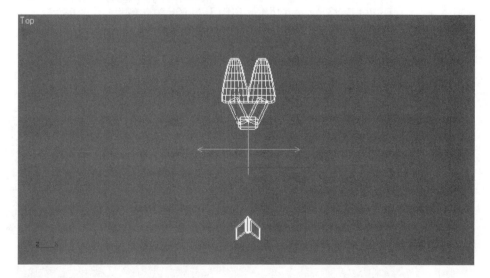

FIGURE 5.32 *The Symmetry modifier seems to have ruined your lobster.*

In the next step, you'll use the Symmetry modifier to adjust the position of the part of the lobster you created.

4. On the Modify panel, in Stack view, expand the Symmetry modifier by click-ing the plus (+) button to the left of the modifier name, and highlight the Mirror sub-object level. In the Top viewport, use the Select and Move tool to click and drag the yellow mirror axis gizmo until the lobster's nose comes to a point (**Figure 5.33**).

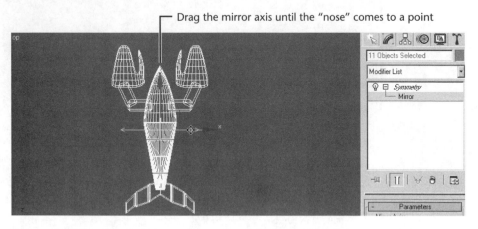

Drag the mirror axis until the "nose" comes to a point

FIGURE 5.33 *Moving the mirror axis too far to the left will result in a gap at the lobster's nose.*

5. In Stack view, highlight Symmetry to exit the sub-object-level mode. Notice that Symmetry in Stack view is italicized to indicate that it is an Instance modifier on a number of selected objects.

6. Save the file. It should already be called Lobster03.max.

Creating a lobster in this manner is much easier than creating both halves. In addition, if you modify the original objects at this point and reapply the Symmetry modifier, you will have a completely new lobster.

tip

To edit the different parts of the lobster, you must remove the Symmetry modifier. Another way to accomplish this would be to select all the objects in the lobster, convert them to a single Editable Poly, apply the Symmetry modifier to the new object, and then navi-gate up and down in Stack view to do your editing.

Summary

This chapter introduced many of the fundamental concepts and work methods for quickly creating complex models while retaining the ability to edit them at many levels. This is the essence of 3ds Max 8. By starting with simple 2D shapes and using modifiers and modeling techniques such as lofting to create complex 3D objects, you can efficiently control the density of your mesh objects and move up and down the modifier stack to make changes at many levels without affecting levels above or below.

In essence, almost everything in 3ds Max 8 can be modified, including mesh objects, polygon objects, shapes, and even modifiers at the sub-object level.

I encourage you to look around the room, find simple objects, and try to re-create them with the techniques you have learned in this chapter.

CHAPTER 6

Cameras

In This Chapter

Creating cameras and adjusting their parameters is simple in 3ds Max 8. However, placing and moving cameras effectively is foreign to almost anyone who isn't formally trained as a photographer. For most 3D animators, the placement and movement of cameras ends up looking more like hit-and-miss experimentation.

In this chapter, you'll learn some of the common techniques of camera placement and movement used by the film industry, which can be applied to your own scenes.

You'll also learn about some of the following topics:

- **Scene composition**—An important element in making the client comfortable with your presentation. You'll learn how to adjust the camera positions so that objects in the scene are composed correctly according to traditional art rules.

- **Camera focal length and field of view**—Two of the technical parameters of cameras that help adjust the camera to focus the viewer's attention on important subjects.

- **Camera angle**—Another important composition tool. You'll learn about affecting the viewer's emotions by pointing the camera up or down.

- **Camera movement**—Using camera movement during animations can help calm or agitate the viewer. You'll learn about techniques to move cameras for maximum impact on the viewer.

Key Terms

- **Focal length**—As it relates to the traditional camera, *focal length* describes the distance from the lens to the film plane, measured in millimeters. However, with cameras in 3ds Max, the term is used differently. It describes whether a wide-angle or telephoto lens has been used to control perspective and only simulates the effect of focal-length adjustments in a real camera.

- **Field of view**—The horizontal width of a camera's view, measured in degrees.

- **Target camera**—Target cameras have two components: the camera, which always points at a target, and the target.

- **Rule of thirds**—An important rule of scene composition, whereby the view is divided horizontally and vertically in thirds.

Camera Basics

Because of the years invested in watching film and television, most people are at least somewhat familiar with camera placement and movement. However, few have actually become students of camera work and spent time analyzing the effects of perspective and movement. If you intend to control the viewer's perception of your scenes, you must make sure you have a thorough understanding of these topics. For example, slight changes in cameras can create a pleasing or disturbing emotional response in the viewer, so you don't want to accidentally mix such disparate emotions as these.

Cameras in 3ds Max 8 are designed to represent a viewpoint similar to that of a typical 35 mm film camera in the real world. It's important to know and remember that 3ds Max 8 cameras represent single-lens cameras that provide no peripheral vision. While most people are aware of the fact that there is no peripheral vision in the real world of film and photography, it's often forgotten when employing cameras in 3ds Max 8. As a result, it's not unusual to see in some projects wild camera positions and camera movement that create tension and make many viewers uncomfortable.

Camera Types

3ds Max 8 features two types of cameras: *target* and *free*. Target cameras have two components: the camera and a target, which are connected to each other to create a single entity. The camera is always pointed toward the target, which is placed some distance away.

In general, target cameras are employed as still cameras or animated cameras that focus on a fixed point in the scene.

Target cameras are analogous to big studio cameras used in film and television that are mounted on heavy tripods or stands and have limited range of movement. Unless you're very comfortable with the coordinate systems and work planes of 3ds Max 8, it's best to create target cameras in the Top viewport of the scene. The Top viewport provides a "ground plane" in which to work comfortably on most scenes. You can adjust the position of the target camera in the other viewports.

You can have as many cameras in the scene as you need, but you can render only one camera at a time. Because each viewport in the graphic display can be set to any camera, it's possible to see up to four camera viewports at any one time.

Scene Composition

You should not be casual about composing your scene in 3ds Max: camera placement and adjustment have a direct impact on the viewer. Almost all of what the viewer feels and perceives is a direct result of how well the camera conveys that information to the viewer's psyche. Moving a camera a few inches in the scene can make or break the visual impact you intend.

Fortunately, there are a few rules you can rely on when making decisions about where to place your cameras and how to adjust them. In all art media, from painting to film, rules for influencing the viewer's perception have developed over the centuries. You must apply these rules of composition to help elicit the emotional response you intend from your viewers, whether it's a pleasing and calming feeling or a tension-filled, excitable state of mind.

Successfully composing a scene involves three basic considerations: the camera field of view, the camera angle, and the positions of objects in the scene.

Camera Field of View

In the first exercise, you'll learn how to set the field of view for a scene. The field of view is the horizontal angle that determines how much of the scene is visible through the camera. A wide-angle view, in which viewers can see much of the surroundings, tends to have a comforting effect; whereas a tightly focused, narrow field of view raises the level of tension because viewers may feel closed in.

Cameras in 3ds Max 8 have a field-of-view setting measured in horizontal degrees; you can also adjust the focal length of the camera lens, as if it were a 35mm film camera.

Exercise 6.1: Setting the field of view

1.   Open the **Camera01.max** file on the CD-ROM and save it to your project
     folder with the name *Camera02.max*.

     This file represents an island with a small fishing enclave, as seen from high
     above in the Perspective viewport (**Figure 6.1**). The scene is very calm and
     peaceful; in fact, it's so calm and peaceful that it's almost boring.

     This calmness arises because the horizon is placed too predictably in the center
     of the scene, and because the view is from above, so the viewer has a full command
     of the scene, making it seem unlikely that something might unexpectedly
     come into view from the sidelines.

     In the next few steps, you'll adjust the camera so that there's a better chance
     the viewer might anticipate some, as yet unknown, event.

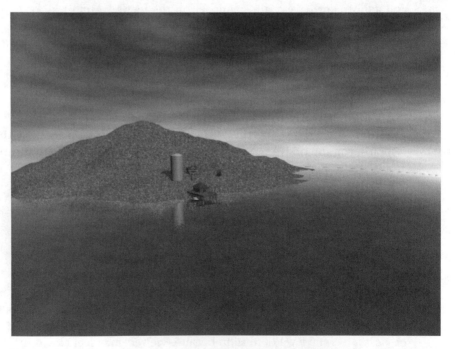

FIGURE 6.1 *This scene as viewed from above, with the objects centered, is almost too
peaceful and quiet.*

2. Create a Target camera from the Perspective view. You can do this from the Create panel, but when you're using the Perspective viewport, there's an easier way. Make sure the Perspective viewport is active and press Ctrl + C.

Notice that the viewport label has changed from Perspective to Camera01, and the eight navigation buttons at the lower right of the display have changed to represent camera controls (**Figure 6.2**). Also notice in the Orthographic viewport a camera icon with a light blue pyramid. This represents the current field of view.

FIGURE 6.2 *A camera viewport has its own navigation buttons.*

note

This chapter's Max Files folder on the CD-ROM includes a bitmap image. 3ds Max always looks for any necessary external files in the same folder as the main Max scene file. If you open a scene file from a location different from the original chapter folder, you may encounter a Missing External Files dialog. If you do, click Browse, and in the Configure External File Paths dialog, click Add. Use the Choose New External Files Path dialog to browse to the location of the CD versions of the Max scene files for this chapter, then click Use Path, and click OK. Click Continue to close the Missing External Files dialog.

3. In the Camera01 viewport, use the Orbit Camera and Truck Camera navigation buttons to position the camera and its target so that they are centered horizontally midway in the scene (**Figure 6.3**). The Orbit Camera control lets you maneuver the camera around its target, while the Truck Camera control lets you move both the camera and the target at the same time. You can double-check the positions of the camera and target in the other viewports (**Figure 6.4**).

Keeping the camera and its target horizontal will help avoid distortion, in the form of convergence or divergence of vertical lines, that can throw the viewer off-balance. However, a horizontal camera is also what's responsible for the calm and peaceful mood of the scene.

Make sure that as you're navigating the camera you stay within the confines of the sky-dome hemisphere so that its backside doesn't accidentally come into the camera's view.

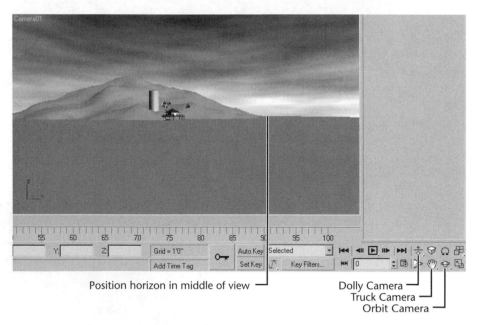

FIGURE 6.3 *Navigate the camera and target into a new position.*

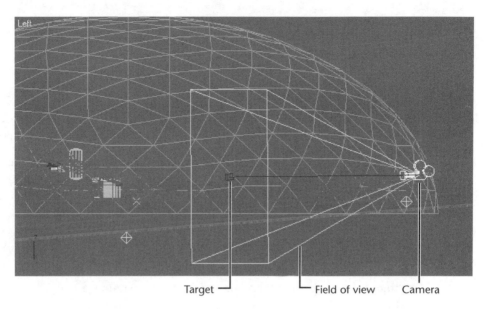

FIGURE 6.4 *The camera, its target, and the field-of-view pyramid are visible in the wireframe viewports, which makes positioning easier.*

4. Make sure that Camera01 is selected. On the Modify panel, Parameters rollout, Stock Lenses area, set Lens to 50 mm.

    This narrows the field of view to roughly 40 degrees, which more closely represents normal human perception (**Figure 6.5**). However, the scene is just as boring as it was before, if not more so, because the horizon is still centered in the scene. Through a series of adjustments, you are slowly navigating the camera into a position that will change the mood of the scene.

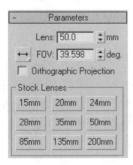

FIGURE 6.5 *You can change a camera's field of view by adjusting the focal length to be the equivalent of a typical film camera's.*

5. Save the file. It should already be called Camera02.max.

As you progress through the steps of camera navigation and parameter adjustment, we'll improve on the scene.

Camera Angle

Just as the camera field of view in the scene influences viewers' perceptions, the camera angle, or the upward or downward angle of view, can also greatly affect perceptions.

For example, Figure 6.1 reflects a bird's-eye view of the scene, which has the effect of making the objects in it seem insignificant because the viewer is positioned above, looking down on them. A bird's-eye view indicates a viewer's power and control over the scene. In contrast, Figure 6.3 reflects a stable and calm scene with the horizon splitting the view vertically, and the objects centered laterally. However, because of the overwhelming balance and calmness, viewers would still tend to lose interest.

In the next exercise, you'll adjust both the field of view and the camera angle to try to inject more excitement and drama into the final image.

Exercise 6.2: Adjusting the camera angle

1. Open the **Camera02.max** file from the CD-ROM or from the last exercise. Save it to your project folder with the name *Camera03.max*.

2. Make sure the Camera01 viewport is active. Then press the H key and, in the Select Objects dialog that appears, select Camera01 by double-clicking it.

3. Click the Dolly Camera button. Drag the mouse upward in the Camera01 viewport to dolly the camera in toward the buildings. At some point, you will notice the camera suddenly flips as it moves beyond its target.

While it's true that dollying the camera to move it directly toward or away from its target is an effective way to move in closer to the subjects in your scene, this step illustrates a common problem that often arises while performing this technique. When the distance between the camera and target isn't sufficient enough to accommodate moving the camera as close as you want, the camera will flip and move beyond the target. You'll adjust the camera to target distance in Step 5 so that you have more room to dolly.

note

A target camera moves independently of its target and must always face the target.

4. While still holding down the left mouse button, click the right mouse button to cancel the dolly operation. If you have already released the mouse button, you can click Undo in the main toolbar to get back to the original camera view.

5. On the Modify panel, in the Parameters rollout, enter 1000 in the Target Distance field and press Enter (**Figure 6.6**).

   This moves the camera target to the middle of the scene without affecting either the depth of field or the camera angle, and it will allow you to move the camera farther forward in the scene.

6. Use the Dolly Camera, Orbit Camera, and Truck Camera buttons to move the camera close to the pier, so that it is glancing upward at the roof of the shack on the pier (**Figure 6.7**).

   Because of the angle of the camera, the scene obviously has a more dramatic feel. In the next step, you'll adjust the field of view to see more of the scene and then enable the Show Safe frame to make sure that what you see in the viewport is what you'll get in the rendered image.

caution

Be careful not to move the camera below the water surface. You can verify its position in the orthographic viewports.

FIGURE 6.6 *Changing the target distance on the Modify panel moves the target toward or away from the camera without affecting the view.*

FIGURE 6.7 *Changing the camera angle to face upward gives the objects in the scene more significance to the viewer.*

7. Select Camera01. On the Modify panel, in the Parameters rollout, click the 28mm Stock Lenses button to obtain a moderately wide-angle lens. Use the Dolly camera to move in a little closer. Right-click on the Camera01 viewport label and choose Show Safe Frame from the menu (**Figure 6.8**).

    The viewport changes to match the aspect ratio of the 640 by 480 rendering output resolution. This shows you what the actual camera sees (**Figure 6.9**).

FIGURE 6.8 *Show Safe Frame is used primarily for video output, and it is the only way you can be sure that the viewport shows what the camera will render.*

FIGURE 6.9 *The outermost yellow boundary of Show Safe Frame indicates what the camera will render. The cyan and orange boundaries are for video titling areas, and are not important for this exercise.*

8. Save the file. It should already be called Camera03.max.

Looking up at the scene places the viewer slightly off-balance and sets up a tension that makes the image a bit more exciting. However, having the water's edge horizontal across the center of the scene and the objects clustered in the middle of the scene is still too stable and boring. Time to apply the rule of thirds.

Rule-of-Thirds Composition

The *rule of thirds* is an age-old rule of traditional composition. It should be the first thing you think of when adjusting your camera viewpoint.

When applying the rule of thirds, you divide the scene into nine areas: three vertical and three horizontal. The important objects in your scene should always be positioned at the intersection of the divisions on the left or right, but not in the center. Objects centered in a scene are very static, so the viewer tends to look directly at them without perceiving the rest of the scene. Moving the important object or objects to the intersections of the grid helps viewers to find them quickly but also notice the context in which the objects are being presented.

tip

It's OK to break the rules of art and visualization occasionally if it serves a purpose in your presentation. Just make sure you are aware of the rules and how they are applied before you break them. Otherwise, you risk creating a scene that doesn't have the effect on viewers that you intended.

In addition, because in western cultures we read from left to right, it's a good idea to keep the important objects to the left side of the scene when you want the viewer to notice them immediately. If you place your major objects at the intersections on the right side of the view, you should also include objects or edges that will lead the viewer's gaze from left to right.

In the next exercise, you'll learn how to use the rule-of-thirds to compose the scene according to traditional art conventions to enhance the viewer's experience.

Exercise 6.3: Composing the camera view

1. Open the **Camera03.max** file from the CD-ROM or from the last exercise. Save it to your project folder with the name *Camera04.max*. Imagine the Camera01 viewport being divided equally by two horizontal lines and two vertical lines (**Figure 6.10**).

    The objects in the scene are centered, and all have somewhat equal importance to the viewer. However, we want to convey the notion that the important objects in this scene are the boat and the shack on the pier.

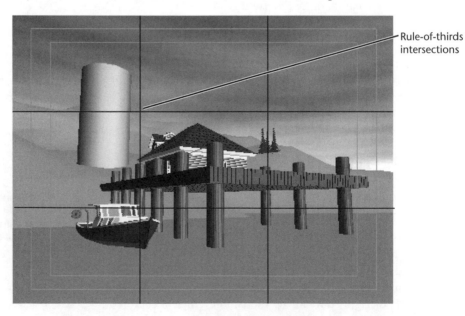

FIGURE 6.10 *The four intersections of the rule-of-thirds lines are the proper locations for the important objects in your scene.*

2. In the Camera01 viewport, use the camera navigation tools to place the bottom center of the shack at the lower left rule-of-thirds intersection (**Figure 6.11**).

The boat and the shack are now more significant in the scene and are the first elements our gaze is drawn to. The left edge of the pier helps bring our attention back to the boat and shack, while the slope of the land and the water's edge keep pulling us to the right. These opposing scene composition elements set up visual tension in the scene, making it more interesting for the viewer.

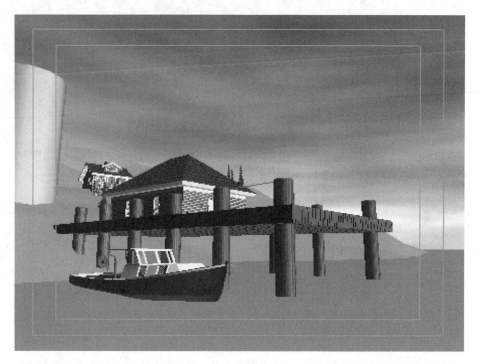

FIGURE 6.11 *While the shack and the boat are now the dominant elements in the scene, other lines keep pulling our gaze to the right to create tension.*

3. Now let's create an even wider view of the scene. Select Camera01, and on the Modify panel, in the Parameters rollout, click the 20mm Stock Lenses button. Use the navigation tools to move the camera more to the left and back slightly, while keeping the shack at the lower left rule-of-thirds intersection (**Figure 6.12**).

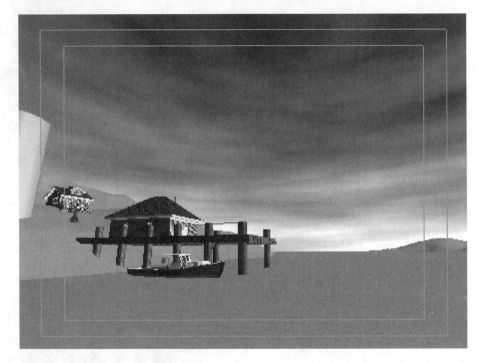

FIGURE 6.12 *Adjust the camera so the water tower is visible at the left and the island is visible at the right.*

Shifting the camera in this way allows the water tower to come into view, and the viewer's eye can now follow the slope of the land down toward the water's edge, out to the sea, and to the land beyond. This view engenders a different perception of the scene because while the island defines the right edge of the scene and brings the viewer's attention back to the center of the composition, it also evokes curiosity as to what might be on the land beyond.

But now we have a different problem. Notice that the distortion caused by the wide-angle lens is making the water tower look as if it's falling onto the house. It has become a distracting element. You'll fix that in the next step.

4. With the camera selected, from the Modifiers drop-down menu, choose Cameras > Camera Correction (**Figure 6.13**).

This modifier converts the camera view to a two-point-perspective view, which corrects the vertical lines in the scene.

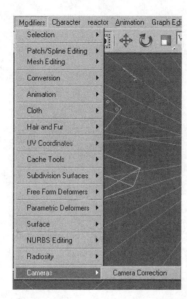

FIGURE 6.13 *The Camera Correction modifier is accessed from the Modifiers drop-down menu.*

5. On the Modify panel, in the 2-Point Perspective Correction and rollout, you can change the perspective angle by adjusting the setting in the Amount or Direction field. Click the Guess button to allow the Camera Correction modifier to perform a best-guess scenario for vertical edges (**Figure 6.14**).

FIGURE 6.14 *The Camera Correction modifier makes a best guess as to what the Amount and Direction settings should be to correct the perspective angle.*

This modifier simulates the corrections available by tilting the lens and film planes in large-format view cameras (**Figure 6.15**).

FIGURE 6.15 *Two-point-perspective camera correction keeps objects at the edge of the view from appearing to fall into the scene when the camera is pointed upward. It also keeps objects from diverging when the camera points downward.*

6. Save the file. It should already be called Camera04.max.

    With proper composition, the scene is much more visually interesting to the viewer. Compare Figure 6.15 with Figure 6.1 in this chapter to see two very different compositions of the same scene.

Summary

Scene composition is a critical part of the storytelling process in visualization. You can control the viewer's perception and comfort level by making relatively minor adjustments in the positions and angles of the cameras in your scene.

You learned how to create a target camera in 3ds Max 8 and make simple adjustments to its field-of-view parameters that determine how much the camera can see horizontally. You then changed the camera angle and position to compose the view using the traditional rule of thirds.

You also learned that a viewer's perception of the scene can be greatly influenced by positioning the main objects at the intersections of the rule-of-thirds lines. This type of composition avoids the boring, static effect that occurs when the objects are dead center and the horizon line runs through the middle of the view.

CHAPTER 7

Basic Lighting

In This Chapter

As I make my rounds training people on 3ds Max, I see far too many offices spending about 90 percent of their time budget on modeling and just 10 percent on lighting and materials. However, it is the lighting and materials, which work in conjunction with each other, that can make or break the success of your final image.

In an ideal production schedule for still images, you should allot one-third of the time for modeling, one-third of the time for materials, and one-third of the time for lighting. If you add a category for animation, you should borrow time from each of these three categories so that about one-quarter of the time budget is allotted for each category.

The lighting of the scene is especially important in creating the illusion of depth in a rendered image. Always keep in mind that the final output of any computer visualization is a 2D image, and the only thing that makes it appear 3D is the perspective created by the camera and, more important, the balance of light and dark in the image.

In this chapter, you'll learn how to place and adjust standard lights to control the amount of light falling on specific surfaces. You'll also learn how to place and adjust a sunlight system to create accurate real-world shadows, which give the objects in a scene "weight" by making them appear to be anchored to the ground. Finally, you'll learn how to gain more control in the scene by excluding objects from the effect of lights.

Key Terms

- **Direct light**—This standard light type in 3ds Max 8 casts its light in a cylinder from the light source.

- **Omni light**—This standard light type in 3ds Max 8 casts its light in all directions.

- **Scanline renderer**—The rendering engine used with standard lights in 3ds Max 8; it renders one horizontal line at a time from the top of the image to the bottom.

- **Angle of incidence**—The angle at which light strikes a surface affects its brightness. At 90 degrees to the surface you have full light; at 0 degrees to the surface you have no light.

- **Max Quadtree Depth**—This parameter of ray-traced shadows can result in significant performance increases when properly adjusted.

- **Bounced light**—In the real world, when light strikes a surface, a portion of that light, depending on the surface, is bounced back into the scene to light other surfaces. This is also sometimes referred to as *radiosity*.

Painting with Light

3ds Max 8 standard lights cannot calculate bounced light, the way lights in the real world do. For instance, if you go outdoors just before the sun comes up over the horizon or just after it has gone down for the evening, you will not need artificial lights to see where you're going. That's because the light you are seeing in this situation is sunlight bouncing from particles and water vapor in the air.

When working in 3ds Max, the position of the light in the scene is not as important as the amount and quality of light striking each surface. So you must approach the lighting in your scene as if you were "painting with light."

When a traditional painter sits down to a new canvas, the first task is usually to create a value sketch, which is a grayscale image that blocks out the darkest, midtone, and brightest areas that add to the illusion of depth. Light areas tend to come forward, while dark areas recede. You must incorporate this concept of a full range of brightness levels and contrast, ranging from almost pure black shadows to the brightest specular highlights.

Using Sunlight to Calculate Shadows

In an outdoor scene rendered in 3ds Max 8, the primary goal of sunlight is to display accurate shadows. While the sun adds direct light to the scene, it cannot be relied on to produce convincing results by itself because the scanline renderer does not calculate light bouncing from surfaces.

In this section of the chapter, you'll perform three exercises that optimize light in a scene using the sunlight system.

The Sunlight System

The sunlight system in 3ds Max 8 comprises a direct light, which is a standard light type that casts its light in a cylinder to create parallel shadows, and a special animation controller that lets you position the light correctly for any location on the earth at any time and date. The sunlight system also contains a compass rose component that lets you adjust the direction of true north to match your scene. In the first exercise, you will place the sunlight system in a scene similar to the fishing-enclave scene you used in the last chapter. The materials of the objects in the scene have been simplified so that you can focus on the lighting effects.

Exercise 7.1: Placing the sunlight system in a scene

1. Open the **Ext_light01.max** file from the CD-ROM. Save it to your project folder with the name *Ext_light02.max*.

   This is essentially the same scene you used in the last chapter to place cameras.

2. Right-click in the Camera01 viewport to activate it, and on the main toolbar, click the Quick Render button.

tip

3ds Max 8 also features a Daylight system, which contains a skylight component that simulates the effects of bounced light in the atmosphere. The skylight limits some of your control by filling in shaded areas for you. It also requires the use of an exposure control utility. Because the purpose of this chapter is to teach you how to utilize standard lights for control and efficiency, we won't delve into the Daylight system here.

note

This chapter's Max Files folder on the CD-ROM includes a bitmap image. 3ds Max always looks for any necessary external files in the same folder as the main Max scene file. If you open a scene file from a location different from the original chapter folder, you may encounter a Missing External Files dialog. If you do, click Browse, and in the Configure External File Paths dialog, click Add. Use the Choose New External Files Path dialog to browse to the location of the CD versions of the Max scene files for this chapter, then click Use Path, and click OK. Click Continue to close the Missing External Files dialog.

The scene renders in just a few seconds with the default lighting (**Figure 7.1**). There is obviously some light coming from behind the camera, but the sky and water are much too dark. Close the Rendered Frame window.

Quick Render

FIGURE 7.1 *With the default lighting, the scanline renderer renders this scene with too little light.*

3. On the Create panel, Systems category, Object Type rollout, click the Sunlight button. In the Top viewport, click in the middle of the pink Skydome01 object and drag very slightly until you see a light gray compass rose expanding as you drag the mouse. When the compass rose is slightly larger than the sky dome, click to set its size. Move the mouse forward to push the white light-source icon until it is a little outside the sky dome, as seen in the Front viewport. Left-click to set the light in position (**Figure 7.2**). If you have problems, delete Sun01 and try again.

note

The size of the compass rose you create is not important, but it must originate in the middle of your scene if it is to accurately determine the direction of true north for the sunlight system.

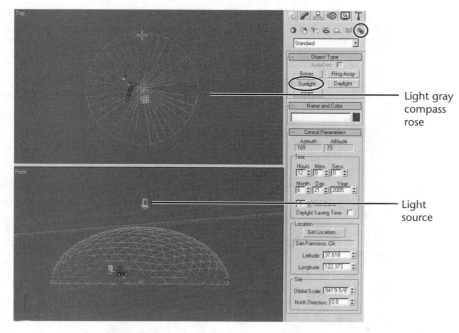

Light gray
compass
rose

Light
source

FIGURE 7.2 *A sunlight system can sometimes take a little practice to place in the scene.*

4. Activate the Camera01 viewport, and click the
    Quick Render button on the main toolbar.

    The scene takes considerably longer to render,
    and only the horizontal and near-horizontal
    surfaces are lit (see **Figure 7.3** on the next
    page). The sun position is set for noon on the
    first day of summer in San Francisco.

    The long render time—2 minutes, 35 seconds
    using a Pentium 4 3.2 GHz processor—is a func-
    tion of the default ray-traced shadows in the
    sunlight system. In the next exercise, we'll work
    to optimize the render time.

tip

Position the light source just
outside your sky-dome object.
If you move the light too far
from your scene, there may
be problems calculating shadows. You can adjust the distance of the light source from
the center of the compass
rose using the Orbital Scale
value on the Create panel.

FIGURE 7.3 *The default sunlight system shines almost straight down in the scene and lights only the horizontal surfaces with full intensity.*

5. Save the file. It should already be called Ext_light02.max.

Now the sky and the objects in the scene are totally black, while the landscape and water are lit with a moderate amount of light.

Simply placing a sunlight system in the scene will not give you a convincing rendered image. The rendering times are too slow, and the objects' vertical surfaces are much too dark. In the next section, you'll learn to place more lights in the scene to simulate atmospheric light that fills in the shaded areas. You'll also learn to adjust shadow parameters for faster rendering.

Sunlight-System Ray-Traced Shadows

As mentioned earlier, shadows are an important part of lighting that give apparent weight to objects and keep them from looking as if they are floating in space.

However, in any scene, shadows can be one of the biggest hindrances to production. The default shadows for the sunlight system (and Daylight system) are ray-traced shadows, which still take a long time to render but do not take a lot of system RAM for temporary storage. The shadows themselves are very dark and hard-edged, so they are good for simulating shadows in bright sunlight.

In the next exercise, you'll work with ray-traced shadows by adjusting the Max Quadtree Depth setting to speed rendering. The Max Quadtree Depth setting determines how a scene is broken down to distribute calculations of ray-traced shadows efficiently. The depth setting ranges from 1 to 10, with 7 being the default. This is almost never the optimum setting.

I highly recommend that when using ray-traced shadows, you try setting the Max Quadtree Depth to 8, then 9, and finally 10 to see which setting is optimal for your scene. The optimal setting depends on such factors as the overall size of the scene, the relative sizes of objects in the scene, and the total number of faces in the scene.

note

I have never seen a situation in which the setting should ever go below the default 7, nor have I seen situations in which the shadows have become unacceptable or even changed noticeably because of higher settings.

Exercise 7.2: Optimizing ray-traced shadows

1. Open the **Ext_light02.max** scene from the CD-ROM or from the previous exercise and save it to your project folder with the name *Ext_light03.max*.

2. In the Left or Front viewport, select the direct light icon called Sun01. Right-click in the Camera01 viewport to activate it, and click the Quick Render button on the main toolbar. Note the render time shown in the Status bar in the upper left corner of the display (2 minutes, 35 seconds on my machine).

3. On the Modify panel, in the Ray Traced Shadow Params rollout, increase the Max Quadtree Depth to 8 and render the camera viewport again.

   This drops the render time to 59 seconds on my machine, increasing productivity significantly.

4. Increase the Max Quadtree Depth setting to 9 and render again, noting the time. Then set it to 10 and render once more (**Figure 7.4**).

    For this scene, the optimal setting appears to be 10 with a render time of 14 seconds. This is less than 10 percent of the original render time and could easily make the difference between a cost-effective project and one in which you lose your shirt.

    You might also notice some minor shadow artifacts on the left side of the landscape and along the water's edge (**Figure 7.5**). These occur when the shadow appears before the object that is casting it. We can fix that by adjusting the Ray Bias setting.

5. In the Ray Traced Shadow Params rollout, increase the Ray Bias setting to 2.0. Render the Camera01 viewport again, and you will see that the artifacts have cleared as the shadow has been moved away from the light.

FIGURE 7.4 *Increasing the Max Quadtree Depth setting for ray-traced shadows can significantly reduce rendering times.*

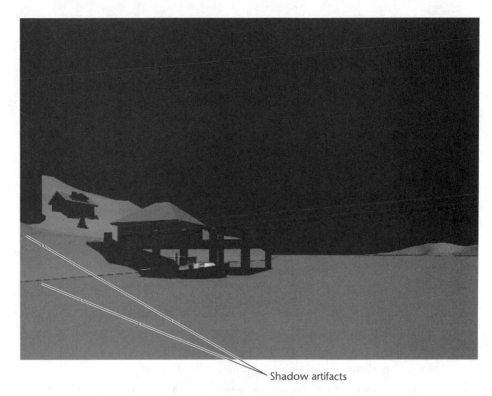

Shadow artifacts

FIGURE 7.5 *In some situations, shadows must be shifted toward or away from the light source to reduce artifacting or to keep objects from appearing to float in space.*

6. Save the file. It should already be called Ext_light03.max.

The scene now renders quickly, and objects are casting hard-edged, dark shadows that might be typical in bright sunlight.

As with so many things in 3ds Max 8, you should strive to get the best possible quality images while at the same time paying close attention to what you can do to increase your efficiency. Shadows, especially ray-traced shadows, are among the most common causes of lost production time that can usually be rectified with a few simple optimizations.

Positioning the Sunlight for Time, Date, and Location

Now that you have the scene rendering quickly enough to make cost-effective tests, it's time to position the sun so that it casts accurate shadows based on the scene's location, time, and date.

I mentioned earlier in the chapter that the sunlight system uses a special animation controller to position the sun accurately based on astronomical data. To maintain correct shadow casting, you cannot simply move the sun with the Select and Move tool; you must use the Motion panel and enter real-world data.

In the next exercise, you'll work with the animation controller to position the sun according to this real-world data. You'll also learn about one of the most important factors in 3ds Max 8 lighting: the *angle of incidence* of light to a surface.

Exercise 7.3: Positioning a sunlight system

1. Open the **Ext_light03.max** file from the CD-ROM or from the previous exercise and save it to your project folder with the name *Ext_light04.max*.

2. Select Sun01 in the Left or Front viewport and go to the Modify panel.

    The parameters on the Modify panel adjust only the quality of the light and shadows and not the sun's position in the sky.

3. With the Sun01 object selected, go to the Motion panel. In the Control Parameters rollout, you'll see the parameters available for adjusting the sun's position accurately. In the Location area, click the Get Location button. In the Geographic Location dialog that appears, choose Portland ME from the City list (**Figure 7.6**). Click OK.

    The Time Zone will automatically adjust itself to Eastern time, the time zone for Portland, Maine.

    Selecting a city from the list is one way to set the location. Another method is to pick on the location of the city in one of the maps of the world in the dialog, or enter the numeric values for the latitude and longitude in the appropriate fields on the Motion panel.

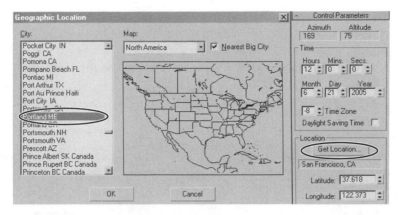

FIGURE 7.6 *Portland, Maine, a small city on the Maine coast noted for its lobster fishing, is the location for the scene we're rendering.*

4. In the Control Parameters rollout, in the Time area, enter the following in the numeric fields: Hours, 7; Mins., 0; Secs., 0; Month, 3; Day, 31; Year, 2006. Render the camera viewport.

    Notice that the water's surface has become considerably darker and the pier is casting long shadows on the ground. The sky is also showing a little color behind the hill because the Sun01 object is lighting it (**Figure 7.7**). In the real world, the sky is not a solid object like it is here, so allowing the sun to shine on it produces unconvincing results. In the next step, you'll exclude the sky dome from the sun.

FIGURE 7.7 *At 7 a.m. on the last day of March on the Maine coast, there would be much more light than is apparent in this rendered image.*

5. With Sun01 selected, go to the Modify panel and, in the General Parameters rollout, click the Exclude button. In the Exclude/Include dialog that appears, highlight Skydome01 in the Scene Objects list and click the double right arrow between the panes to send it into the Exclude column (**Figure 7.8**). Click OK.

    The sky dome is no longer affected by the sunlight. This is an extremely powerful feature of lights that gives you explicit control not available in the real world.

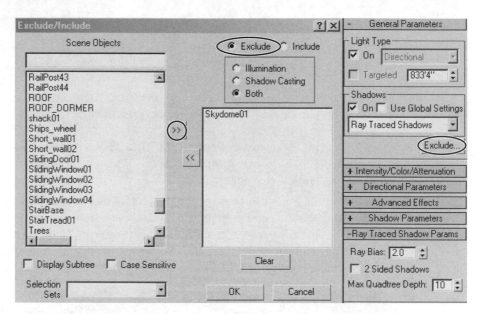

FIGURE 7.8 *The ability to exclude objects from the influence of lights gives you more control over the scene.*

6. Render the camera viewport. Notice that the sky is completely black again.

    Even though you have positioned the light to generate accurate shadows for a specific time, day, and location, the absence of bounced light in 3ds Max 8 scanline rendering results in a scene that is too dark.

7. Save the file. It should already be called Ext_light04.max.

The primary purpose of the sun is to cast shadows, and in this exercise you have applied the sunlight system and optimized the shadows for faster rendering. Now we need to work to make the overall scene more convincing.

Using Omni Lights to Simulate Bounced Light

The early-morning sun in our scene is low on the horizon. The scene is fairly dark, which can be attributed to the angle of incidence. The angle of incidence at which a light strikes a surface has a direct bearing on the amount of light on that surface (**Figure 7.9**). Only the surfaces that are perpendicular to the direction of the light are bright. Surfaces that are parallel to the direction of the light are very dark or black.

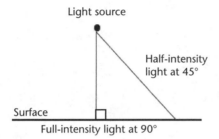

FIGURE 7.9 *This diagram shows the effect of angle of incidence and light intensity on the surface.*

In the next two exercises, you'll practice using omni lights to correct the dark areas caused by the angle of incidence and use another omni light to light the sky evenly.

Simulating Atmospheric Light for Landscape and Water Surfaces

The first light you'll add to this scene will simulate the light bouncing in the atmosphere to raise the levels of illumination on the horizontal surfaces in the scene. This will be similar to the light that is apparent just before sunrise or just after sunset in the real world. There is no noticeable shadow casting, and the light seems to come from everywhere.

Exercise 7.4: Lighting horizontal surfaces

1. Open the **Ext_light04.max** file from the CD-ROM or from the previous exercise, and save it to your project folder with the name *Ext_light05.max*.

2. Use the Quick Render button on the main toolbar to render the Camera01 viewport so you can see the scene with only sunlight as a light source. In the Rendering drop-down menu, choose RAM Player. In the RAM Player dialog that appears, click the teapot button for Channel A, and click OK to accept the defaults in the RAM Player Configuration dialog. Minimize the RAM Player. Close the rendered frame window.

3. In the Front viewport, zoom out and pan so that the entire scene is fairly small at the bottom of the viewport. On the Create panel, Lights category, Object Type rollout, click the Omni button, and then click in the Front viewport to place the omni light high above and centered to the sky dome (**Figure 7.10**). In the Top viewport, make sure the omni light is centered on the sky dome.

FIGURE 7.10 *The omni light must be placed high above the horizontal surfaces of your scene. Because of the angle of incidence, the light will be evenly distributed over the landscape and water.*

4. Right-click in the Camera01 viewport, and then click the Quick Render button to render the scene. Maximize the RAM Player and use the teapot button for Channel B to open the last rendered image. Click OK to accept the defaults in the RAM Player Configuration dialog, and then click and drag in the RAM Player window to compare the two images.

The horizontal surfaces are much brighter and the shadows are lighter. That's because lights in 3ds Max 8 are additive, so the scene is brighter than either light by itself. However, the vertical surfaces are still very dark because of the angle of incidence of the lights (**Figure 7.11**). You'll now add omni lights at the sides of the scene to light the vertical surfaces.

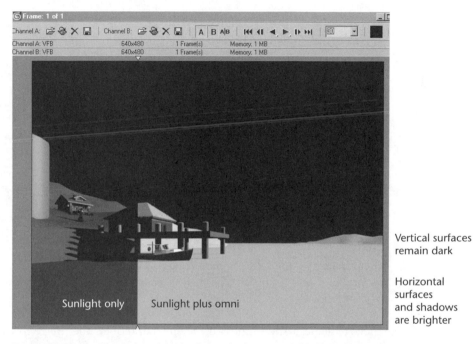

Vertical surfaces remain dark

Horizontal surfaces and shadows are brighter

FIGURE 7.11 *An omni placed high above the scene simulates the light bounced in the atmosphere.*

5. Minimize the RAM Player and close the rendered frame window. Zoom out in the Top viewport. Place a new omni light about 45 degrees below and to the right of the landscape. It should be approximately two times the width of the objects in the scene away from the landscape.

6. On the Modify panel, in the Intensity/Color/Attenuation rollout, enter 0.4 in the Multiplier field to reduce the light's intensity (**Figure 7.12**).

Because of a very low angle of incidence, this light does not brighten the water surface or the vertical sides of the pier and buildings facing the camera. It boosts the feeling of sunlight on the landscape and the fronts of the buildings.

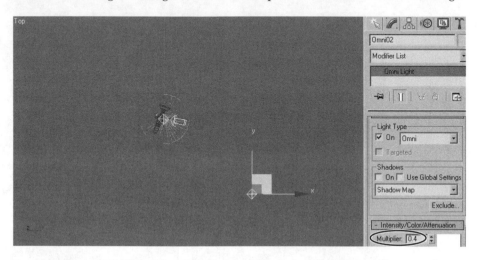

FIGURE 7.12 *An omni light placed in the top viewport brightens the sunlit areas of the landscape and the buildings without affecting the water surface, because of the angle of incidence.*

7. Click the Render the Camera01 viewport and open the image in Channel A of the RAM Player to compare it with the previous rendering. Minimize the RAM Player and close the Rendered Frame Window.

8. On the Modify panel, in the General Parameters rollout, click the Exclude button for this omni light. Highlight Skydome01 in the Scene Objects list, and use the double right arrow button to move it into the right column. Make sure the Exclude radio button at the top right of the Exclude/Include dialog is selected (**Figure 7.13**). Click OK.

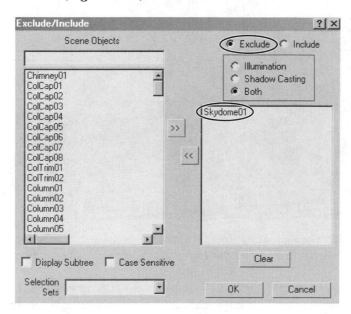

FIGURE 7.13 *This light should not affect the sky dome because it will cause uneven, and unconvincing, lighting.*

9. Activate the Top viewport. Click the Select and Move button on the main toolbar, hold down the Shift key, and drag the clone of the omni light to the left until it is shining at about a 90-degree angle to this light. Make sure that the Copy radio button is chosen in the Clone Options dialog that appears (see **Figure 7.14** on the next page). Click OK. On the Modify panel, in the Intensity/Color/Attenuation rollout, enter 0.1 in the Multiplier field.

    This provides a low level of light from behind the viewer's left shoulder. It brightens the sides of the building enough to see some detail while still retaining contrast with the other visible sides of the buildings.

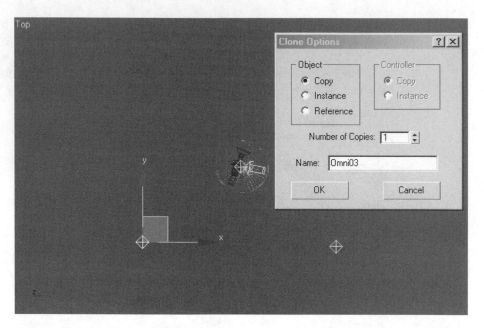

FIGURE 7.14 *Cloning the omni light 90 degrees to the left and lowering the intensity lets you fill in the shaded side of the buildings to a level where you can just make out the detail.*

10. Render the Camera01 viewport and load it into Channel B of the RAM Player to compare the new lighting with the previous rendering. Close the RAM Player and save the file. It should already be called Ext_light05.max.

The scene now has brightly lit areas to simulate direct sunlight, and filled-in shaded and shadow areas to simulate bounced light in the atmosphere.

For this particular scene, the three omni lights are sufficient to create the effect you want. If the camera were to move around the scene, you would need more omni lights to fill in those areas, based on the angle of incidence of existing lights. The important point here is to light the scene adequately while keeping a good range of contrast levels, from the darkest areas to the brightest areas. This adds to the illusion of 3D depth in the scene.

You'll probably need to adjust the lights in the scene after you have applied materials to the objects—remember how I mentioned earlier that materials and lights go hand in hand? For now, however, you've painted the scene with your lights to get the brightest light in the areas that would be hit by direct sun, and much lower levels in shaded areas. Now you need to light the sky with an even distribution of light that isn't affecting other objects in the scene.

Lighting the Sky

All the lights placed in the scene up to this point have excluded the sky dome. It remains completely black in the rendered image. In the real world, the sky dome is not actually an object, but sunlight being reflected and refracted in the atmosphere. At all times of the day except at sunrise and sunset, a clear blue sky would be consistently lit.

To simulate this smooth lighting in 3ds Max 8, you will dedicate a single omni light to the sky dome, placed in the scene so that the angle of incidence provides even lighting over the entire dome.

It's also important that no objects in the scene cast shadows on the sky dome and that the sky dome doesn't cast shadows on the scene. This will be accomplished using object properties.

Exercise 7.5: Using the angle of incidence to evenly light the sky

1. Open the **Ext_light05.max** file from the CD-ROM or from the previous exercise, and save it to your project folder with the name *Ext_light06.max*. In the Front viewport, zoom in to fill the viewport with the Skydome01 object.

2. On the Create panel, Lights category, Object Type rollout, click the Omni button and click just below the center of the sky dome (**Figure 7.15**). In the Top viewport, make sure the omni light has been placed in the scene so that it is centered in all directions.

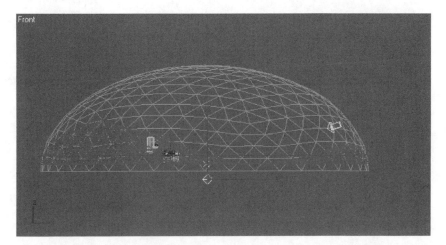

FIGURE 7.15 *An omni light placed near the bottom center of the sky-dome hemisphere will distribute its light evenly because of the angle of incidence.*

3. On the Modify panel, in the Intensity/Color/
    Attenuation rollout, set the Multiplier to 1.0.
    Notice in the Camera01 viewport that the land-
    scape and water tower and the underside of the
    roof trim are extremely bright. You'll exclude
    these objects from the new light.

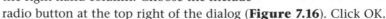

tip

If you are continuing from
the last exercise, you'll notice
that the lights have the same
intensity and other settings
from the previous light you
adjusted.

If you are opening the scene
after having exited or reset
3ds Max 8, all new lights will
have the default light settings.

4. On the Modify panel, in the General Parameters
    rollout, click the Exclude button. In the
    Exclude/Include dialog that appears, highlight
    the Skydome01 object in the Scene Objects list,
    and use the double right arrow to move it into
    the right-hand column. Choose the Include
    radio button at the top right of the dialog (**Figure 7.16**). Click OK.

This omni light illuminates only the sky dome and nothing else. Including
just one object is easier than excluding all other objects and then remembering
later to exclude any new objects that are added to the scene.

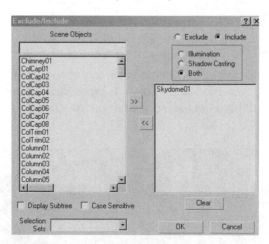

FIGURE 7.16 *The Include option for
lights often makes it easier to keep
track of what is excluded. However, it
has the same end result.*

5. Render the Camera01 viewport. You should see an evenly lit and bright sky.

   Now you'll set the properties so that the sky dome won't cast or receive shadows.

6. On the main toolbar, make sure that the Select Objects button is active, and, in the front viewport, select Skydome01 and right-click on it. Choose Properties in the quad menu, and, in the Object Properties dialog, General tab, Rendering Control area, clear the check boxes for both Receive Shadows and Cast Shadows (**Figure 7.17**). Click OK.

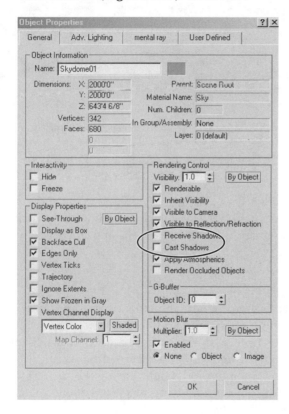

FIGURE 7.17 *You would never want your sky dome to cast or receive shadows.*

7. In the Tools drop-down menu, choose Light Lister. The Light Lister dialog appears (**Figure 7.18**).

The Light Lister dialog gives you access to settings that let you easily adjust any light in the scene to fine-tune the balance of lighting.

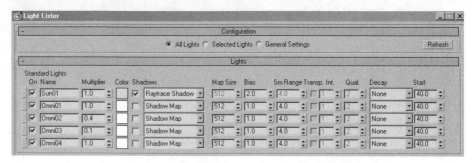

FIGURE 7.18 *All lights in the scene can be accessed using the Light Lister tool.*

8. Close all windows and dialogs. Save the file. It should already be called Ext_light06.max.

Lighting the sky independently of all other objects allows greater control and flexibility. Using the Light Lister tool, you can quickly fine-tune adjustments for any light in the scene to set the light levels to make the scene appear the way you want it to.

Summary

You learned in this chapter how to light an outdoor scene and generate fairly accurate shadows using the sunlight system, and how to place omni lights around the scene to raise the illumination on darker surfaces and compensate for 3ds Max 8's inability to calculate bounced light. You also learned how critical a tool angle of incidence is in controlling the intensity of light hitting the surfaces of a scene, and how including or excluding objects from lights extends that control far beyond what would be possible in the real world.

CHAPTER **8**

3D Lighting

In This Chapter

In this chapter, you'll learn how to light a simple interior scene using some of the same principles of standard lighting as you used in Chapter 7, with a focus on "painting with light."

First you'll learn how to *attenuate* light, or cause the intensity of light to decay over a distance, by adjusting a single omni light to simulate the effect in 3ds Max 8. You'll do this by adjusting and scaling the light's attenuation ranges to set the brightness levels in the corners of the room, thereby establishing the base lighting that you can build on.

This method of setting a dark base level of illumination in your scene and building up light levels from this base is similar to the way traditional painters set a baseline in a painting. First they block out the darkest areas on the canvas with a value sketch, then they paint darker color in the shadow areas, and finally they apply progressively lighter paint to bring up the midtone areas and highlights.

Once you've attenuated the light, you'll add accent lights that draw the viewer's attention to objects in the scene and adjust the softness at the edge of the spotlights.

Finally, you'll learn how to generate shadows to give objects apparent weight. Shadows in interior scenes have softer edges because of the diffuse nature of the light, so you'll work with shadow-mapped shadow types, the default for omni lights and spotlights in 3ds Max, to simulate that effect.

Because calculating shadows in 3ds Max 8 can take up an enormous amount of resources and rendering time, you'll also learn how to simulate potentially costly shadows by projecting images through lights that simulate shadows.

The scene you'll use in this exercise is the interior of the shack on the pier that we worked with in the last chapter. There are several objects in the scene that will cast shadows, including barrels and tables, and you'll simulate sunlight casting shadows through the windows.

Key Terms

- **Attenuation**—The natural decay of light from its source, based on the inverse square law of physics. Light intensity diminishes based on the inverse of the square of the distance from the light source (the formula is $1/d^2$, or one divided by the distance squared).
- **Hotspot**—A cone emanating from a spotlight source that describes an area of full-intensity light.
- **Falloff**—An outer cone for a spotlight, within which light falls off laterally. There is no light outside the falloff cone.

Attenuating Light Using Standard Omni Lights

Setting up the attenuation or decay of standard lights in 3ds Max 8 is accomplished manually. By default, all standard lights shine to infinity, and while enabling shadow casting will stop the light at a surface, you must still do the calculations necessary to check if there are other objects in World space beyond the shadow-casting surface. This can be computationally expensive, so learning to apply attenuation will make your renderings more efficient. Your task in the first exercise is to establish a base level of illumination for the darkest areas in the interior scene by using attenuation to control light intensity; the darkest areas will typically be the corners of the room.

Exercise 8.1: Using Far Attenuation and scaled omni lights

1. Reset 3ds Max 8 and then open the **Int_light01.max** file from the CD-ROM. Save the file to your project folder with the name *Int_light02.max*.

2. Right-click in the Top viewport to activate it, and then zoom in on the shack at the back of the pier so that the shack fills the viewport.

    Zooming in close to your work area makes it easier to select objects in the scene.

3. On the Create panel, in the Lights category, in the Object Type rollout, click the Omni button and click in the middle of the shack in the Top viewport.

The omni light is created on the World grid, which is located near the bottom of the long pilings, far below the shack.

4. On the main toolbar, click the Select and Move button, and, in the Left or Front viewport, move the light up so that it's centered in the room (**Figure 8.1**).

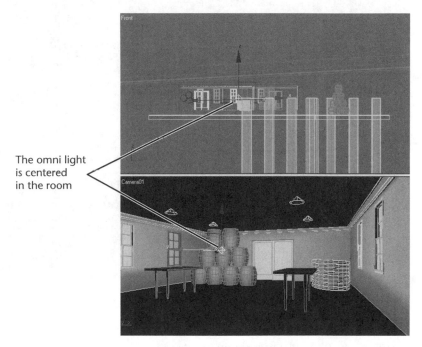

The omni light is centered in the room

FIGURE 8.1 *Place an omni light in the shack, equidistant from the walls, floor, and ceiling, so that it lights the room evenly.*

5. Right-click in the Camera01 viewport to activate it. Click the Quick Render button on the main toolbar, and then, from the Rendering drop-down menu, choose RAM Player and open the last rendered image in Channel A (**Figure 8.2**).

FIGURE 8.2 *Placing a single omni light in the middle of the room results in a boring scene that has no apparent depth.*

Using the RAM Player lets you compare your renderings as you make changes. Notice that the room appears featureless and flat. In the next few steps, you'll learn how to place a light that will light the walls, floor, and ceiling, while leaving the corners of the room darker for contrast.

6. Minimize the RAM Player and close the rendered frame window.

7. On the Modify panel, Intensity/Color/Attenuation rollout, Far Attenuation area, check the Use box.

Far attenuation, or the diminishment of light over distance, displays two ranges around the omni light in the viewports—a tan inner range and a brown outer range (**Figure 8.3**). The light has full intensity from the source to the tan Start range. It then decays in linear fashion to the brown End range. Beyond the End range, there is no light and calculations are not performed.

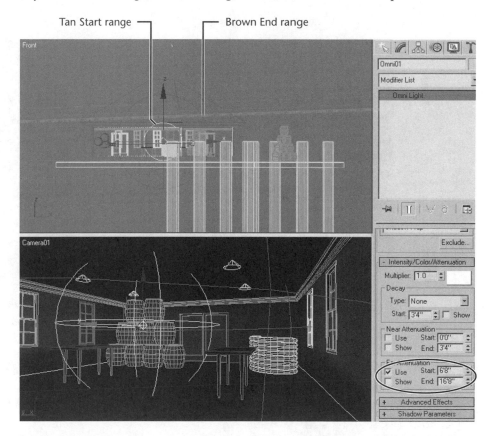

FIGURE 8.3 *The Far Attenuation Start range denotes the beginning of light decay. There is no light beyond the End range.*

8. Render the Camera01 viewport. Notice that the walls of the room have disappeared in darkness, and only some of the floor and a few objects are visible. You'll adjust the attenuation ranges to remedy this.

Don't forget that the CD-ROM contains full-color images of all the figures used in the exercises, which you can use for reference.

9. On the Modify panel, in the Intensity/Color/ Attenuation rollout, in the Far Attenuation area, enter 14'6" in the Start field. This causes the tan range to touch the side walls, as seen from the Top viewport (**Figure 8.4**).

The tan Start range should touch the side walls

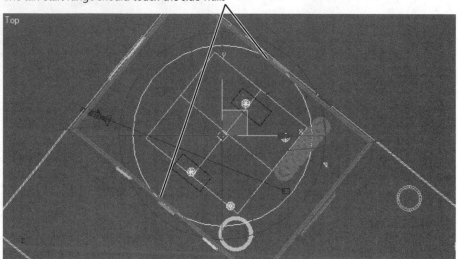

FIGURE 8.4 *The side walls now have full intensity of the Omni light near their centers. The strength of the light diminishes toward the corners because of attenuation and angle-of-incidence.*

10. Render the Camera01 viewport. The points on the walls where the tan range touches them will have full intensity of light, but the back wall has become extremely dark with an abrupt transition, because the light dies out before reaching it (**Figure 8.5**).

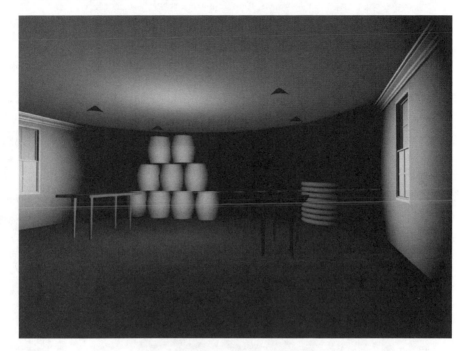

FIGURE 8.5 *The back of the room abruptly turns dark because the Start and End attenuation ranges are so close together and because both ranges end before the wall.*

Next, you need to scale the attenuation ranges into an oval shape to touch the back walls. To do this accurately, you will need to use the Pick reference coordinate system to scale along the axis of the pier.

11. On the main toolbar, click the Select and Scale button. Click the reference-coordinate-system drop-down menu to the right of the Scale button and choose Pick (**Figure 8.6**). In the Top viewport, pick on the edge of the pier.

FIGURE 8.6 *You can pick a reference coordinate system from other objects in the scene.*

The reference coordinate system shows pier_shape, and the scale gizmo axes are aligned with the room and the pier (**Figure 8.7**).

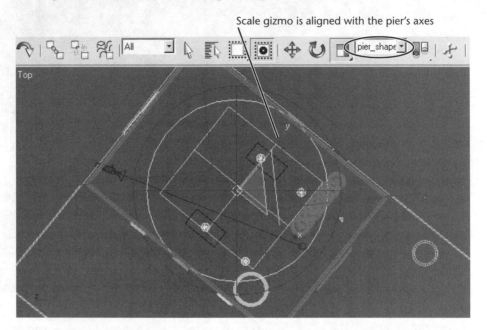

Scale gizmo is aligned with the pier's axes

FIGURE 8.7 *The attenuation ranges can now be scaled along the axes of the shack.*

12. In the Top viewport, click and drag on the X axis of the scale gizmo until the tan Start range touches the end walls of the shack. In the Left viewport, scale the ranges in the Z axis until the tan range touches the floor and ceiling (**Figure 8.8**).

    This ensures that the centers of the walls, floor, and ceiling will have the same light intensity.

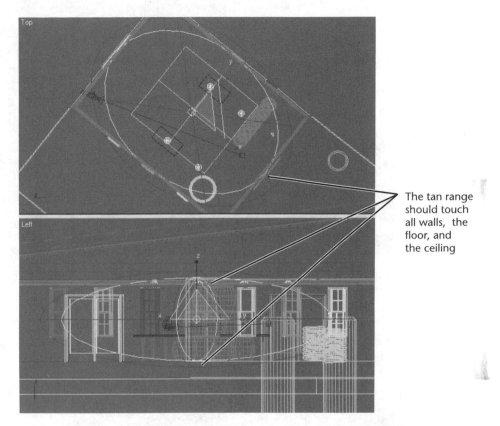

The tan range
should touch
all walls, the
floor, and
the ceiling

FIGURE 8.8 *Scale the attenuation ranges to touch the walls, floor, and ceiling.*

13. On the Modify panel, in the Far Attenuation
area, enter 25'0" in the End range numeric
field and then render the Camera01 viewport.
This brightens the corners of the room without
affecting the surfaces perpendicular to the light
(see **Figure 8.9** on the next page).

Figure 8.9 *Increasing the End range distance lightens the corners of the room without affecting the walls.*

14. Maximize the RAM Player and open this image in Channel B. The room with the darker corners appears longer than the room with the light that has no attenuation (**Figure 8.10**).

Without attenuation   With scaled attenuation

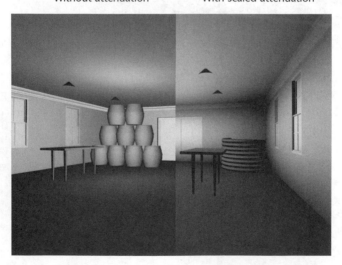

Figure 8.10 *Making the corners of the room darker increases the room's apparent depth.*

15. In the Intensity/Color/Attenuation rollout, enter 0.5 in the Multiplier field. The room now has a base level of illumination to which other lighting can be applied. The Far Attenuation End range is now the primary brightness control in the scene.

16. Save the file. It should already be called Int_light02.max.

Light and dark are being used to create an illusion without actually changing geometry.

Scaling omni lights with attenuation enabled allows control of the shape of attenuation. In this case you are creating the impression of 3D depth simply by darkening the corners of the room. Is it realistic? Not really—lights don't function that way in the real world—but it can be extremely convincing.

Adding Spotlights to the Scene for Accent

The single attenuated omni light in the scene is now the base level from which you can begin to "paint your scene" with accent lights. In the next exercise, you'll learn how to use spotlights that allow more control of coverage because the light is cast from the source within a cone, rather than in all directions as with the omni light.

You'll also adjust the far attenuation for the spotlight to control just how much light strikes the surfaces within the cone, and adjust hotspot/falloff settings to make the edge of the light beam more consistent with the appearance of real interior lights and to enable shadow casting.

Exercise 8.2: Placing and adjusting spotlights

1. Open the file called **Int_light02.max** from the CD-ROM or from the last exercise and save it to your project folder with the name *Int_light03.max*. Rightclick in the Top viewport to activate it.

2. Press the H key to bring up the Select Objects dialog, and highlight objects Light_fixture01 through Light_fixture04 (**Figure 8.11**). Click the Select button. These are four light shades near the shack's ceiling. Press Alt + Q to isolate the four fixtures.

Isolating the object or objects you want to work on is more productive than working in cluttered viewports.

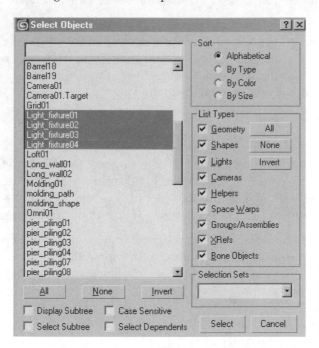

FIGURE 8.11 *You can select a series of objects in the list by clicking the first object you want and dragging to the last.*

3. On the Create panel, Lights category, Object Type rollout, click the Free Spot button. Click anywhere in the Top viewport to place the free spot. You'll see light blue and dark blue circles representing the hotspot and falloff, respectively. Make sure the Multiplier is set to 0.5 in the Intensity/Color/Attenuation rollout for this new light.

You can use a free spot because these lights are always pointing downward and you won't need to aim them at other objects.

4. On the main toolbar, click the Align button, and, in the Top viewport, pick the fixture on the left. In the Align Selection [Light_fixture01] dialog, in the Align Position (Screen) area, make sure that all three axes' boxes are selected, the Pivot Point radio button is selected in the Current Object column, and the Center radio button is selected in the Target Object column (**Figure 8.12**). Click OK.

Aligning the light with its fixture makes this accent light more convincing.

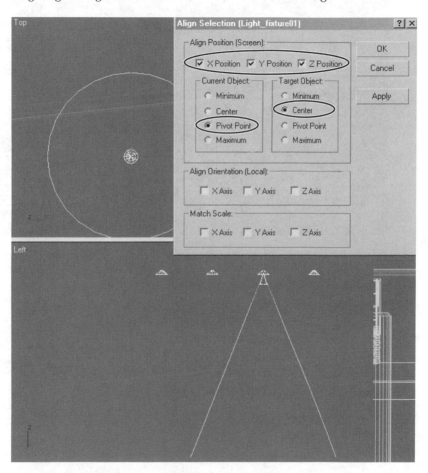

FIGURE 8.12 *The Align tool makes positioning lights in fixtures an easy task.*

5. On the main toolbar, click the Select and Move button, hold down the Shift key, and move in any direction to create three Instance clones in the Top viewport a short distance from each other (**Figure 8.13**). Click OK, and then use the Align tool to place the clones in the other three fixtures.

Instance cloning lets you edit any one of the lights to affect them all.

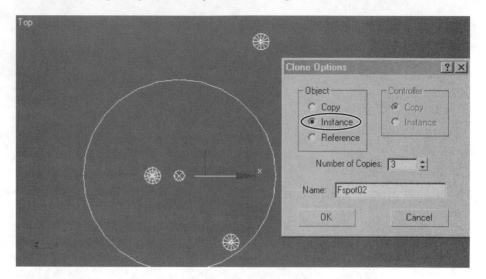

FIGURE 8.13 *Make sure the Instance radio button is chosen before cloning the lights.*

6. Click the large yellow Exit Isolation Mode button to reveal all other objects in the scene, and render the Camera01 viewport. You'll now see four hard-edged light pools on the floor of the shack. On the Modify panel, in the Spotlight Parameters rollout, enter 80.0 in the Falloff/Field numeric field and press Enter. Render the Camera01 viewport again, and you will see that the edges of the light pools are much softer. There are also bright areas where the lights overlap (**Figure 8.14**).

tip

The settings in the Align Selection dialog will be remembered from the last alignment, allowing you to quickly place the lights in the fixtures.

Bright areas where lights overlap

FIGURE 8.14 *The greater the angle between the hotspot and falloff cones, the softer the edge of the light pool. Lights are additive, and where they overlap, the area is brighter.*

7. In the Tools drop-down menu, choose Light Lister. At first glance, it will appear that there are only two lights in the scene. If you click the drop-down list for Fspot01, you will find that all four free spots are listed. This is because they are instances, and adjusting one will adjust all. Check the Shadows box for the free spots to enable shadow-mapped shadows for all four lights (**Figure 8.15**). Render the Camera01 viewport to see that the tables now cast shadows on the floor (see **Figure 8.16** on the next page).

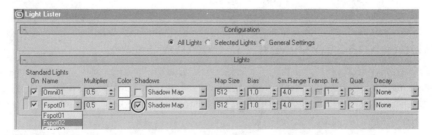

FIGURE 8.15 *Instance clone lights display only one set of controls in the Light Lister.*

FIGURE 8.16 *Increasing the falloff angle relative to the hotspot angle softens the edges of the light pools and minimizes the brightness in overlapping areas.*

8. Close all dialogs and render windows and save the file. It should already be called Int_light03.max.

   These spotlights are accenting the tables and casting shadows on the floor, but they do not add much overall light to the scene.

Spotlights can be used to carefully control which objects in the scene are lit and to cast shadows, drawing the viewer's attention where you want it. You are continuing to paint the scene with light.

Adjusting Shadow-Mapped Shadows

Shadow-mapped shadows, the default shadow type for standard lights, are black-and-white bitmaps that have been calculated by looking down the light to see what objects obscure other objects in the scene; the shadow bitmaps are then composited into the image at render time.

The ray-traced shadows you learned about in Chapter 7 can only have hard, sharp edges, but the shadow-mapped shadows can be adjusted for edge quality. In the next exercise, you'll make several adjustments that will result in softer-edged shadows that are more convincing for typical interior scenes.

Exercise 8.3: Using shadow-mapped shadow controls

1. Open the scene called **Int_light03.max** from the CD-ROM or from the previous exercise, and save it to your project folder with the name *Int_light04.max*. From the Tools drop-down menu, choose Light Lister. In the Map Size field for Fspot01, enter 75 and press Enter. Render the Camera01 viewport. The tables cast softer-appearing shadows, but if you look closely, you will see that the shadows are quite ragged (**Figure 8.17**).

    The shadows have ragged edges because the Map Size is the resolution of the shadow map in pixels—here, 75 by 75 pixels, which is too low a resolution for compositing over this 640-by-480 rendering.

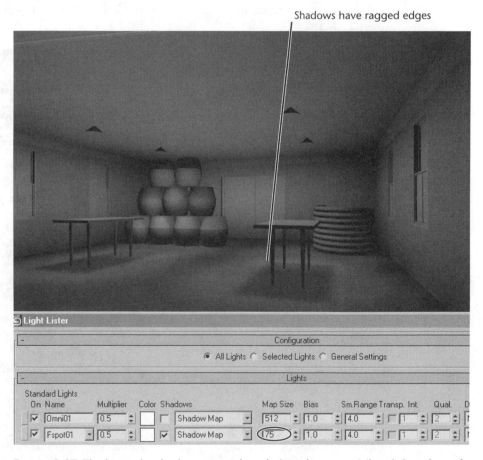

FIGURE 8.17 *The lower the shadow-mapped resolution, the more pixilated the edges of the shadows will become.*

2. In the Light Lister, set the Map Size back to 512, the default, and then enter 20 in the Sm. Range (sample range) field and press Enter. Render the Camera01 viewport, and you'll notice that the shadows have become a bit softer without any sign of pixelization or ragged edges. This setting averages several iterations of the shadow edges to produce the soft-edged effect. However, high sample-range settings can significantly increase the render times of scenes with lots of shadow-mapped shadows.

    Increasing the map size sharpens the edges, and increasing the sample range softens the edges.

3. Because the sample range and the map size work against each other, it is best to compromise on the settings. Set the Map Size to 128 and the Sm. Range to 8.0, and render the Camera01 viewport to see that the shadows are acceptably soft (**Figure 8.18**).

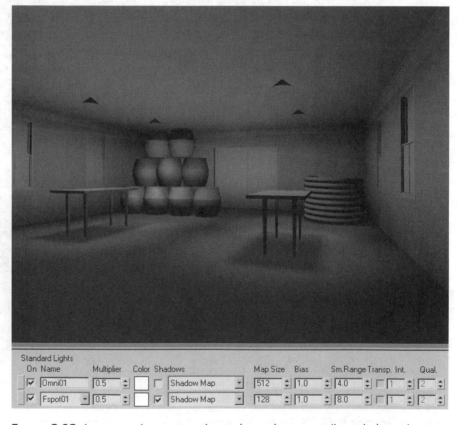

FIGURE 8.18 *A compromise on map size and sample range strikes a balance between shadow quality and efficiency.*

4. Close all windows and dialogs and save the file. It should already be called Int_light04.max. Shadows are an important part of any rendering, but they must be used efficiently.

The hard edges of ray-traced shadows are not appropriate for lights coming from most light fixtures, and shadow-mapped shadows are a good alternative. However, you must always be aware of the potential cost in computer resources for any kind of shadow-casting light; shadow-mapped shadows tend to use more RAM, while ray-traced shadows take longer to calculate. Let's have a look at more-efficient ways of simulating shadows.

Simulating Shadows Using Projector Maps

Sometimes you'd like to have complex shadows in a scene, but the overhead of generating those shadows would be very expensive. A good example is the shadows on the ground cast by sunlight passing through the leaves of a tree, or the sun shining into a room through window blinds.

3ds Max 8 lights can project bitmap images—either still images or animations—from any light source. In the next exercise, you'll learn how to apply and adjust those projector maps to simulate shadows.

The scene contains multipaned windows through which the sun should beam into the room, creating a grid pattern of light and shadows on the floor. Instead of placing a light outside the window to cast the shadows, you'll use a projector map in a target spot to accomplish a similar effect. You'll also use a rectangular spotlight to make the effect more convincing.

Exercise 8.4: Creating and adjusting target spotlights

1. Open the file from the CD-ROM or from the last exercise called **Int_light04.max**. Save it to your project folder with the name *Int_light05.max*. Right-click in the Top viewport to activate it, and zoom out so that you have a little room to place lights on the right side.

2. On the Create panel, Lights category, Object Type rollout, click the Target Spot button. In the Top viewport, pick a little way outside a window in the right wall to set the light, and drag to the center of the floor to set the target (**Figure 8.19**).

    You want to place the light outside the building to simulate sunlight shining through the window.

Click here to set the light

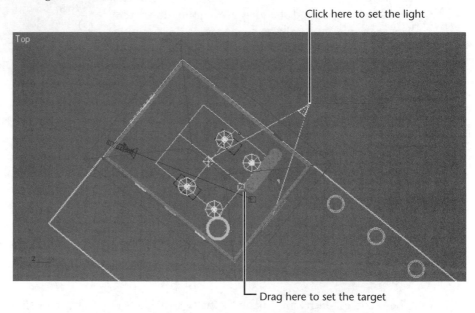

Drag here to set the target

FIGURE 8.19 *The light source must be placed in the scene first, and then you can drag the mouse to find the target position.*

3. Click the Select Object button on the main toolbar, and then click anywhere in the Top viewport to deselect everything. In the Top viewport, pick the light blue line that connects the spotlight and target. This selects both with one pick. Press the spacebar to lock the selection. A yellow padlock button, the Lock Selection button, will also be toggled at the bottom center of the display when you press Spacebar. In the Left or Front viewport, use Select and Move to move the light and target up to the level of the shack floor (**Figure 8.20**). Press the spacebar to toggle the Lock Selection off.

    The Lock Selection toggle lets you easily select objects in one viewport and then transform them in another viewport without losing the selection.

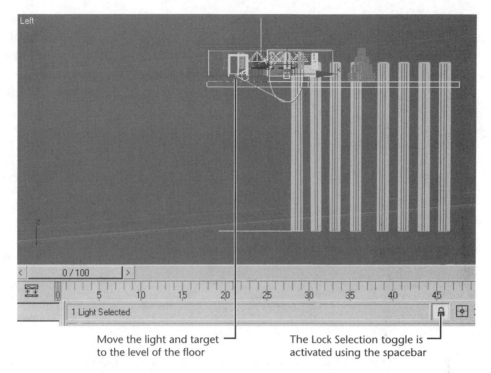

Move the light and target
to the level of the floor

The Lock Selection toggle is
activated using the spacebar

FIGURE 8.20 *Lock the selection before trying to move it. Remember to toggle it off when you are finished.*

4. Right-click in the Camera01 viewport to activate it, press Shift + 4, and then double-click Spot01in the Select Light dialog (**Figure 8.21**).

   This changes the Camera01 viewport to a light view using the Spot01 light. The viewport now shows what the spotlight is looking at and changes the navigation buttons at the lower right corner of the display to light navigation controls.

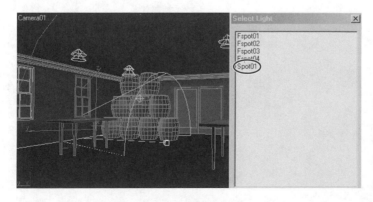

FIGURE 8.21 *The Select Light dialog lets you select the light that will become the viewport's view.*

5. Click the Orbit Light button, located in the light navigation button area, and adjust the Spot01 viewport so that you are looking at the window from slightly above with the window centered in the hotspot/falloff circles (**Figure 8.22**).

The light navigation buttons behave similarly to the camera navigation buttons you used in Chapter 6, but you need to aim the light as you change the view.

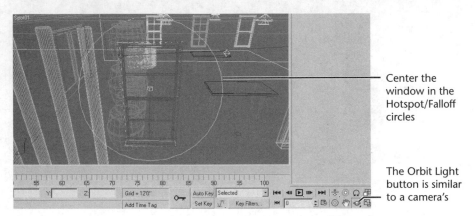

Center the window in the Hotspot/Falloff circles

The Orbit Light button is similar to a camera's

FIGURE 8.22 *Orbit the spotlight to aim through the window.*

6. Make sure that Spot01 is selected, and, on the Modify panel, in the Spotlight Parameters rollout, choose the radio button for Rectangle. In the Hotspot/ Beam field enter 25.0, and then enter 27.0 in the Falloff/Field field. In the Aspect field, enter 0.5. In the Spot01 viewport, use the navigation buttons to make the light blue hotspot rectangle slightly larger than the window (**Figure 8.23**).

This causes the light beam to fit both the shape and size of the window opening and cast a rectangular beam onto the floor.

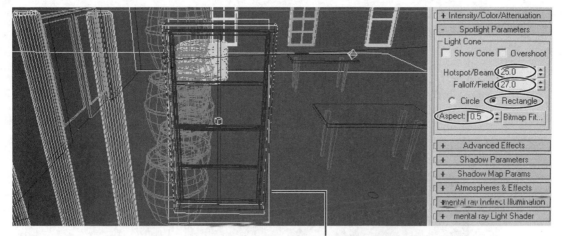

Navigate so that the hotspot rectangle
is slightly larger than the window

FIGURE 8.23 *Adjust the spotlight to a rectangular shape and a specific size and aspect ratio.*

7. Save the file. It should already be called Int_light05.max.

   Using a spotlight view can make aligning lights easier.

Reshaping and resizing spotlights and direct lights can make them more useful than just typical light fixtures. They can be used to simulate light streaming through a window, as in this case—or the same process can be used to simulate film or video projectors. The next step is to provide the image to be projected.

Projecting Maps for Efficiency

The spotlight has been turned into a rectangular shape and resized to fit the window so that it appears as though sunlight is shining through the window. This is done without needing to actually cast shadows, which could be expensive in terms of computer resources and rendering time.

The window has multiple panes, but the beam of sunlight is currently solid on the floor and wall, resulting in an unconvincing effect. Your next task is to project a map that simulates the multiple panes through the spotlight.

Lights can project any type of image in the same way as a movie projector functions.

Exercise 8.5: Creating and adjusting a projector map

1. Open the file called **Int_light05.max** from the CD-ROM or from the last exercise, and save it to your project folder with the name *Int_light06.max*. In the Top viewport, select Spot01, and, on the Modify panel, in the Intensity/ Color/Attenuation rollout, enter 2.0 in the Multiplier field. Right-click in the Spot01 viewport and press C to switch to the Camera01 view. On the main toolbar, click the Quick Render button (**Figure 8.24**).

    This will help simulate bright sunlight at a low angle of incidence to the floor.

FIGURE 8.24 *The bright light shining through the window is solid, with no apparent shadows from the window mullions. Remember that the light is not actually casting shadows; therefore, the opaque windows do not play a role in this exercise of simulating shadows for efficiency.*

2. On the Modify panel, in the Advanced Effects rollout, click the None button in the Projector Map area. In the Material/Map Browser, double-click Tiles to load it into the map slot (**Figure 8.25**).

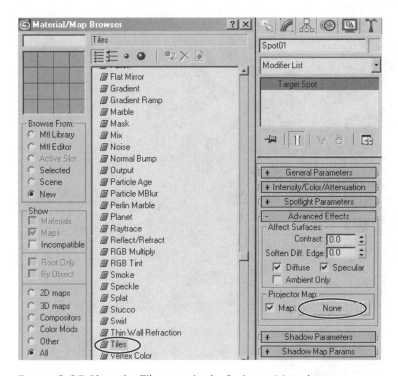

FIGURE 8.25 *Place the Tiles map in the Projector Map slot.*

3. To adjust the map so that it projects correctly, you must use the Material
    Editor. On the main toolbar, click the Material Editor button, or press the
    M key. On the Modify panel, click the Projector Map slot, and drag it to the
    Material Editor and drop it on the first sample window there. Make sure that
    the Instance radio button is chosen in the Instance [Copy] Map dialog (see
    Figure 8.26 on the next page).

    It is important to use instance cloning, so that you can easily change the prop-
    erties of the map in the projector slot.

Drop here   Drag from here

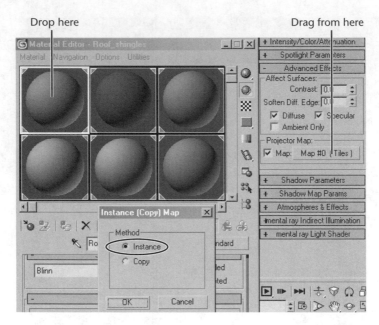

FIGURE 8.26 *You can drag and drop the map from the projector slot on the right to the sample window.*

4. In a projector map, white allows light to shine through and black obscures it, so you must change the map's colors and pattern. In the Material Editor, in the Advanced Controls rollout, in the Tiles Setup area, click on the light gray Texture color swatch, and, in the Color Selector dialog that appears, change the color to pure white. Enter 2.0 in the Horiz. Count field and press Enter. In the Grout Setup area, click the Texture color swatch and set it to pure black in the Color Selector. This creates the illusion of eight panes of glass with mullions. In the Grout Setup area, enter 4.0 in the Horizontal Gap field, and press Enter (**Figure 8.27**).

    Adjusting the layout and dimensions of the map causes it to more closely resemble the actual window.

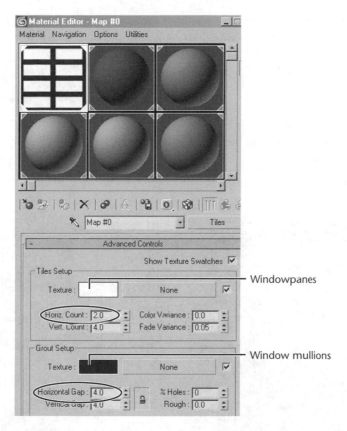

FIGURE 8.27 *Change the sizes and colors of the map.*

5. Close the Material Editor. Make sure that the Select Object button is toggled on in the main toolbar, and click in an empty space in the Top viewport to de-select everything. Click the blue line that connects the source of Spot01 to its target. Click the Select and Move button on the main toolbar, and then change the reference coordinate system to Local. Hold down the Shift key, and clone the spotlight in its target to the next window. The spotlight will rotate erratically, so either right-click to cancel the operation or click the Undo button in the main toolbar.

note

The grout's horizontal and vertical settings are locked together, so you need to change only one or the other to have them both use the same setting.

This step illustrates a common point of confusion that new users of 3ds Max 8 will encounter and must be aware of. You have a Grid object in the scene that will help you to move the spotlight accurately.

caution

If two or more selected objects have different Local reference coordinate systems, transforming them can create unpredictable behavior.

6. Press H, and, in the Select Objects dialog, double-click on Grid01. Right-click in the Top viewport, and choose Activate Grid in the quad menu (**Figure 8.28**).

   Before using a new grid, it must first be activated.

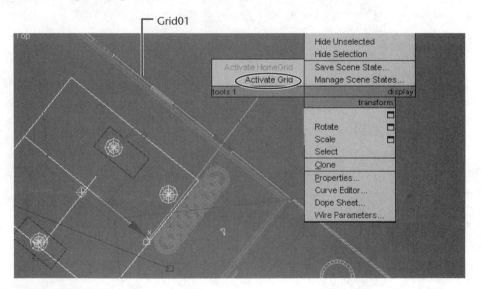

FIGURE 8.28 *You must select a grid object in the scene before it can be activated.*

7. Make sure that Select and Move is still active on the main toolbar, and set the reference coordinate system to Grid. Click the blue line for Spot01 to select both it and its target. Hold down the Shift key, and clone the light and target to the next window. In the Clone Options dialog, choose the Instance radio button. Click OK. Clone an Instance of the new light and target once more to the next window (**Figure 8.29**). Select Grid01 in the scene in the Top viewport, and then right-click in the viewport and choose Activate Home Grid in the quad menu.

   Even though you need a spotlight and projector map for each window, simulating shadows with a projector map can still be more efficient than casting actual shadows.

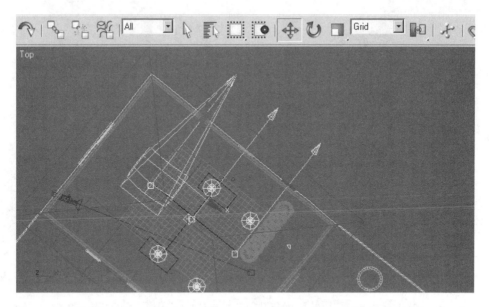

FIGURE 8.29 *Clone the spotlight and target for each window on that side of the shack, for a total of three.*

8. Render the Camera01 viewport, and notice that the spotlights are extra-bright where they overlap on the right-hand wall, resulting in an unconvincing effect. Select either of the spotlights in the Top viewport. On the Modify panel, in the Intensity/Color/Attenuation roll-out, check the Use option of Far Attenuation, enter 25'0" in the Start field, and enter 42'0" in the End field. Press Enter and render the Camera01 viewport again. The sunlight is still bright on the floor near the windows but no longer makes the wall too bright (see **Figure 8.30** on the next page).

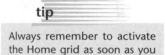

tip

Always remember to activate the Home grid as soon as you are finished with custom grids.

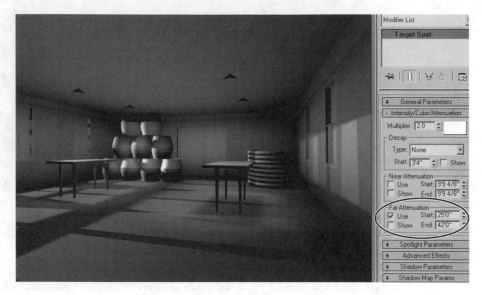

FIGURE 8.30 *Attenuation counteracts the adverse effect of angle of incidence and overlapping lights in this scene.*

9. Close all windows and dialogs, and save the file. It should already be called Int_light06.max.

Faking shadows is often much more efficient and just as effective.

Using lights in 3ds Max 8 can do more than just provide extra light in a scene. Projector maps are a simple example of some of the time-saving effects that you can generate using lights.

Summary

This chapter has provided you with a foundation in a very important aspect of 3D visualization: the ability to control how light decays over distance. This attenuation, combined with the ability to shape lights and project images through the lights, is a powerful technique that you should practice so that it becomes second nature in your production workflow. All light types can use projector maps for special effects or to simulate complex shadows.

The ability to control lights far beyond what is possible in the real world lets you fine-tune your rendered images to make them more convincing and efficient.

CHAPTER 9

Rendering

In This Chapter

You've already rendered a few images using the Quick Render button on the main toolbar of 3ds Max 8, but you have not yet rendered the scene in any form that can be sent to the client. The default rendering engine in 3ds Max 8 lets you create images that may be used as still images in print, on the Web, or as sequences of images in animations.

This chapter shows you how to use the Render Scene dialog to set the rendered image's resolution in pixels, and then save the rendered images to your hard drive. The image you see on your display at render time is called the *rendered frame window*, and you'll learn how to access some of the options that let you compare two images, save the files directly from the dialog, and view files as grayscale images for contrast analysis.

Choosing the proper output file type is important for optimum results, so you'll learn about a few of the more commonly used file types rendered from 3ds Max 8. You also learn how to set up rendering parameters for printing hard-copy images at the correct resolution for different printers.

Key Terms

- **Scanline renderer**—This is the default 3ds Max 8 rendering engine, which calculates the rendered image one horizontal line at a time and is known in the industry for its rendering speed.

- **Render resolution**—The horizontal and vertical size of a rendered image in pixels.

- **Color depth**—A numeric value of the total possible number of colors in an image.

- **Overscan/underscan**—When determining file output, you must compensate for the degree to which television recording devices change the size and aspect ratio of your rendered image.

- **Codec**—This software compresses and decompresses animations. Several codecs ship with 3ds Max 8, and many more are available on the Internet.

- **Anti-aliasing**—A computer image is a pattern of discrete points of color or light arranged in a grid pattern. To smooth diagonal edges, the computer applies anti-aliasing to avoid any stair-stepped effects.

- **Pixel aspect ratio**—A width-to-height ratio of pixels in rendered output that counteracts image stretching that is inherent when using television recording equipment. The pixel aspect ratio for print images should always be 1.0, or square pixels.

- **Alpha channel**—Transparency pixels stored in certain file types for compositing images or maps.

Rendering Options

The default renderer in 3ds Max 8 is called the scanline renderer. It is noted in the industry for being a very fast and efficient renderer that produces good-quality images. The scanline renderer is also used in the Material Editor to preview materials.

Other rendering tools come built into 3ds Max, such as the radiosity renderer and the mental ray renderer. You can also purchase third-party rendering engines. This chapter will focus on the scanline renderer only, but keep in mind other options are available.

tip

If at first you do not achieve satisfactory results with the scanline renderer, avoid the temptation of trying other renderers to correct the problem. Because the scanline renderer is fast, it is ideal for quickly fine-tuning and testing your work and is therefore conducive to learning the skills necessary to produce good-quality images.

Although you have already rendered images in 3ds Max 8 to check your progress while modeling a scene or developing materials, you have nothing to show for your effort. You have not saved and stored these images anyplace where they can be retrieved and viewed. In this chapter you'll render images and learn about a variety of parameters and file types that will allow you to share your work with clients or pass it on for further post-processing.

The Render Scene Dialog

Rendering scenes requires some planning to determine where the rendered images will be used, what file types the client can access, and whether they will be multiuse images—for example, for the Web and for print.

You must first know the rendering output necessary to obtain the quality for the type of files you will be sending the client. Web and video animations require much lower resolution than printed images, for example. Some video equipment and some post-processing requires certain file types to be effective, and all of these parameters are set in the Render Scene dialog in 3ds Max 8.

Exercise 9.1: Setting the output resolution for the Web

1. Reset 3ds Max 8 and open the **Render01.max** file from the CD-ROM. Save it to your project folder with the name *Render02.max*. This is the outdoor scene from Chapter 7, with a few materials added.

2. On the main toolbar, click the Render Scene button to open the Render Scene dialog. Say, for example, your client needs a high-resolution image that can be posted to a Web site for its client to view. In the Common Parameters rollout, in the Time Output area, make sure that the radio button for Single is selected.

   This means that you will be rendering the Camera01 viewport scene as only a single image, and not a sequence of images that are required for animations.

3. Most people who access Web sites on a desktop or laptop computer can view images that are 1024 by 768 pixels, so you'll set up the rendering for typical full-screen display. In the Output Size area, enter 1024 in the Width field and 768 in the Height field (see **Figure 9.1** on the next page).

   Rendering your images at the correct size in the beginning of a project avoids any problems with file conversion later.

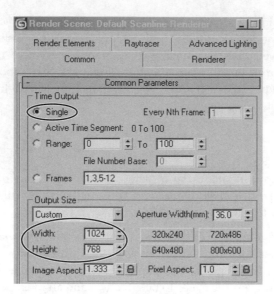

FIGURE 9.1 *Enter the rendered pixel size for the width and height of the image you want.*

4. Make sure that the Camera01 viewport is selected in the Viewport drop-down list at the bottom center of the Render Scene dialog, and click the Render button (**Figure 9.2**).

    The rendered image will be about 2.5 times larger than what you have previously seen with the default 640-by-480-pixel resolution. It will also take longer to render.

FIGURE 9.2 *Always double-check to see that the correct viewport is being rendered before rendering the scene.*

5. Close all windows and dialogs and save the file. It should already be called Render02.max. You just rendered the image at a larger resolution, but you still haven't saved the file so that the client will have access to it.

The rendered frame window cannot be accessed by programs other than 3ds Max 8; therefore, there is no way for the client to post this rendered image on the company Web site because you have not saved the file to your hard drive. Let's save the rendered image to a file that can be viewed on other computers.

Exercise 9.2: Setting the output file type

1. Open the **Render02.max** file from the CD-ROM or from the previous exercise and save it to your project folder with the name *Render03.max*.

2. Click the Render Scene button on the main toolbar. In the Render Scene dialog that appears, Common Parameters rollout, Render Output area, click the Files button.

    You may need to pan or scroll down in the Render Scene dialog to access it.

3. In the Render Output File dialog that opens, access your project folder in the Save In navigator. Enter Render_test01 in the File Name field, click in the Save As Type field, and choose PNG Image File [*.png] from the drop-down list (**Figure 9.3**). Click the Save button.

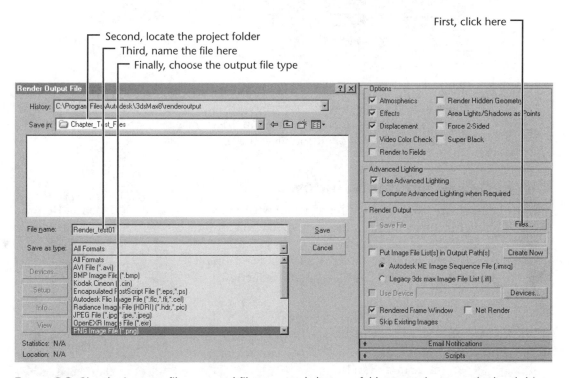

FIGURE 9.3 *Give the image a filename and file type, and choose a folder to render to on the hard drive.*

4. In the PNG Configuration dialog, choose the RGB 24-bit [16.7 Million] radio button and uncheck the Alpha Channel box (**Figure 9.4**). Click OK and, in the Render Scene dialog, click the Render button.

As the white scanline progresses downward in the Rendered Frame Window, the scanline render is rescanning the Window and saving the image to the location you specified.

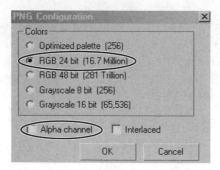

FIGURE 9.4 *Set up the PNG file type for the parameters you want before rendering.*

5. Close all windows and dialogs and save the file. It is already named Render03.max.

The rendered image may now be viewed from within 3ds Max 8 with the RAM Player or from the File pull-down menu, View Image File option; or you may use other software to open and view the file.

The Rendered Frame Window

You've used the rendered frame window throughout earlier chapters of this book only to view the results of your test renderings. There is, however, functionality in the rendered frame window beyond simply viewing images that can speed your production.

In the next exercise, you'll learn how to use some of the window's options and discover how these tools can help you to save files directly from the window, to clone renderings to compare two images, and to view an image in grayscale.

This chapter's Max Files folder on the CD-ROM includes a bitmap image. 3ds Max always looks for any necessary external files in the same folder as the main Max scene file. If you open a scene file from a location different from the original chapter folder, you may encounter a Missing External Files dialog. If you do, click Browse, and in the Configure External File Paths dialog, click Add. Use the Choose New External Files Path dialog to browse to the location of the CD versions of the Max scene files for this chapter, then click Use Path, and click OK. Click Continue to close the Missing External Files dialog.

Exercise 9.3: Using the rendered frame window to speed production

1. Open the **Render03.max** file from the CD-ROM or from the previous exercise and save it to your project folder with the name *Render04.max*.

2. On the main toolbar, click the Render Scene button and, in the Common Parameters rollout, Output Size area, click the 640x480 resolution preset button for a smaller image (**Figure 9.5**). In the Render Output area, clear the check box for Save File; otherwise you will overwrite your previously saved PNG image.

    Rendering smaller images, especially when testing, will result in faster renderings and greater productivity.

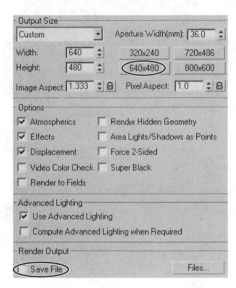

FIGURE 9.5 *Render to a lower resolution and don't save the rendered file.*

3. Click the Render button in the Render Scene dialog to render the Camera01 viewport in the rendered frame window. On the window's main toolbar, click the Save Bitmap button, which looks like a diskette. This brings up the Browse Images for Output dialog, which looks similar to the Render Output file dialog you used in the previous exercise (**Figure 9.6**). You can name a new image file, choose a folder, and choose a file type with which to save the image as it appears in the rendered frame window. Click Cancel.

    You don't need to save this image again, but it is important to know, especially if you're doing long renderings, that you can save the file directly from the rendered frame window if you have forgotten to set it up before rendering.

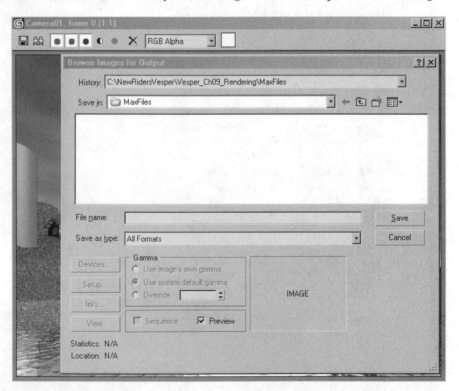

FIGURE 9.6 *Files may be saved to the hard drive directly from the rendered frame window. The resolution is predetermined, but a new file type can be chosen.*

4. Click the Clone Rendered Frame Window button, which looks like twins, on the main toolbar of the rendered frame window. You can now make changes to your scene, render again, and compare the two images side by side (**Figure 9.7**).

Evening-sky test in new rendering   Original rendered image in clone window

FIGURE 9.7 *Clone the Rendered Frame Window, make changes, and render again to compare changes made in the scene.*

5. Click the Monochrome toggle button, which looks like a gray circle, on the rendered frame window toolbar. This converts the render window to a grayscale image and is very useful for checking contrast levels in a scene. Right-click on the rendered image, hold down the mouse button, and move the eyedropper cursor around to see important information about the pixel under the cursor (**Figure 9.8**). Useful for checking contrast, the Mono level lets you see the relative brightness of pixels. Toggle Monochrome off.

Viewing images in grayscale gives you a much better perception of the contrast than you get in the colored image.

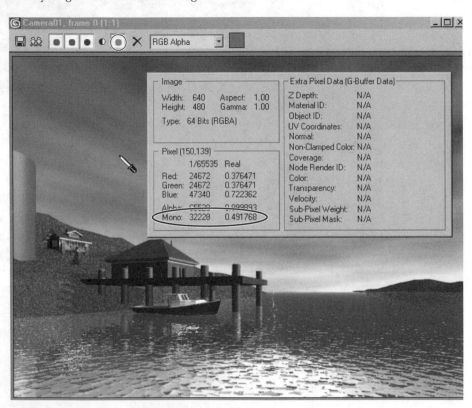

FIGURE 9.8 *Convert the image in the rendered frame window to grayscale, and sample pixel information.*

6. Close all windows and dialogs and save the file. It should already be called Render04.max.

While it certainly has been convenient for viewing the rendered images, the rendered frame window has a tool set that makes it particularly useful in production, especially for comparing changes to scenes and for checking the all-important contrast in your images.

Rendering for Animations

To create animation sequences, you need to do a bit more planning before starting the rendering. For example, rendering animations for television requires different setup parameters than for Internet playback, and DVD animations require yet other settings. Here are some of the things we'll look at in this section:

- Recording equipment, if any
- Required resolution and pixel aspect
- Output file type

Animation output for television and film often requires special recorders to perform a process called *overscan* or *underscan* so that the animation fits the screen correctly. In the Rendered Scene dialog, Common Parameters rollout, Output Size area, you can click the drop-down list that has presets for many different film and television standards (**Figure 9.9**).

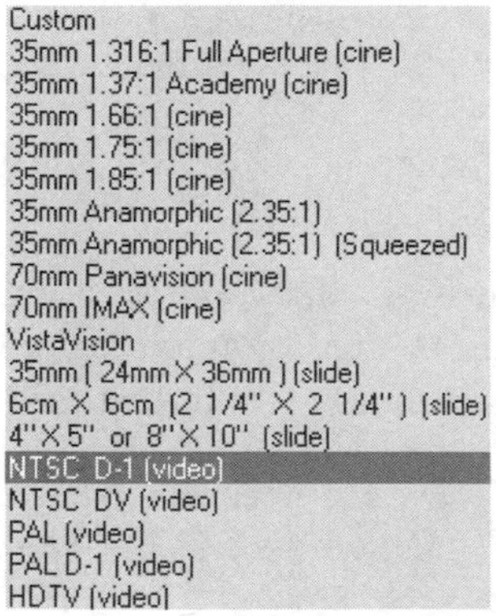

FIGURE 9.9 *3ds Max 8 has many render output presets for film and television recording devices.*

If you should choose, for example, NTSC D-1 [video], you will notice that a resolution of 720 by 486 is set with a pixel aspect ratio of 0.90000 (**Figure 9.10**). This pixel aspect ratio ensures that circles will show up as circles in the rendered image, and not be deformed into ovals.

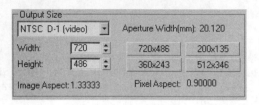

FIGURE 9.10 *NTSC D-1 is an animation output format commonly used in U.S. television and can be chosen from a list of standards.*

Choosing an animation output file type is a two-part process; it is *highly recommended* that you always render animations to a sequence of still images. These might be TGA, TIF, or PNG images. If the client is then going to play back the animation on his or her computer or on the Internet, you'll need to convert the sequence of still images to an animation file type; AVI and MOV are two of the more popular.

When converting to AVI or MOV files, you will be required to choose a *codec*—a compression utility that converts the image sequence into a playable animation. It is beyond the scope of this book to address codecs, but you need to check with your client to make sure their equipment will play the codecs you render to.

tip

If you have a client who needs animations for television, make sure that you check and double-check both the required rendering resolution and the pixel aspect ratio before rendering anything. You may use custom settings when your equipment is not listed in the presets.

In the next exercise, you will choose a camera in the scene that has been animated moving along the pier. It starts moving at frame 0 and finishes by frame 50, so you don't need to render the full 100-frame sequence that is currently set on the timeline.

You'll choose a low-resolution, PNG output file type to render the sequence of still images, and then use the RAM Player to convert those still images to an AVI file that can be played back on almost any computer.

Exercise 9.4: Rendering animations for computer playback

1. Open the **Render04.max** file from the CD-ROM or from the last exercise and save it to your project folder with the name *Render05.max*.

2. Make sure the Camera01 viewport is active, and press the C key to switch to a camera viewport. Because there is more than one camera in the scene, you are presented with the Select Camera dialog. Double-click Camera02 in the dialog, and your viewport will look like that shown in **Figure 9.11**.

FIGURE 9.11 *Camera02 looks down the pier to the water tank and is animated along a path.*

3. On the main toolbar, click the Render Scene button. In the Common Parameters rollout, Time Output area, is a radio button that allows you to render the Active Time Segment, but in this situation the camera is animated for only the first 50 frames and not the entire 100-frame segment. Choose the Range radio button, enter 50 in the To field, and press Enter (see **Figure 9.12** on the next page).

It's not necessary to render the 50 frames at the end of the animation with the camera not moving, and there are no other animated events visible in the scene.

note

It is possible to render directly to animation codecs from 3ds Max 8. However, codecs render using delta compression, in which the first frame of an animation is recorded completely, and then subsequent frames only record pixels that have changed. This reduces file size and often speeds playback performance. If something should go wrong during the rendering process, individual segments or frames cannot be rerendered and reassembled into the animation.

More important, you cannot use the built-in network rendering feature of 3ds Max 8 to render to delta-compressed file types.

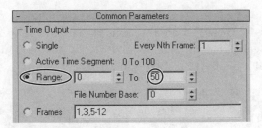

FIGURE 9.12 *Set to 3ds Max 8 to render a range of images from frame 0 to frame 50.*

4. In the Common Parameters rollout, Output Size area, click the 320x240 resolution preset button. The pixel aspect ratio will remain 1.0 for computer playback (**Figure 9.13**).

    This lower-resolution image will render faster and play back on most computers, and the quality is good enough for testing.

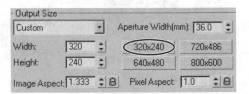

FIGURE 9.13 *Set the render resolution to a low setting of 320 by 240 pixels.*

5. In the Render Scene dialog, click the Render button. You'll receive a warning that no files are going to be saved, and be asked, "Do you want to continue?" Click No to cancel the rendering. In the Common Parameters rollout, Rendered Output area, click the Files button. In the Render Output File dialog, navigate to your project folder and enter Animation.PNG in the File Name field (**Figure 9.14**). Click Save.

    3ds Max 8 will warn you if you try to render an animation sequence without saving it to your hard drive.

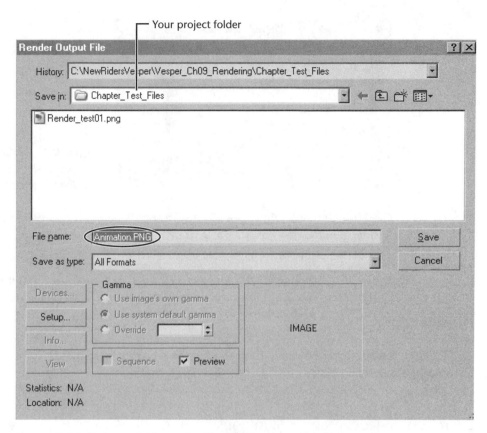

FIGURE 9.14 *Choose a folder and a filename for the animation.*

6. In the Render Scene dialog, click the Render button. The rendered frame window will begin scanline rendering each frame, and the Rendering dialog will display the progress and the estimated time remaining for the entire animation (see **Figure 9.15** on the next page).

The Time Remaining figure can change throughout the animation process, depending on many variables, such as the visibility of dense objects, the amount and quality of shadows in the scene, and whether reflections are being rendered.

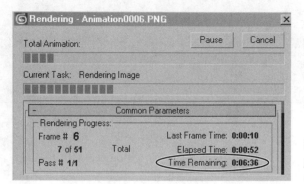

FIGURE 9.15 *Rendering progress is shown in the Rendering dialog.*

7. Close all windows and dialogs and save the file. It should already be called Render05.max. Exit 3ds Max 8.

    The sequence of PNG images has been saved to the hard drive.

Rendering to a sequence of still images gives you the opportunity to network render, which distributes individual images in a sequence over a network of computers; to render individual frames to make corrections; and to use the files in post-processing with other software.

In the next exercise, you will learn how to convert the sequence of still images into a single compressed file that can then be passed on to your client for viewing.

Exercise 9.5: Converting still images to animation

1. Start 3ds Max 8 from scratch with an empty scene or reset the current session.

    You've already rendered a sequence of images, so you don't need to have the Max file loaded in order to convert them to an animation.

2. From the Rendering pull-down menu, choose RAM Player. In the RAM Player dialog, click the Open Channel A button. In the Open File, Channel A dialog, locate your project folder and highlight the **Animation0000.PNG** file, which is the first still image in the sequence you rendered (**Figure 9.16**). Make sure that the Sequence box at the bottom of the dialog is checked. Click the Open button.

3ds Max will create a new file called Image File List, which has some options you'll see next.

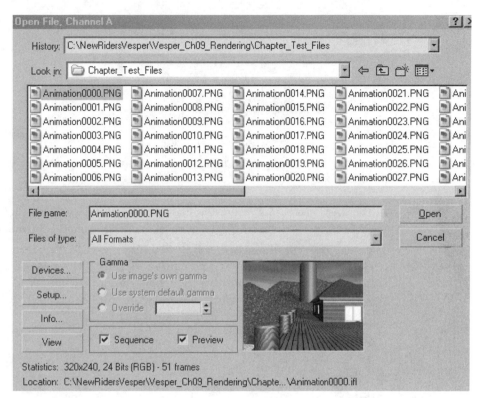

FIGURE 9.16 *For you to be able to convert all the images into an animation, it is imperative that the Sequence option be selected.*

3. In the Image File List Control dialog, click the OK button to accept the default settings to place the animation in your project folder and to use the entire sequence of image files (see **Figure 9.17** on the next page).

    The default settings are set to render each frame from frame 0 to frame 50.

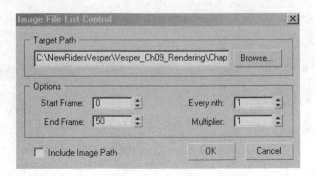

Figure 9.17 *You can save the complete animation to your project folder, which comes up because you have saved files there previously.*

4. In the RAM Player Configuration dialog, click OK to accept the defaults for the animation resolution and the number of frames rendered (**Figure 9.18**).

    The sequence of still image files is loaded into the RAM Player, and you may click the Play button to see the animation play back. However, this is still not an animation you can send your clients, but just a preliminary step in the conversion process that allows you to preview the still images as an animation.

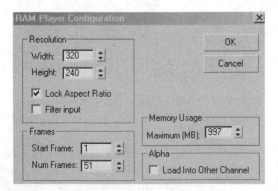

Figure 9.18 *The default settings in the RAM Player Configuration dialog are fine for this example.*

5. In the RAM Player, click the Save Channel A button. In the Save File, Channel A dialog, in the File Name field, enter `test.AVI`, and click Save. In the AVI File Compression Setup dialog, click OK to accept the default Cinepak codec (**Figure 9.19**).

    Nothing will appear to happen for a few seconds, but when the computer frees up again, you will have written your AVI file to your hard drive.

tip

What has been created in your project folder is a new file called Animation0000.Ifl. This is simply an image file list that can be opened in any text editor to view or to edit a list of the names of all the files opened in the RAM Player.

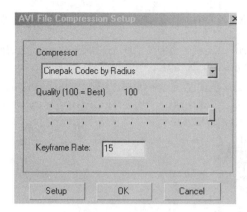

FIGURE 9.19 *The Cinepak codec creates a very common AVI file output type that almost anyone can play back on any computer; the default settings are usually sufficient.*

6.   Reset 3ds Max 8; you only needed to open it to access the RAM Player to convert the still images into an animation. You could also have used other software, such as Adobe Premier, to convert the still images into an animation file. The other software packages would allow much more complex video editing features, whereas 3ds Max 8 is a simple conversion with no editing capability.

The RAM Player loads the individual still-image sequence and creates the new Image File List file type, which can then be saved to any other file output format.

Rendering for Print Output

Many people are often confused by the terminology that is used to describe the process of outputting rendered images for printing. Many common printer types process ink on paper using a measurement called *dpi* (dots per inch). Computers, on the other hand, work with pixel resolution. The two measurement terms have nothing to do with each other directly, so you must interpolate from resolution to dpi to get acceptable printed results.

The formula for determining resolution for printing at a certain dpi is simple enough: resolution = paper size × dpi. If you want an 8-by-10-inch print from a 300-dpi printer, the resolution is 2400 (8 × 300 = 2400) pixels by 3000 (10 × 300 = 3000) pixels.

To ease the process of determining the correct resolution for the print size and printer's dpi in 3ds Max 8, you can use the Print Size Wizard, which you'll learn about in the next exercise.

tip

The formula presented in this section suggests only a starting point for determining rendering resolution. Variables such as the printer's ability to "dithe," or blur, the dots for smoother output, the types of ink and paper used, and the viewing distance of the image will also have an effect on the required resolution. For example, some highway billboards are printed at 12 dpi and look just fine when viewed from a distance.

Exercise 9.6: Using the Print Size Wizard

1. Open the **Render05.max** scene from the CD-ROM or from Exercise 9.4. Make sure that the Camera02 viewport is active.

2. In the Rendering drop-down menu, choose Print Size Wizard (**Figure 9.20**). It will allow you to choose combinations of different print sizes and dpi's, and then render the image to the hard drive.

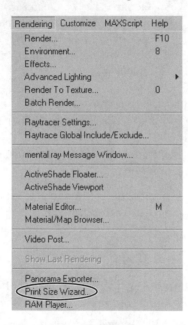

FIGURE 9.20 *The Print Size Wizard simplifies the math involved in calculating resolution for printing.*

3. In the Print Size Wizard dialog, from the Paper Size drop-down list choose A - 11x8.5in (**Figure 9.21**). Click the 300 button in the Choose DPI Value area, and you'll notice that the resolution has been changed to 3300 by 2550 pixels.

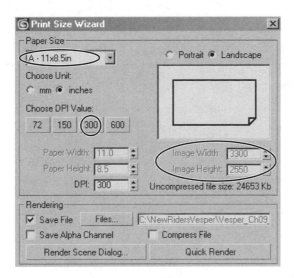

FIGURE 9.21 *Choose the paper size and your printer's dpi value to calculate the render resolution in the Print Size Wizard.*

4. In the Print Size Wizard dialog, in the Rendering area, click the Files button. In the Select TIFF File dialog, make sure that you're rendering to your project folder and in the File Name field enter Print_test. Click Save.

    The Print Size Wizard will render directly only to TIFF files, a file type commonly used in the print industry.

5. In the Print Size Wizard dialog, Rendering area, click the Render Scene Dialog button. This opens the Render Scene dialog, which you are already familiar with. In the Common Parameters rollout, Render Output area, click the Files button. In the Render Output File dialog, Save As Type drop-down list, choose JPEG, and click Save. Click OK in the JPEG Image Control dialog to accept the defaults. In the Render Scene dialog, click the Render button.

6. Exit 3ds Max 8 without saving the file. The image has been rendered to your hard drive and can be opened using other software.

Again, the Print Size Wizard is only a starting point for a trial-and-error process to determine what resolution works best with your printer, paper, and ink. You'll need to make adjustments as necessary for efficiency and quality.

caution

The codec that saves JPEG images in 3ds Max 8 tends to produce images that are a bit on the soft side. To maintain crisp anti-aliasing throughout your visualization process, you'd be better off rendering to PNG files.

Summary

You've learned the fundamentals of rendering to still images, to animations, and to still images specifically for printing. Always check with your clients to see what their requirements are, especially for resolution and file type, and allow some time in the process for experimentation.

CHAPTER 10

Creating Convincing Materials

In This Chapter

Materials define all of the surface attributes in 3ds Max 8—things like color, shininess, texture, reflectivity, and more. You can think of materials in 3ds Max 8 like frosting on a cake—cake can be quite good, but it is always much, much better with frosting.

In this chapter, you'll learn how to work with the Material Editor, which is analogous to the artist's palette, where you'll create materials and maps and apply them to the surfaces of objects in the scene.

First you'll learn how to create and apply solid colors within the default Standard material, which makes objects appear homogeneous with no discernible patterns. Then you'll learn how to adjust the parameters of *specular highlights*, or the light scattered from surfaces. You'll also learn how to create materials with patterns that require you to assign and adjust mapping coordinates, so that the patterns are the right size and fit for your intended material.

In addition, you'll practice a technique called *bump mapping*, which lets you simulate geometry in the scene using materials so that you can reduce the overhead of extra geometry. Finally, you'll learn how to create reflections in materials and optimize them to increase performance while maintaining a convincing appearance.

While this chapter focuses on the mechanics of creating materials, knowing the mechanics is not all there is to the process. You must train yourself to look at the world around you with a more critical eye.

Without an understanding of how light reacts with surfaces, you will not be able to reproduce convincing effects in 3ds Max 8. As with lighting, you must view the world as an artist and interpret reality with the materials in 3ds Max 8 to satisfy your client's requirements.

Key Terms

- **Material Editor**—This is the workspace in 3ds Max 8 where you create and adjust all materials.

- **Materials**—Materials are applied to objects and define all of the visual attributes that make up the surface.

- **Maps**—Maps are simply patterns within materials. They cannot be applied directly to objects.

- **Specular highlights**—Light strikes the surface of materials and is either bounced back from the surface or absorbed by it. The highlights are an indicator of the material's hardness and provide key bright areas in the scene to enhance contrast.

- **Mapping coordinates**—These determine how map patterns are sized and repeated over surfaces.

The Material Editor: Interactive Editing

As with so many other things in 3ds Max 8, it is important to create materials that can be easily edited to keep up with the demands of clients, so in this chapter you'll learn how to use the Material Editor in ways that provide maximum flexibility.

The Material Editor is made up of sample windows where you can visualize the results of various layers of surface attributes as you create them.

The first step in working with the Material Editor is to learn its basic functionality for controlling surface color and shininess, the two primary components of materials that meet the viewer's eye and create a first impression. In the next exercise, you'll use the Material Editor to change materials that have already been assigned to some of the objects in the fishing shack from Chapter 8, to give the scene a more convincing look.

note

The result you see in the sample windows of the Material Editor provides a good idea of how the materials will appear in the scene. But because materials react to lighting and surroundings, it is only an approximation.

Exercise 10.1: Getting acquainted with the Material Editor

1. Open the file called **Int_matl01.max** from the CD-ROM. Save it to your project folder with the name *Int_matl02.max*.

   This is the fully lit fishing shack from Chapter 8.

2. On the main toolbar, click the Material Editor button, or press the M key, which is the keyboard shortcut that opens the Material Editor.

   You will see six sample windows (**Figure 10.1**). The first contains the projector map from Chapter 8 that simulates sunlight shining through windows in the room. The other five windows contain very basic materials with random colors that have been assigned to objects in the scene.

   You'll now adjust the number of sample windows visible in the Material Editor.

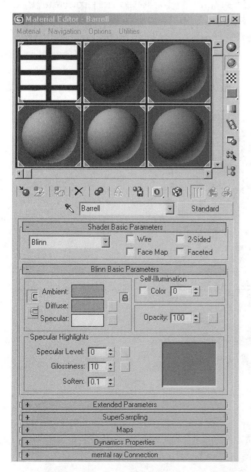

FIGURE 10.1 *Open the Material Editor to gain access to the sample windows, where materials are created before being assigned to objects in the scene.*

3. Right-click on any sample window in the Material Editor, and choose 6 x 4 Sample Windows from the contextual menu (**Figure 10.2**).

You now see a total of 24 sample windows, the maximum number you can view in the Material Editor at any one time.

FIGURE 10.2
Change the number of sample windows in the Material Editor to the maximum 24.

4. Right-click on a sample window again, and switch back to the 3 x 2 Sample Windows display. Use the horizontal scrollbar to scroll right in the sample windows, and click in the sample window that contains a dark red sphere.

A white border appears around the sample window to indicate the sample window is active. The white triangles in the corners indicate an object in this scene has this material assigned to it. A sample window with white triangles is known as a hot material: changing its parameters in the Material Editor will automatically update the object in the scene. Finally, the material name Floor will appear in the name field (**Figure 10.3**). (The material was given the name Floor previously, and it is important that materials have logical names.)

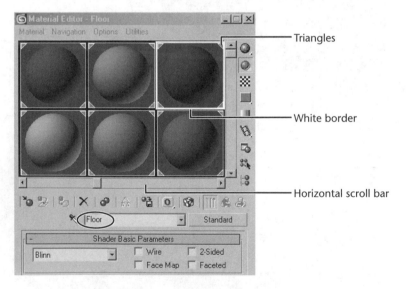

FIGURE 10.3 *Click on a sample window to make it active.*

5. In the Material Editor, in the Blinn Basic Parameters rollout, click the Diffuse color swatch to open the Color Selector (**Figure 10.4**). There you can change the base color of the material to update the scene. Make sure the Camera01 viewport is active and press Ctrl + L, the keyboard shortcut that toggles default lighting on in the shaded viewport, so that you can see the materials in this dark room. In the Color Selector, click in the middle of the green stripe in the Hue field.

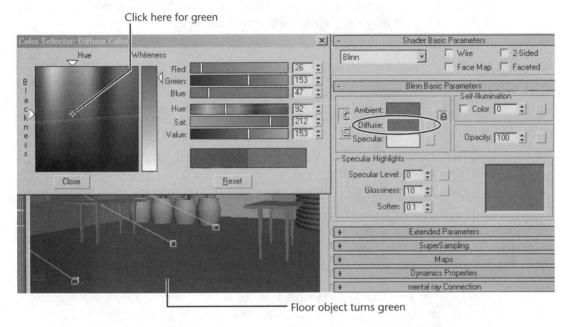

FIGURE 10.4 *Open the Color Selector to see that hot materials in the Material Editor can be changed, and the result will immediately show in the scene.*

6. Close all windows and dialogs and save the file. It should already be called Int_matl02.max.

This simple exercise illustrates the important interactivity of the Material Editor and the materials in the scene.

The Diffuse and Ambient color swatches control the color of solid homogeneous materials, such as plastic or paint. Because of their homogeneous nature, the solid colors do not require mapping coordinates to make them fit the objects to which they are applied, so the results can be seen immediately.

caution

By default, the Diffuse color (color in direct light) is locked to the Ambient color (color in shaded areas) for consistency when using the radiosity renderer. It is best to leave it that way until you are very comfortable with 3ds Max 8, because any variations may make advanced lighting materials unpredictable.

Specular Highlights

Specular highlights, the light scattered from a surface, is one of the least understood and most neglected components of materials, yet it is critical for creating convincing materials.

If you look around you in the real world, you can almost always accurately guess what material an object is made of. Is it because of the color? Is it because of the texture? No, the first indicator of the nature of a material comes from its specular highlights, which indicate the hardness of a material.

When light strikes a surface, it is either absorbed or scattered back into the atmosphere. Hard materials have molecules that are very close together, causing most of the light that strikes the surface to scatter back, creating a bright, small specular highlight. Soft materials, on the other hand, have molecules that are far apart, so that some of the light is absorbed, and the remaining light is widely scattered, resulting in a broad, soft specular highlight.

This section addresses three primary controls for specular highlights: color, specular level, and glossiness.

The floor material in the scene will eventually become ceramic tiles, which will have a moderately rough, antislip surface.

Exercise 10.2: Adjusting the parameters of specular highlights

1. Open the **Int_matl02.max** file from the CD-ROM or from the last exercise, and save it to your project folder with the name *Int_matl03.max*.

2. Open the Material Editor from the main toolbar or by pressing the M key. Make sure the material called Floor is the active sample window.

3. In the Blinn Basic Parameters rollout, click the Specular color swatch. In the Color Selector, drag the Whiteness slider to the bottom to make the color pure white (**Figure 10.5**).

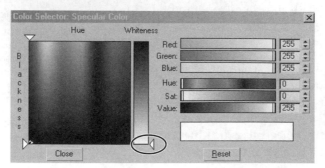

FIGURE 10.5 *Drag the Whiteness slider to its lowest point to create a pure white material color.*

4. In the Blinn Basic Parameters rollout, Specular Highlights area, enter 100 in the Specular Level field (**Figure 10.6**). Press Enter.

The specular highlights on the sample window become large and bright with soft edges, but the bright specular highlights should have hard edges and be quite small. The specular level value controls the brightness of the specular highlight; higher values indicate a harder material, in which more of the light that strikes the surface is scattered back to the viewer.

tip

Most materials, regardless of color, have white specular highlights. The main exceptions are the pure metals—such as gold, lead, and copper—and materials like anodized aluminum, in which the color is baked in at the molecular level.

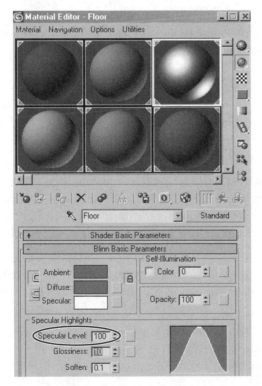

FIGURE 10.6 *Increase the Specular Level setting to give the appearance that much of the light striking the surface is scattered back. However, the highlight is unconvincing because it's so broad and bright.*

5. In the Specular Highlights area, enter 60 in the Glossiness numeric field and press Enter.

This setting controls the size of the specular highlight and usually increases or decreases as the Specular Level setting increases or decreases. The harder the surface, the more the light is scattered straight back from it.

6. Ceramic and terra-cotta floor tiles can vary widely in their surface condition and hardness; therefore, you must decide how you want the specular highlights to be represented in your scene. In this fishing shack, you'll want a low-gloss nonslip surface, so set Specular Level to 40 and Glossiness to 20.

   This results in a broad, dull specular highlight on the sample sphere.

note

The Material Editor sample window is only a representation of how your material looks. Factors such as lighting and the curvature of the object's surface will play a big role in the material's appearance in the final rendered image.

7. Close all windows and dialogs, and save the file. It should already be called Int_matl03.max.

Simulating specular highlights in the Material Editor can be a fairly subjective process, and you must experiment a bit with lighting and the specular-highlights adjustments to achieve the results that are most convincing to your viewers.

Creating Patterned Materials

A common misperception among new users of 3ds Max 8 is that materials and maps are the same thing. It's important to keep in mind that materials are applied to surfaces, and maps are patterns within materials.

The material you have just created for the floor would be fine if the floor were a painted surface or any other homogeneous, solid color. However, the floor in this case is to be of terra-cotta tile, a reddish-brown tile, with light tan cement grout between the tiles. This will require you to apply a tile pattern instead of the solid color.

It would be possible to photograph actual tiles with a digital camera and import the image directly into 3ds Max 8 to be used as a "bitmap" for the color of the material, but that is not a particularly flexible solution if the client wants to change the color or size of the tiles later.

There are many types of maps available in 3ds Max 8, but in this chapter you will use a procedural map type—a pattern that is mathematically generated and therefore offers a high degree of flexibility for making edits on the fly.

In the next exercise, you will apply color to the floor's surface, which will be represented by 1-by-1-foot-square terra-cotta tiles with the Tiles map type in 3ds Max 8.

Exercise 10.3: Using maps as color patterns

1. Open the file called **Int_matl03.max** from the CD-ROM or from the last exercise, and save it to your project folder with the name *Int_matl04.max*.

2. Press the M key to open the Material Editor, and make sure that the sample window for the material called Floor is active, it's the fourth sample window in the top row.

3. In the Blinn Basic Parameters rollout, click the gray button to the right of the Diffuse color swatch. This is the map shortcut button that takes you directly to the Material/Map Browser. Double-click Tiles in the browser list (**Figure 10.7**).

   Double-clicking on a map loads it into the current map slot—in this case, Diffuse. You could also highlight Tiles in the list and click OK to load the map. You are now automatically at the Tiles map level in the material hierarchy.

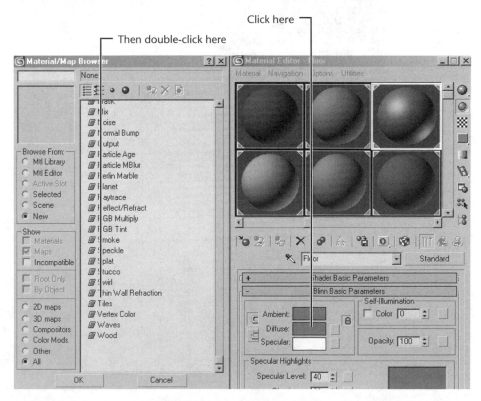

FIGURE 10.7 *Use the Material/Map Browser to load a map into the Diffuse color slot. When you place a map in the Diffuse color slot, it completely controls the color of your material by overriding the previously assigned solid color.*

4. Click the Material/Map Navigator button at
    the lower right corner of the sample windows
    (**Figure 10.8**).

    Using the Material/Map Navigator is a critical
    tool for efficiently moving around within the
    different levels of materials.

note

Just as the Diffuse and
Ambient solid colors are locked
together, so are the Diffuse
and Ambient maps locked
together, so that the entire
material is colored by the
map, whether it be in directly
lit or shaded areas.

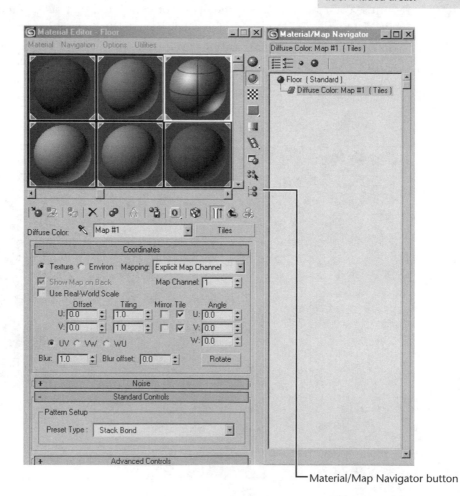

Material/Map Navigator button

FIGURE 10.8 *Open the Material/Map Navigator for a hierarchical view of the current
material, so that you can pick any level in the navigator to display it in the Material Editor.*

5. At the Tiles map level, you can click the Show Map in Viewport button at the bottom of the sample windows to see a representation of the map in the shaded viewport (**Figure 10.9**).

The map is stretched over the entire floor, as seen in the shaded viewport, resulting in tiles that are much too large, but you'll correct that in the next exercise.

The tiles in the scene and in the sample window are gray with black grout, not the colors you want.

If the Tiles map appears distorted in the Camera01 viewport, you can right-click on the viewport label and choose Texture Correction from the contextual menu.

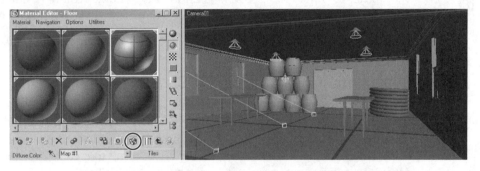

FIGURE 10.9 *The Show Map in Viewport button will enable you to view most maps in the shaded viewport.*

6. In the Tiles map, expand the Advanced Controls rollout. In the Tiles Setup area, click the Texture color swatch. In the Color Selector, enter 200 in the Red numeric field, 105 in the Green numeric field, and 80 in the Blue numeric field to create a terra-cotta color (**Figure 10.10**).

The Tiles map has color swatches for both the tile color and the grout color that can be adjusted at any time to update the map in the scene.

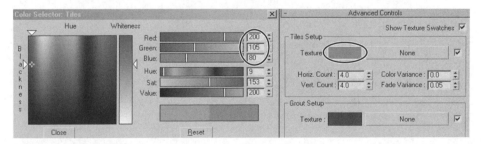

FIGURE 10.10 *Set the Tiles color to a reddish brown.*

7. In the Advanced Controls rollout, in the Grout Setup area, click the Texture swatch and change it to a light tan; RGB values of around 200, 165, and 90 would be fine.

    The floor colors in the Camera01 viewport automatically update to reflect the changes.

8. Close all windows and dialogs, and save the file. It should already be called Int_matl04.max.

    It is now the Tiles map colors that control the color of the floor.

Most materials you create will have maps that define the patterns within the material, rather than just solid colors. So far in this example, you have changed only the color with the map, but many other aspects of materials, such as bumpiness, can also be affected by maps, as you will learn next.

Using Mapping Coordinates to Size Maps

When most objects are created, they automatically receive general mapping coordinates, so that maps will show in the scene when Show Maps in Viewport is enabled. In order for maps to look convincing, however, the map size must be adjusted to reflect real-world sizes of the material you are trying to create. Two simple steps will ensure that your maps are sized correctly:

- Analyze the map to see how much real-world area one repetition would cover.
- Apply a UVW Map modifier, and adjust its size to match one repetition of the map.

The UVW Map modifier acts as a projector for the map and can be adjusted for both shape and size. In the next exercise, you will apply a UVW Map modifier to the floor so that the Tiles map is projected directly down onto the surface, and then you'll adjust the modifier's height and width for correct coverage.

Exercise 10.4: Applying and adjusting a UVW Map modifier

1. Open the **Int_matl04.max** file from the CD-ROM or from the last exercise, and save it to your project folder with the name *Int_matl05.max*.

2. Click the Select Object button on the main toolbar, and, in the Camera01 viewport, pick on the shack_floor object in the scene to select it. You can also press the H key and select it by name if that is easier.

3. On the Modify panel, in the Modifier List, double-click UVW Map near the bottom of the list.

   By default, the UVW Map modifier projects in Planar mode along the Local Z axis of the object and fits the length and width so that it is slightly larger than the object (**Figure 10.11**). Because of this automatic sizing of the UVW Map modifier, the map will look the same in the shaded viewport because it is still stretched over the entire floor.

4. Open the Material Editor and make sure the floor material sample window is active. Use the Material/Map Navigator to navigate to the Diffuse Color Map #1 [Tiles] level. In the Material Editor, click the Show End Result button below the sample windows to toggle it off (**Figure 10.12**).

   When Show End Result is toggled on, you see the end result of all maps in the sample window, and when this is off, you see only the map at the current map level—in this case, the Tiles map of the diffuse color. The default Tiles pattern is four tiles horizontally by four tiles vertically.

   Presuming that each tile, as measured from center of grout to center of grout, is 1 by 1 foot, then the real-world area covered by one repetition of this pattern is 4 by 4 feet.

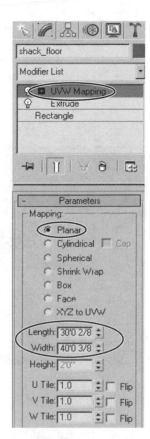

FIGURE 10.11 *Applying a UVW Map modifier controls how the current maps in the material are projected onto the object's surface.*

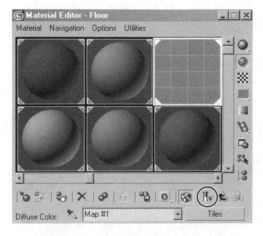

FIGURE 10.12 *The Show End Result toggle allows you to analyze the pattern of the current map in the sample window.*

5. On the Modify panel, in the Parameters rollout, enter 4'0" in both the Length and Width fields (**Figure 10.13**). Make sure to press Enter to finalize the numeric entry.

   Each tile on the floor in the Camera01 viewport is exactly 1 by 1 foot.

FIGURE 10.13 *Set the pattern of four horizontal tiles by four vertical tiles to cover an area of 4 by 4 feet to size the tiles correctly.*

6. Right-click in the Camera01 viewport to make sure it is active, and click the Quick Render button on the main toolbar.

   The rendered image shows a properly sized color pattern on the floor (**Figure 10.14**).

7. Close all windows and dialogs, and save the file. It should already be called Int_matl05.max.

Many maps that are applied to materials require mapping coordinates in order to resize them for correct appearance; a common method of resizing the map patterns is to use the UVW Map modifier.

FIGURE 10.14 *When the scene is rendered, the floor pattern has the correct color and size.*

Creating the Illusion of Geometry Using Bump Maps

Throughout this book, I've emphasized the importance of efficient modeling, and one of the best techniques in 3ds Max 8 to accomplish this efficiency is the use of bump mapping.

Bump mapping is an illusion that occurs at render time, in which white pixels in the map make the surface appear to be raised, while black pixels have no effect, and gray pixels have an effect somewhere in between. It's not actually the color of the pixels in the bump map, but the luminance value (brightness) of each pixel that creates the effect.

In the next exercise, you'll use bump mapping to make it appear as though the tiles are raised above the grout in the shack floor material.

Exercise 10.5: Using bump maps for raised tiles

1. Open the **Int_matl05.max** file from the CD-ROM or from the last exercise, and save it to your project folder with the name *Int_matl06.max*.

2. Open the Material Editor, and activate the sample window for the material called Floor.

3. In the Material Editor, expand the Maps rollout to view all the map slots available for this material, all of which are empty except Diffuse Color, which has the Tiles map. Clone the Tiles map from the Diffuse Color slot to the Bump slot by dragging it from one slot to the other. Release the mouse button when the pointer changes to show an arrow over None in the map slot (**Figure 10.15**).

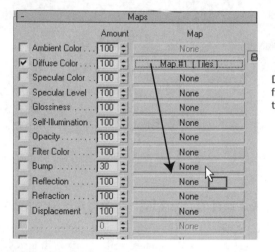

Drag the map from one slot to the other

FIGURE 10.15 *The mouse pointer must appear as a box and arrow cursor with the arrow positioned over the slot on which you want to drop the map.*

4. In the Copy [Instance] Map dialog that appears, make sure that the Copy radio button is selected and click OK (**Figure 10.16**).

    The map in the Bump slot should be a copy of the map, because you want its colors to be changed without affecting the map in Diffuse Color.

FIGURE 10.16 *Choose the Copy option in the Copy [Instance] Map dialog.*

5. In the Material Editor, click the Material/Map Navigator button, and highlight the bump map in the navigator to go to that level (**Figure 10.17**). Expand the Advanced Controls rollout.

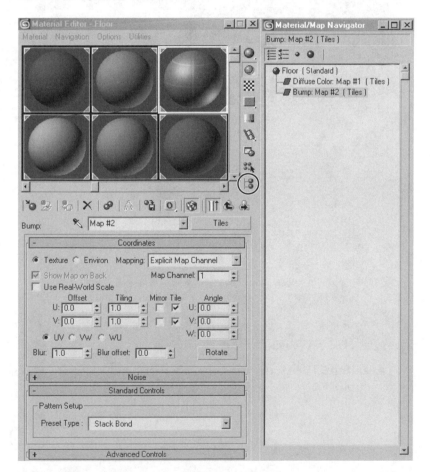

FIGURE 10.17 *The Material/Map Navigator allows you to quickly jump through the hierarchy of materials for editing at the appropriate level.*

6. In the Advanced Controls rollout, in the Tiles Setup area, click the Texture color swatch and change it in the Color Selector to pure white to make those areas appear raised. In the Grout Setup area, click the Texture color swatch and change it to pure black to have no effect on the areas with grout on the floor (**Figure 10.18**).

The brightness levels of the pixels in the map are important in order to achieve maximum results with the bump map.

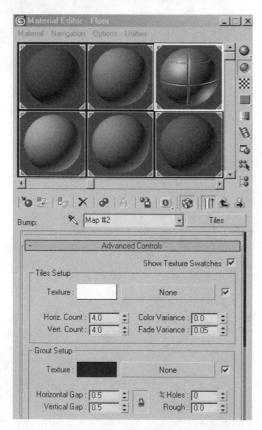

FIGURE 10.18 *Change the Tiles and Grout colors for the bump map.*

7. Right-click in the Camera01 viewport to make sure it is active, and then click the Quick Render button on the main toolbar.

    The floor tiles in the rendered image appear to be three-dimensional and no longer just a flat colored surface (**Figure 10.19**).

FIGURE 10.19 *Just like in the real world, bumps are more apparent in areas where light is raking across the surface.*

8. Close all windows and dialogs and save the file. It should already be called Int_matl06.max.

    The illusion of raised tiles is convincing to the viewer without adding extra geometry and, therefore, extra overhead.

Colored maps can be used in the bump slot of materials, but it is difficult to judge the luminance value of the colors. By using grayscale images you can more easily predict the results you'll get from the map.

Generating Reflections in Materials

The correct color and the apparent bumpiness of the material are beginning to make the floor look convincing, but there is still something missing: reflections.

Good reflections are an important material component, especially when they represent hard surfaces, but reflections can also be expensive in terms of computer resources, so they must be used judiciously.

You'll learn how to use Raytrace map reflections because they are the most accurate and versatile reflection map type in 3ds Max 8. Raytrace map reflections can be applied to either curved or flat surfaces, unlike Flat Mirror maps, which can be applied only to coplanar, contiguous faces, or Reflect/Refract maps, which can be applied only to curved surfaces.

Exercise 10.6: Applying Raytrace map reflections

1. Open the **Int_matl06.max** file from the CD-ROM or from the last exercise, and save it to your project folder with the name *Int_matl07.max*.

2. Open the Material Editor, if it is not already opened, and activate the Floor material sample window.

3. Open the Material/Map Navigator and choose the top level of the material in the navigator. In the Material Editor, in the Maps rollout, click the None button to the right of Reflection and double-click Raytrace in the Material/Map Browser (**Figure 10.20**).

Make absolutely sure that you place the Raytrace map in the Reflection slot. There is a Refraction slot, just below Reflection, that won't work for this exercise.

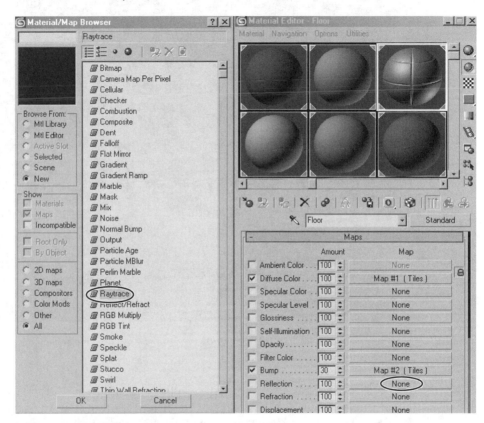

FIGURE 10.20 *Load the Raytrace map in the Reflection slot.*

4. Activate the Camera01 viewport if it is not already active, and click the Quick Render button on the main toolbar.

   In the rendered image, you'll see that the reflections are too intense to be convincing (**Figure 10.21**).

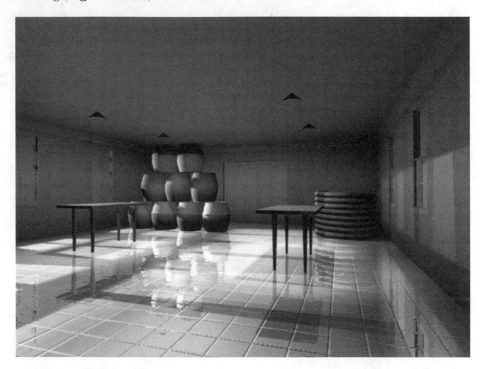

FIGURE 10.21 *Render the Camera01 viewport to see that full reflections are not appropriate for this material.*

5. To reduce the reflection amount, you'll use attenuation. In the Material Editor, at the Raytrace map level, expand the Attenuation rollout. In the Falloff Type drop-down list, choose Exponential. In the Ranges End field, enter 250, and press Enter (**Figure 10.22**).

   The Exponential falloff type is the most efficient option, and the ranges indicate where the reflection will start and end. With 0.0 as the Start value, the reflections start right at the surface and then attenuate, or die out, exponentially until 250 inches.

   The settings you will use in your scenes is subjective, based on how you want the floor reflections to look.

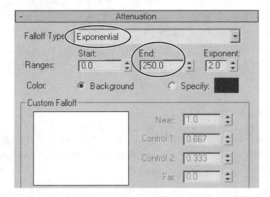

FIGURE 10.22 *Set the end attenuation range to stop calculating materials after 250 inches from the surface.*

6. Render the Camera01 viewport, and you will see that the reflections on the floor are rather clear near the objects but diminish where the objects are farther away from the floor surface (**Figure 10.23**).

FIGURE 10.23 *Render the scene to see that attenuated Raytrace reflections result in a more convincing floor surface.*

7. Close all windows and dialogs, and save the file. It should already be called Int_matl07.max.

Because Raytrace reflections will work effectively on any type of surface, they are a logical choice. But you must use attenuation to make the reflections look more convincing. Another benefit of using attenuation is that it reduces calculation time when rendering, because any objects beyond the Exponential End range are ignored.

Summary

To create convincing materials in 3ds Max 8, you must train yourself to look at materials in the real world with an eye toward identifying important components such as color, specular highlights, texture, and reflections.

You must then use the parameters and maps in the Material Editor to make materials that look good and are efficient, as you've learned in creating the floor material. You could now quickly change the material to represent almost any rectangular tile, simply by adjusting a few parameters.

While 3ds Max 8 comes supplied with many materials, it's a good idea to spend the time necessary to learn how to construct your own materials so that you can give your scenes a signature look and distinguish your work from your competition's.

CHAPTER 11

3D Materials

In This Chapter

In Chapter 10, you learned how to create materials in 3ds Max 8 using the Standard material type with maps applied one level deep, at the Diffuse Color level and the Bump level, which are both just below the topmost level of the material. This was clearly evident when you were using the Material/Map Navigator to move up and down the levels.

In this chapter, you'll go a bit deeper into the hierarchy of materials to learn a technique called *masking*, which is applied on both the map and the material levels to gain more flexibility, such as using more than one map in Diffuse Color. Masking enables you to hide or reveal selected areas of maps or materials with other maps based on the luminance value of pixels in the mask map.

You'll also learn about new material types that will allow you to combine multiple materials into a single, more complex material for greater editing flexibility. The Blend material type allows you to mix two materials together or to use masking to reveal one material through the other. The Multi/Sub-Object material type enables you to place multiple materials on a single object, using Material ID numbers assigned to faces. Double-sided materials allow "open" surfaces, such as flat planes, to have different materials on each side of faces. They could be used to create a single triangular face for the leaf of a low polygon tree that would have a shiny dark green on one side and a dull light green on the other.

As you learned in Chapter 10, the Material Editor allows you to view a maximum of 24 material sample windows at any one time, but you'll learn how to create material libraries that are stored in special files on your hard disk and can be opened from any other 3ds Max 8 scene, so that any scene can have an unlimited number of materials. You are, of course, still limited to viewing only 24 of those materials at any one time.

Key Terms

- **Material ID numbers**—Each face or polygon of a surface automatically has a number assigned to it that can be used to control placement of the sub-materials of a Multi/Sub-Object material type.

- **Face normals**—Each face or polygon has an invisible vector perpendicular to its surface. If the vector points toward the viewer, the face or polygon is visible; if the vector points away, the face is invisible.

Masking Techniques

The floor material that you created in Chapter 10 looks pretty good except for one particular issue: the tiles and grout have the same reflectivity. In the real world, this wouldn't be the case because grout is a form of cement that isn't reflective.

You'll learn how to use a mask map, which can be applied to existing maps to mask out or reveal the underlying map. The white pixels allow 100 percent of the underlying map to show; black pixels show none of the underlying map, and gray pixels show a mixed effect.

Applying the Mask Map Type

Masks can be applied at either the map level or the material level in 3ds Max 8. In the next exercise, you will apply the Mask map type to the reflection map of the floor material that you created in Chapter 10.

White pixels in the mask will cause reflections to show, and black pixels in the mask will hide reflections, so that the grout between the floor tiles appears dull.

Exercise 11.1: Masking at the map level

1. Reset 3ds Max 8; open the **Int_matl2_01.max** file from the CD-ROM and save it to your project folder with the name *Int_matl2_02.max*.

2. Right-click in the Camera01 viewport to make sure it is active and, in the main toolbar, click the Quick Render button to render the viewport (**Figure 11.1**).

   In the rendered image, you can see that the grout has the same reflectivity as the tiles.

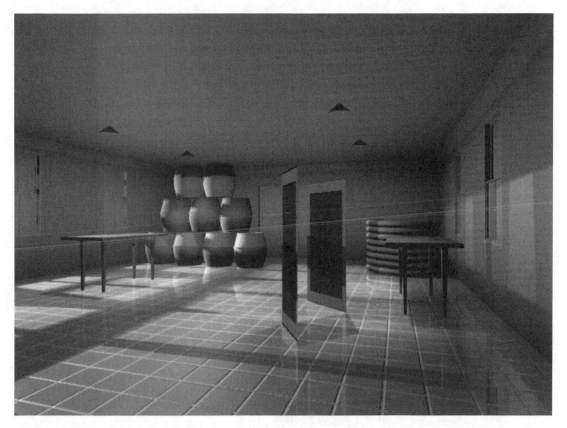

FIGURE 11.1 *Render the Camera01 viewport to review the floor material.*

3. From the Rendering drop-down menu, choose RAM Player. In the RAM Player
    dialog, click the Open Last Rendered Image in Channel A button (**Figure 11.2**),
    and click OK in the RAM Player Configuration dialog to accept the defaults.
    Minimize the RAM Player.

    The RAM Player will allow you to make a before-and-after comparison of the
    affect of the mask map that you will apply to the reflections.

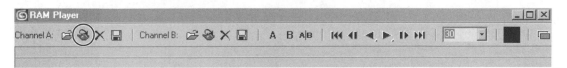

FIGURE 11.2 *Click the Open Last Rendered Image in Channel A button in the RAM Player.*

4. Open the Material Editor by clicking the button on the main toolbar or by pressing the keyboard shortcut M. Make sure the sample window for the Floor material is active. Click the Material/Map Navigator button at the bottom right of the sample windows, and, in the navigator dialog, highlight the Reflection map to go to the Raytrace level (**Figure 11.3**).

Use the Material/Map Navigator to move up and down the hierarchy of materials. This navigation method is very important as the materials become more complex.

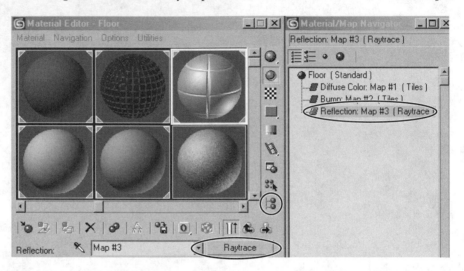

FIGURE 11.3 *Use the Material/Map Navigator to go to the Raytrace reflection map level, where a mask will be applied.*

5. In the Material Editor, below and to the right of the sample windows, click the Raytrace button. In the Material/Map Browser, double-click the Mask map in the list. In the Replace Map dialog, make sure that the "Keep old map as sub-map?" radio button is selected, and click OK (**Figure 11.4**).

You must keep the old map so that the mask is applied on top of that to reveal reflections only in areas of white pixels in the mask. Discarding the old map with simply replace reflections with an empty mask map.

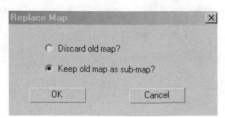

FIGURE 11.4 *You must keep the Raytrace reflection map, when prompted, so that the new mask map is applied to it.*

6. The mask map must have white pixels for the tiles and black pixels for the grout in order to function correctly. In Chapter 10, you applied a map exactly like that to create the bumps in the floor, and you can use that same map for this mask. In the Material/Map Navigator, drag the Bump level Tiles map onto the None button in the Mask Parameters rollout of the Material Editor (**Figure 11.5**). In the Instance [Copy] Map dialog, make sure that the Instance radio button is selected and click OK.

Existing maps within the same material can be cloned from the Materials/Map Navigator into the Material Editor.

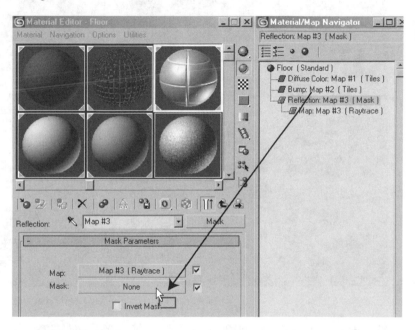

FIGURE 11.5 *Drag the Bump map from the navigator to the None button in the Mask Parameters rollout.*

7. Use the Quick Render button in the main toolbar to render the Camera01 viewport. Maximize the RAM Player, and click the Open Last Rendered Image in Channel B button. In the RAM Player, click in the image area and drag the mouse back and forth. In this scene, the reflection masking effect will be most noticeable in the dark area along the right wall (**Figure 11.6**).

Masking reflections is a cost-effective method of making materials like tile floors look more convincing.

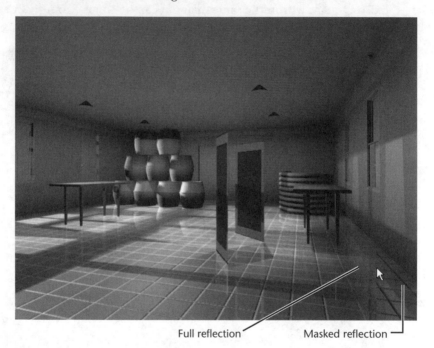

Full reflection   Masked reflection

FIGURE 11.6 *Drag the mouse on the image in the RAM Player to reveal Channel A on the left and Channel B on the right, and compare the two images.*

8. Close all windows and dialogs and save the file. It should already be called Int_matl2_02.max.

The Mask map type modifies previously assigned maps to hide or reveal the underlying map's visibility—in this case, the reflection map.

While many viewers might not have recognized specifically that the grout had the same reflectivity as the tiles, they would probably have perceived that something was wrong.

This same fundamental masking technique could be used to create, for example, the illusion of puddles on a street or dirt on a polished surface.

Using Masking in Materials

Masking at the map level is perfect for modifying the behavior of a single map, and it might be feasible to have several masks in a single material—for example, a mask for the diffuse color and a mask for glossiness. But there will also be times when mask maps are just too restrictive to get the job done.

In the next exercise, you'll learn how to use masking at the material level to create a floor surface that has tiles running down the center with carpet on either side. Because tiles and carpet material are different in so many ways—such as color, texture, and shininess—it would be very difficult to create and manage a single material with masks for the task.

You'll learn how to replace the Standard material type with a new material type, called Blend, that contains two sub-materials with a mask option.

Exercise 11.2: Masking at the material level

1. Open the **Int_matl2_02.max** file from the CD-ROM or from the previous exercise and save it to your project folder with the name *Int_matl2_03.max*.

2. Open the Material Editor with the M keyboard shortcut, and make sure the sample window for the Floor material is active. You can see that this material is a Standard material type (**Figure 11.7**).

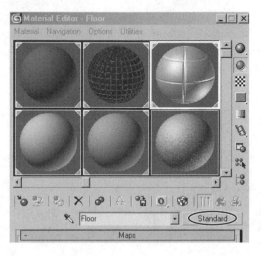

FIGURE 11.7 *The button to the right of the name field indicates the material type.*

3. To change the material type of an existing material, click the Standard button in the Material Editor to open the Material/Map Browser. Double-click Blend in the browser list (**Figure 11.8**), and make sure that the "Keep old material as sub-material?" radio button is selected in the Replace Material dialog; click OK.

This process is similar to applying the mask to the reflection map in the previous exercise, but here you're replacing the whole material, while keeping the previous as a sub-material.

FIGURE 11.8 *Double-click the Blend material type in the Material/Map Browser list. Material types are indicated by a blue sphere to the left of the name. Maps would have a green or red parallelogram.*

4. In the Material Editor, rename the Blend material *Shack floor* and open the Material/Map Navigator. The original Floor material is now the first sub-material, and the second sub-material contains an unnamed Standard material type that will become the carpet material (**Figure 11.9**).

5. In the sample window just below the window for Floor material is a speckled blue carpet material that you'll want to copy into Material 2 of the Blend material. In the Material Editor, click the Get Material button at the bottom left of the sample windows to open the Material/Map Browser. In the Browse From area, choose the Mtl Editor radio button to see a list of all materials currently in the Material Editor (**Figure 11.10**).

You don't have to create all new materials from scratch—you can clone existing materials into new materials by using the Material/Map Browser.

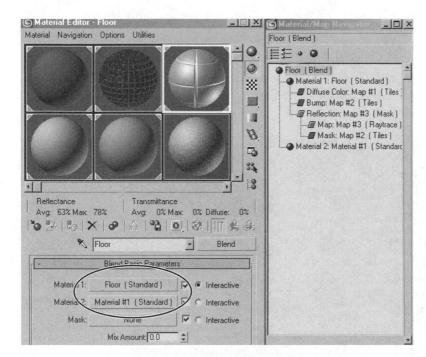

FIGURE 11.9 *The Material/Map Navigator clearly shows that the Blend material contains two other materials.*

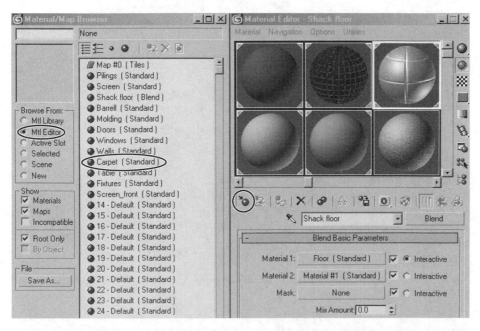

FIGURE 11.10 *The Material/Map Browser can be used to find materials and maps outside the current material.*

6. Drag and drop the Carpet material from the browser list to Material 2, the second Blend material slot; make sure that the Instance radio button is chosen in the Instance [Copy] Material dialog, and click OK (**Figure 11.11**).

You can drag and drop from the browser to clone maps into a new slot; or you could also have dragged the Carpet sample window and dropped it onto the new material slot.

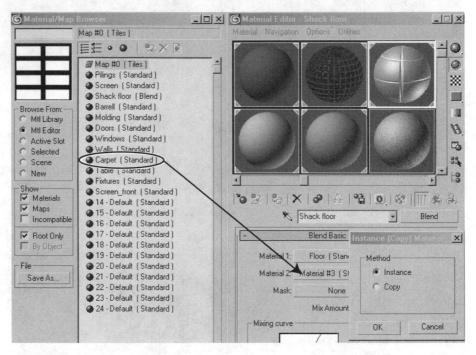

FIGURE 11.11 *Drag and drop the Carpet material from the browser to the Material Editor.*

7. If you render the scene now, the floor will still show all tiles (Material 1 slot), because the Mix Amount is set to 0.0 and there is no mask. In the Material Editor, in the Blend Basic Parameters rollout, click the None button in the Mask slot. In the Material/Map Browser list, double-click Gradient Ramp. Render the Camera01 viewport and you will see a soft-edged banding from tiles to carpet, every 4 feet (**Figure 11.12**).

tip

You can clone maps from the Material/Map Navigator, but materials must be cloned in the Material/Map Browser.

The Gradient Ramp map is a linear gradient which uses the same 4'0" by 4'0" UVW Map coordinates as the tiles. White pixels in the map reveal carpet and black pixels reveal tile, while gray pixels reveal a mix depending on their brightness.

Figure 11.12 *Applying the Gradient Ramp map to the Mask slot reveals one material blending into another.*

8. The mask needs hard edges and needs to be rotated to run the length of the floor. It should also be distributed over the entire floor, not tiled every 4 feet. In the Material Editor, in the Gradient Ramp Parameters rollout, change the Interpolation from Linear to Solid (**Figure 11.13**). Right-click on the middle flag in the gradient and choose Edit Properties from the menu. In the Flag Properties dialog, click the color swatch located to the right of Color. In the Color Selector, change the color from gray to pure white.

Solid interpolation creates a hard edge from one color to the next. Changing the flag to white eliminates the mixing of the two materials.

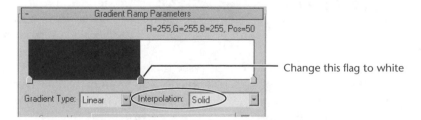

Figure 11.13 *Set the Gradient Ramp type to Solid interpolation for a hard transition between the colors, and change the middle flag to white.*

9. In the Material Editor, in the Coordinates rollout, change the Mapping type from Explicit Map Channel to Planar from Object XYZ, and enter 90.0 in the Z field in the Angle column (**Figure 11.14**).

The gradient ramp was repeating every 4 feet on the floor, because it was set to use the Explicit Map Channel that corresponds with the UVW Map modifier used to adjust the size of the tiles. Changing to Planar from Object XYZ ignores the UVW map modifier and uses the objects own coordinate system to fit the map over the entire surface.

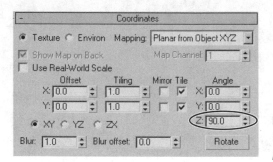

FIGURE 11.14 *Rotate the Gradient Ramp 90 degrees and set it to project along the object's Z axis.*

10. In the Gradient Ramp color field in the Material Editor's Gradient Ramp Parameters rollout, click in the black area to create a new black flag, and drag the new flag into the white area. Reposition the flags by dragging them, so that the right flag is at position 60 and the left flag is at position 40 (**Figure 11.15**).

The flags in the gradient can be moved to positions of 0 through 100, in whole numbers only. The position numbers are shown at the upper right of the gradient.

Position this flag at 40   Position this flag at 60

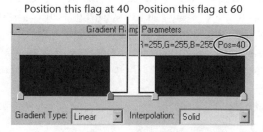

FIGURE 11.15 *Create and reposition flags in the gradient ramp to create a solid black, white, black pattern.*

11. Render the Camera01 viewport to see that the carpet runs down the center of the floor; however, you want tile in the center and carpet on the sides. In the Material Editor, expand the Output rollout and check the Invert box. Render the Camera01 viewport again (**Figure 11.16**).

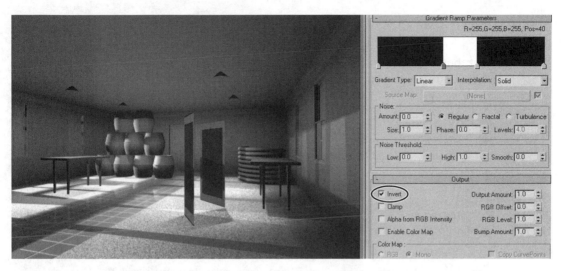

FIGURE 11.16 *Invert the black and white colors of the map in the Output rollout.*

Inverting a map reverses the effect of each color without changing the original map. The tile is positioned correctly along the length of the room, but it can still be easily edited to satisfy the client's needs.

12. Close all windows and dialogs, and save the file. It should already be called Int_matl2_03.max. Again, the procedural maps in 3ds Max 8 allow a high degree of flexibility.

By using the Blend material with a procedural map in the mask slot, you have an unlimited range of materials and layouts for the shack floor.

tip

If you invert a colored image—for example, a digital photo—it will appear as a photographic negative. The Invert option works best for grayscale images.

tip

A Blend material can be made up of any other material types; therefore, it would be possible to use a Blend material with a Blend material, each with its own mask.

Assigning Materials to Objects at Face Level

It is a general rule in 3ds Max 8 that each object can have only one material assigned to it, but you have learned in the last exercise that the Blend material type contains two or more materials that can be applied to a single object.

Let's take a look at a method of assigning materials to individual faces or polygons in the objects. The material type is called Multi/Sub-Object and can contain any number of sub-materials of any other material type.

Each face or polygon in 3ds Max 8 is automatically assigned a Material ID number that corresponds to the sub-materials in a Multi/Sub-Object material.

Material ID numbers can be assigned to objects at face, polygon, patch, and element sub-object levels by converting the selected object to the appropriate Editable Mesh, Editable Poly, or Editable Patch, or by applying the appropriate Edit modifier type.

tip

Material ID numbers are automatically assigned to objects depending on their construction. For example, the faces of a sphere primitive object all have Material ID 1 assigned to them, but a primitive box object has six material IDs, one for each pair of faces that makes up the side.

Preparing an Object for a Multi/Sub-Object Material

For a Multi/Sub-Object material to function correctly, the object must have Material ID numbers assigned to the appropriate faces or polygons. In the next exercise, you will edit a barrel so that one material will be assigned to the majority of the barrel, but another material will be assigned to rectangular areas at the front and back of the barrel.

Exercise 11.3: Assigning Material ID numbers

1. Open the **Int_matl2_03.max** file from the CD-ROM or from the previous exercise, and save it to your project folder with the name *Int_matl2_04.max*.

2. In the Camera01 viewport, select one of the barrels at the back of the room. They already have a material assigned, and the barrels are instances, so it doesn't matter which barrel you select. Press the keyboard shortcut Alt + Q to isolate the selection.

   Isolating selections can make editing easier, especially when scenes are large.

3. Click the Zoom Extents All Selected button at the lower right corner of the display to fill the orthographic viewports with the barrel. Go to the Modify panel, and you'll see that the barrel started as a cylinder primitive, has a Taper modifier for the curvature, and has an Edit Poly modifier that was used to create the rim around the body and the inset top (**Figure 11.17**).

There is also already a UVW Map modifier at the top of the stack, which won't be necessary for this material but also won't do any harm.

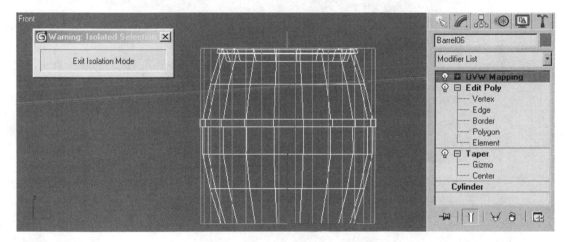

FIGURE 11.17 *The barrel objects have an Edit Poly modifier that you can use to access sub-object levels.*

4. On the Modify panel, in stack view, highlight the Element sub-object level of the Edit Poly modifier. Click on the barrel in the Front viewport, and it will turn red to indicate that the barrel contains only one element. On the Modify panel, in the Polygon Properties rollout, enter 1 in the Set ID field and press Enter. This ensures that all polygons in the object have Material ID 1 (see **Figure 11.18** on the next page).

As mentioned earlier, different primitive objects have different Material ID assignments, so it's a good idea to make sure that all polygons are set to the same Material ID number before making specific assignments.

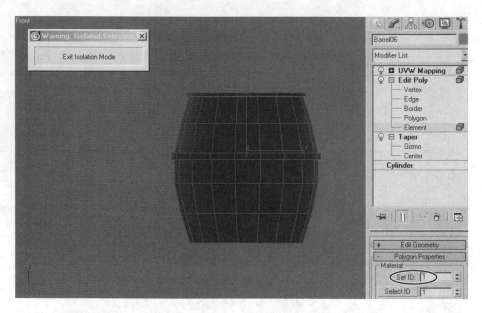

FIGURE 11.18 *A cylinder primitive has three Material ID numbers assigned by default—for the body and the two end caps. You want to set all polygons to Material ID 1, which is easy to do at the Element sub-object level.*

5. On the Modify panel, in stack view, highlight the Polygon sub-object level and pick anywhere in the empty space in the Front viewport to unselect everything. In the Selection rollout, make sure the Ignore Backfacing box is unchecked, so that you can select polygons on the front and back of the barrel. In the main toolbar, make sure the Select Object button is toggled on and Crossing selection mode is current on the Window/Crossing button. In the Front viewport, drag a crossing window through the faces in the middle of the barrel (**Figure 11.19**).

    The result will be that 30 polygons are selected, 15 on either side of the barrel, and they will have turned red to indicate that they are selected.

caution

Do not enter 1 in the Select ID field by mistake. This allows you only to select polygons that already have a Material ID number assigned to them.

note

The Set ID field was blank initially, because the Element selection set had three Material IDs assigned, and the field can display only one number.

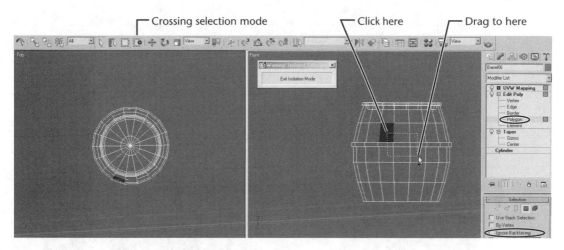

Crossing selection mode   Click here   Drag to here

FIGURE 11.19 *Select a group of polygons in the middle of the barrel.*

6. On the Modify panel, in the Polygon Properties rollout, use the spinner arrows to the right of the Set ID field to increment the number to 2, or enter 2 in the field. Also on the Modify panel, in stack view, highlight Edit Poly to exit sub-object mode, and then highlight UVW Mapping to return to the top of the modifier stack.

   The selected polygons will now receive the second material in a Multi/Sub-Object material because they have Material ID 2.

7. Click the large yellow Exit Isolation Mode button in the Warning dialog to display all objects and save the file. It should already be called Int_matl2_04.

Assigning Material ID numbers to polygons or faces simply prepares objects to receive Multi/Sub-Object materials.

Creating the Multi/Sub-Object Material

In the next exercise, you will edit a Standard material that has already been assigned to the barrels in the scene to become a Multi/Sub-Object material with two sub-materials. The Material ID numbers that you assigned in the previous exercise will result in a red-painted barrel with a green rectangle on its face.

Exercise 11.4: Converting a Standard material to a Multi/Sub-Object material

1. Open the **Int_mapl2_04.max** file from the CD-ROM or from the previous exercise, and save it to your project folder with the name *Int_matl2_05.max.*

2. Press the keyboard shortcut M to open the Material Editor, and activate a sample window in the top row with a material called Barrel.

3. In the Material Editor, click the Standard button to the right of the material name, and double-click Multi/Sub-Object in the Material/Map Browser list (**Figure 11.20**). Make sure that the "Keep old material as sub-material?" radio button is selected in the Replace Material dialog, and click OK.

This is the same process you used to change from a Standard material type to a Blend material type earlier in the chapter.

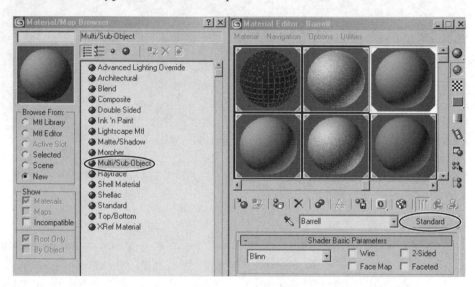

FIGURE 11.20 *Change the material type from Standard to Multi/Sub-Object.*

4. By default, the material has ten sub-materials, but you need only two. In the Material Editor, in the Multi/Sub-Object Basic Parameters rollout, click the Set Number button. In the Set Number of Materials dialog, enter 2 in the Number of Materials field and click OK (**Figure 11.21**).

You can add new materials at any time—they'll simply be added to the end of the list. However, reducing the number of materials could discard existing sub-materials at the end of the list, so make sure the number of sub-materials includes all those you want to use in the scene.

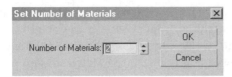

<figure>FIGURE **11.21** *Reduce the number of sub-materials to 2; the unused materials are discarded.*</figure>

5. In the Material Editor, click the Material/Map Navigator button to open the navigator, and highlight the first sub-material. In the Material Editor, rename this material *Paint Red*. In the Blinn Basic Parameters rollout, click the Diffuse color swatch, and in the Color Selector, choose a bright red color. In the Specular Highlights area, enter 30 in the Specular Level field and 20 in the Glossiness field to create dull, broad specular highlights (**Figure 11.22**).

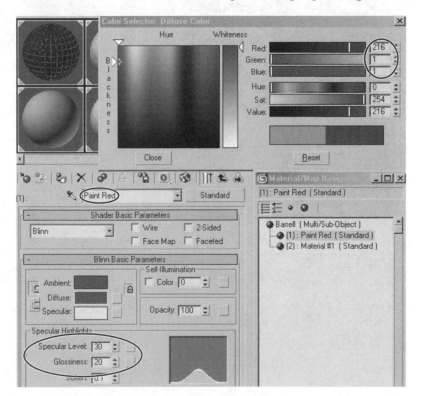

FIGURE **11.22** *Create a new material for a bright red semigloss paint that will be applied to most of the barrel.*

6. Highlight the second sub-material in the Material/Map Navigator and, in the Material Editor, rename the material *Paint Green*. Change the Diffuse color to any color green you like, and in the Blinn Basic Parameters rollout, set the specular highlights similarly to Paint Red. In the Material/Map Navigator, return to the top level of the material, and you will notice that the sample window shows a checkerboard pattern of green and red to indicate that this is a Multi/Sub-Object material (**Figure 11.23**).

    Paint Green is the material that will be applied to the faces with Material ID 2.

FIGURE 11.23 *Create a green material that is similar to the red paint material, except for the color.*

7. Right-click in the Camera01 viewport to activate it. Click the Quick Render button on the main toolbar, and you'll notice that each barrel is red with a green rectangle in the left center, and that the sub-materials in the Material Editor have the proper ID numbers (**Figure 11.24**).

FIGURE 11.24 *The Multi/Sub-Object material is applied to the object according to the Material ID number assignment that is listed in the Multi/Sub-Object Basic Parameters rollout.*

8. Close all windows and dialogs, and save the file. It should already be called Int_matl2_05.max.

   All you have to do is match sub-materials in a Multi/Sub-Object material to the Material ID numbers of faces of polygons in the object.

Multi/Sub-Object materials offer a lot of flexibility in applying materials to objects. You could very quickly drag and drop different materials into the sub-material slots to show a client options, and you can easily add more materials and then edit the Material ID numbers to apply them where you want on the object.

Assigning Different Materials Based on Face Normals

The face normals of an object control the visibility of faces and polygons: if the face normal points in the viewer's direction, the face is visible, and if the face normal points away, the face is invisible.

A material type called Double Sided also uses face normals to assign two different materials to objects. The side with the face normal gets one sub-material, and the side without the face normal gets the other sub-material. This can be an efficient method of applying materials and keeping an object's total number of faces to a minimum if the object's walls don't need to have a thickness.

In the next exercise, you will fix a problem with a folding screen in the middle of the shack and assign a material at the same time. The folding screen has a Standard material currently assigned that uses a Gradient Ramp map in both the Diffuse and Bump slots to give the illusion that it is a red frame with a blue inset. However, you might have noticed in the final rendered image of the last exercise that the screen appears to be simply two panels rather than a folding screen made up of four panels.

Exercise 11.5: The Double Sided material type

1.   Open the file called **Int_matl2_05.max** from the CD-ROM or from the previous exercise, and save it to your project folder with the name *Int_matl2_06.max*.

2.   In the Camera01 viewport, you'll see what appears to be two freestanding panels in the middle of the room. Select the object, which is called Screen01, and click the Zoom Extents All Selected button at the lower right of the display to fill all viewports with the screen. In the top viewport, you will see that it is actually a W-shaped line that has been extruded (**Figure 11.25**).

A line that is extruded has no thickness and the faces are invisible when the face normals point away from the viewer.

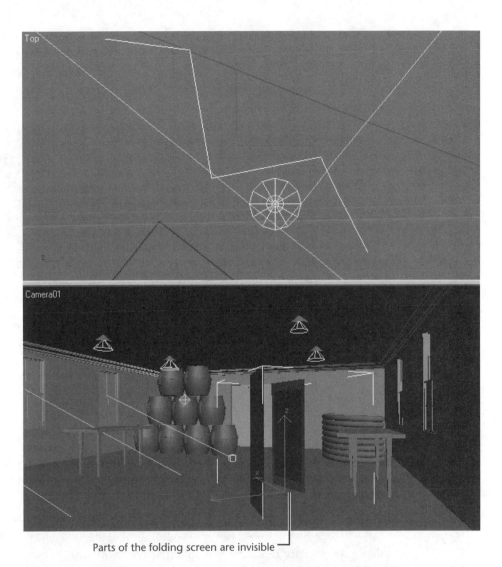

Parts of the folding screen are invisible

FIGURE 11.25 *Render the scene to compare the folding screen with the W-shaped line from which it was derived.*

3. Open the Material Editor, and locate the blue and red material sample window called Screen in the top row. In the Material Editor's Shader Basic Parameters rollout, check the 2-Sided box and notice that the screen appears complete in the Camera01 shaded viewport (**Figure 11.26**). However, this applies the same material to both sides of the object. Uncheck the 2-Sided box.

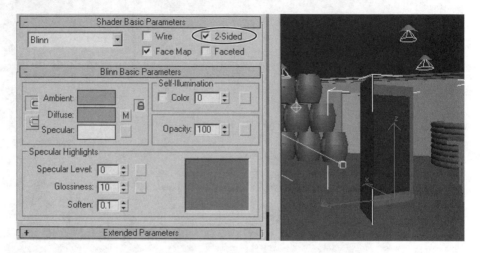

FIGURE 11.26 *When the 2-Sided option is selected in any material, face normals are ignored and the flat surface has the same material applied to each side.*

To apply different materials to each side of the screen, you'll need to use the Double Sided material type.

4. In the Material Editor, click the Standard button and double-click Double Sided in the Material/Map Browser list. Make sure that the "Keep old material as sub-material?" radio button is selected, and click OK.

The Screen material becomes the Facing Material that is applied to the side with face normals, and a new default material has been applied in the Back Material.

Once again, you are replacing one material type with another while retaining the old material as a sub-material.

5. In the Material Editor, in the Double Sided Basic Parameters rollout, drag the button that says Screen [Standard] from the Facing Material and drop it onto the slot for the Back Material (**Figure 11.27**). Click the Copy radio button in the Instance [Copy] Material dialog, and then click OK. You can copy materials from one slot to another by dragging and dropping so that both material slots contain the same material.

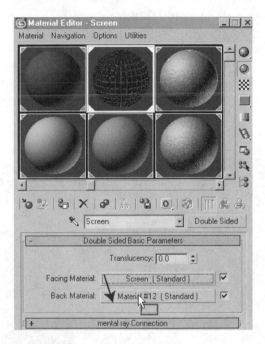

FIGURE 11.27 *Making the material a Copy clone will allow you to change the colors on the Back Material.*

6. In the Material Editor, click the Material/Map Navigator button to open the navigator, and highlight Diffuse Color in the Back: Screen [Standard] material (see **Figure 11.28** on the next page). In the Material Editor, in the Gradient Ramp Parameters rollout, right-click on the left-most flag of the gradient and choose Edit Properties from the menu. In the Flag Properties dialog, click the Color swatch, and, in the Color Selector, change the color to a bright yellow.

You now have two different materials for the folding screen with no thickness: one for the front and one for the back.

FIGURE 11.28 *Make sure you highlight the Diffuse Color for the Back material in the navigator and change it to yellow.*

7. Close all windows and dialogs, and right-click in the Camera01 viewport to activate it. Click the Quick Render button on the main toolbar to render the scene (**Figure 11.29**).

    The folding screen is now visible, and both sides have different materials.

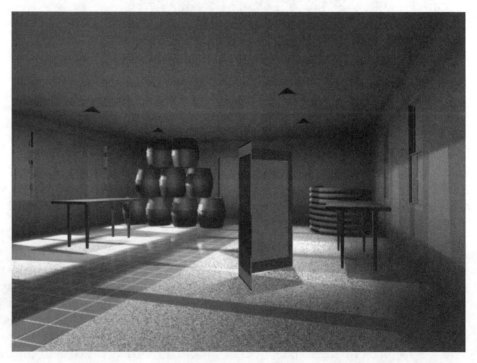

FIGURE 11.29 *When you render the scene, you see that even though the screen has no thickness, it appears to have a different material on each side.*

8. Close the rendered frame window and save the file. It should already be called Int_matl2_06.max. The Double Sided material allows you to use efficient geometry.

The Double Sided material can be used to create leaves on trees or bushes that are efficient and have a material on one side that is lighter than material on the other. You could also use it to create different refractive and reflective qualities on the inside and outside of window glass, for example.

Material Libraries: A Management Tool

In the exercises so far in this book, you've been creating materials and assigning them to objects for each individual scene. If you were to start a new scene or open an unrelated scene, you would have only the default materials in the Material Editor and would have no way to access the materials you'd already created.

In 3ds Max 8, you can create *material libraries*—files, containing materials, that are saved to your hard drive and can be accessed from any other 3ds Max 8 file by any user. Let's create a project material library for the scene you've been working on in this chapter.

tip

Material library files contain only a description of your materials and take up very little space on your hard drive, so it is feasible to have any particular material in multiple libraries. For example, your floor material may be in the project library as well as another library that contains a number of floor-tile materials.

Exercise 11.6: Building and saving material libraries

1. Open the **Int_matl2_06.max** file from the CD-ROM or from the previous exercise. You don't need to save it with a new name, because you won't be creating anything that needs to be stored in a new file.

2. Press the M keyboard shortcut to open the Material Editor. In the Material Editor, click the Get Material button below the sample windows, to the left. In the Material/Map Browser dialog, in the Browse From area, choose the Mtl Library radio button (**Figure 11.30**).

The browser displays all of the maps and materials available in the current default library called 3dsmax.mat, as seen at the top of the browser. These materials and maps are not in your Material Editor. Next you'll clear the browser list to make room for your materials, which can be saved to your hard drive.

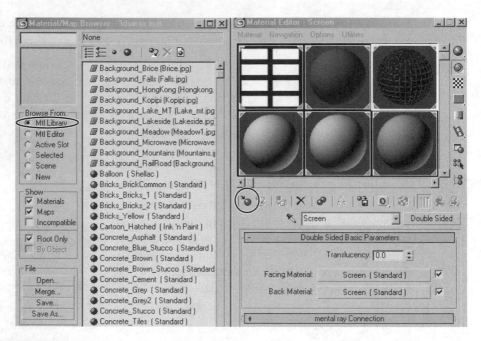

FIGURE 11.30 *Use the Material/Map Browser to open a material library called 3dsmax.mat.*

3. In the Material/Map Browser dialog, click the Clear Material Library button just above the list. When asked, "Are you sure you want to delete all materials in the library?" in the Material/Map Browser, click the Yes button (**Figure 11.31**).

FIGURE 11.31 *Clearing all the materials in the current library does not delete the materials; they are still in the file on the hard drive.*

This operation will not cause you to lose any information; it only clears this list of the materials in the current library. You'll notice there is no name at the top of the browser now—you have an empty library browser.

4. In the Material/Map Browser, in the File area, click the Save As button. In the Save Material Library dialog, navigate to your project folder and enter Chapter 11 in the File Name field (**Figure 11.32**). Click the Save button to save the new empty library to your project folder.

    Newly named material libraries are automatically appended with the .*mat* file-name extension when you save them.

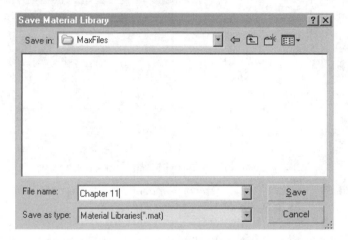

FIGURE 11.32 *Save the new material library to your project folder, so that it may be opened from any other 3ds Max 8 scene.*

5. In the Material Editor, right-click on any sample window, and choose 6 x 4 Sample Windows in the menu to display all the materials in the Material Editor. Drag and drop each of the sample windows in the first two rows into the browser list area (see **Figure 11.33** on the next page).

    This places all of the "hot" materials, as indicated by the triangles in the corners of the sample windows, into the browser list.

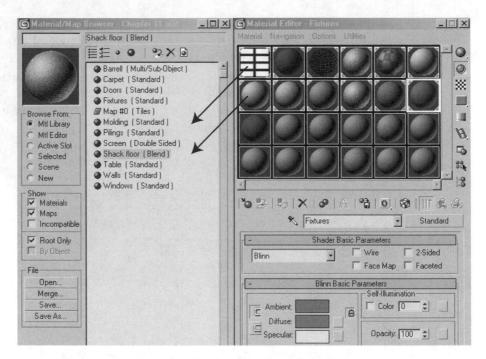

Figure 11.33 *Drag and drop the sample windows from the Material Editor into the browser list, so that they may be saved in the library.*

6. In the Material/Map Browser, in the File area, click the Save button to save these materials to your hard drive in the file called Chapter 11.mat. Close all windows and dialogs, and exit the 3ds Max 8 file without saving.

    It's not important to save this file, because you haven't really changed it.

Material libraries are important management tools that allow you to organize and distribute materials for all your projects.

Summary

Materials that are made up of one or more sub-materials can make it easier to manage your projects and to reduce the overall number of objects in the scene, which increases efficiency and rendering speed.

The Blend material type allows you to put materials anywhere on an object and reveal one or the other with a mask map. The Multi/Sub-Object material is assigned to faces of objects by changing the Material ID numbers associated with the face. Double Sided materials are applied to objects based on face normal direction. As you build your own materials, start with simple Standard materials that you can later assemble using the techniques learned in this chapter for applying multiple materials to single objects.

Always remember to make material libraries for each project, so that the materials you create can be saved and used on other projects.

Efficiency, project management, and ease of editing are the primary goals when using these more complex materials.

CHAPTER 12

Global Illumination

In This Chapter

All the rendering you have done in previous chapters has relied on standard lighting and the scanline renderer, which only calculates direct illumination, or the light that travels from the light source to the surfaces of objects in the scene.

In the real world, however, light that strikes object surfaces is bounced back into the atmosphere to light other nearby surfaces, according to laws of attenuation, until the light is too weak to see. (You accomplished the illusion of bounced light in previous chapters by adding fill lights throughout the scene.)

Global illumination is the computer's method of calculating the effect of bounced light from surface to surface. Using global illumination in rendering, you can make a scene more convincing by filling in the shaded portions normally left completely black with standard lighting techniques.

In this chapter, you will learn a method of simulating global illumination in 3ds Max 8, called *radiosity rendering*. Essentially, polygons in the scene are treated as secondary light sources that derive their intensity from the lights in the scene and other nearby surfaces.

Key Terms

- **Global illumination**—Computer simulation of light bouncing from surfaces.

- **Radiosity rendering**—A method of global illumination used in 3ds Max 8 that calculates the intensity of light emanating from all surfaces.

- **Photometric lights**—A light type for radiosity rendering that uses calculations for intensity and attenuation based on real-world light sources.

- **Meshing**—The process of subdividing surfaces to ensure that vertices are no more than a given distance apart for even distribution of lighting.

- **Color bleeding**—As 3ds Max 8 simulated light energy bounces photons from the surface, the photons also pick up the color from that surface and tints neighboring objects.

Simulating Bounced Light Using Global Illumination

It is important to note that modeling can play a very important role in the efficiency of radiosity calculations because the radiosity rendering solution is stored in the vertices of objects and distributed across adjacent faces.

If vertices are too far apart, the quality of light distribution across large distances is poor, and the rendering is not convincing. Likewise, if two adjacent objects don't have vertices at a common location in the model, the radiosity distribution is also poor.

For example, if a round column sits in the middle of a floor, the vertices at the bottom of the column must interpolate lighting all the way to the corners of the floor, resulting in an even distribution. 3ds Max 8 radiosity rendering has tools to overcome lighting problems caused by geometry, but each application of the tools has the potential to decrease productivity.

The exercises in this chapter will lead you through a series of important processes that will result in a satisfactory radiosity rendering. All the processes work together in balance.

Radiosity Rendering

The scanline renderer, which is the default renderer and the one you learned about in Chapters 7 and 8, is designed to render scenes quickly and efficiently using the direct lighting of standard light types. However, another light type, called *photometric lights*, is frequently used with radiosity rendering. Photometric lights use real-world physical properties for calculating intensity and attenuation.

In the first exercise, you'll learn how to set the scanline renderer to use radiosity rendering and photometric light types that closely mimic lights in the real world. The scene you'll use is already set up with four point-type photometric light sources centered in the four fixtures at the ceiling of the fishing shack.

Exercise 12.1: Changing renderers in 3ds Max 8

1. Reset 3ds Max 8, and then open the **Radiosity01.max** file from the CD-ROM. Save it to your project folder with the name *Radiosity02.max*.

2. Right-click in the Camera01 viewport to make sure it is active and, in the main toolbar, click the Quick Render button.

   The rendered image shows four hotspots near the light fixtures at the ceiling and a minimal amount of light elsewhere in the scene (**Figure 12.1**). The lights in the ceiling are photometric lights. The current renderer is the default scanline renderer, which cannot calculate the effects of photometric lighting or light bouncing from surfaces.

FIGURE 12.1 *Render the scene to see that photometric lights rendered with the scanline renderer produce unacceptable results.*

3. You can change the renderer that 3ds Max 8 uses by going to the Rendering pull-down menu and choosing Advanced Lighting > Radiosity (**Figure 12.2**). In the Radiosity dialog, you'll be prompted to choose whether to use a Camera Exposure Control with the radiosity renderer. Click the Yes button.

   Exposure control must be used to compensate for the brightness levels of the physically correct photometric lights in much the same way as you must adjust the aperture of a real-world camera to control the amount of light striking the film.

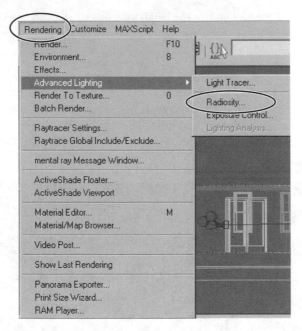

FIGURE 12.2 *Switching from the default renderer to another can be accomplished through the Rendering pull-down menu.*

4. Render the Camera01 viewport again, and notice that the scene is much brighter but is certainly not convincing.

   Radiosity rendering is a mathematically complex solution that needs to be calculated and then stored in mesh objects before rendering the results.

5. In the Rendered Scene dialog, on the Advanced Lighting tab, in the Radiosity Processing Parameters rollout, click the Start button to calculate the initial radiosity solution (**Figure 12.3**).

   The radiosity will be calculated within about 85 percent of its full potential and may take a while to process, depending on your computer.

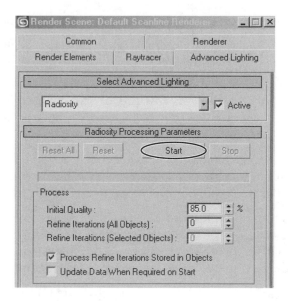

FIGURE 12.3 *Click the Start button in the Radiosity Processing Parameters rollout to calculate the radiosity solution.*

6. Render the Camera01 viewport again, and compare the rendered frame window with the Camera01 viewport (**Figure 12.4**).

By default, the shaded viewports show a representation of the radiosity solution without the need to do a full render.

An approximate representation of the radiosity solution shows in the Camera01 viewport, and in the rendered image you can clearly see that light is being bounced from the floor and walls, and that the bounced light is affecting the overall color as well as illumination values.

Rendered image   Camera01 viewport

FIGURE 12.4 *Render the scene to see the extra light bounced from surfaces by the radiosity calculations.*

7. Close all windows and dialogs and save the file. It should already be called Radiosity02.max.

Photometric lights must be rendered using the radiosity renderer to simulate light bouncing from surfaces.

Radiosity rendering not only calculates the intensity of light bounced from surfaces, but it also calculates the color bleeding from one surface to the next, which is why all the materials appear to be quite green.

Photometric lights differ from standard lights in that their intensity and attenuation are accurate according to the laws of physics, but otherwise they have similar adjustments and controls. Standard lights have no physical properties related to the real world.

In the next exercise, you'll learn how to change the type of photometric light from point to spotlight distribution, and then you'll learn how to adjust the intensity, based on real-world lighting parameters. The light from the spotlight will be confined to a cone pointing at the floor and will greatly affect the amount of light bounced back into the scene.

Anytime you change lighting parameters when using the radiosity renderer, you must reset and recalculate the radiosity solution before rendering the scene again.

Exercise 12.2: Working with photometric lights

1. Open the **Radiosity02.max** file from the CD-ROM or from the previous exercise, and save it to your project folder with the name *Radiosity03.max*.

2. Press the 9 key, which is the keyboard shortcut to open the Rendered Scene dialog. On the Advanced Lighting tab, in the Radiosity Processing Parameters rollout, click the Reset button if necessary.

3. In the Reset Radiosity Solution dialog, check the "Do not ask me this again box," and click the Yes button (**Figure 12.5**).

The radiosity solution is discarded, and the shaded viewport is returned to normal. It doesn't matter whether you reset the radiosity solution before or after making changes to lighting parameters, but it must be done before rerendering.

note

The exercise files on the CD-ROM have been saved without the radiosity solution. The Reset button is grayed out and you won't need to reset those files before calculating the solution.

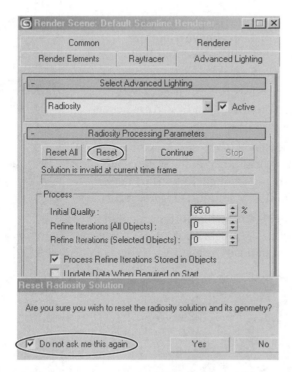

FIGURE 12.5 *Reset the radiosity solution to clear the existing lighting information, and then render the scene again.*

4. Make sure the Select Object button is highlighted on the main toolbar, and press the H key. In the Select Objects dialog, highlight FPoint01 in the list and click the Select button.

    This is one of the four Free Point lights near the ceiling; the others are instance clones, so changing one will affect them all.

note

The Reset All button clears the lighting solution and the meshing geometry created by the radiosity renderer. The Reset button clears only the lighting solution, which is appropriate for this situation because you have not made any changes to the meshing parameters.

5. On the Modify panel, in the Intensity/Color/
    Distribution rollout, pick on the Distribution:
    Isotropic drop-down list and choose Spotlight
    (**Figure 12.6**).

    This changes the light distribution from casting
    light in all directions to casting light within a cone
    that is pointed straight down at the floor.

6. In the Render Scene dialog, Radiosity Processing
    Parameters rollout, Process area, enter 50.0 in the
    Initial Quality field, and then click the Start button
    to recalculate the radiosity solution (**Figure 12.7**).

    Reducing the Initial Quality will shorten calculation
    times and still provide reasonable quality for testing
    in the early stages of radiosity rendering.

FIGURE 12.6 *Change
the light's distribution
pattern from omni-
directional to a cone.*

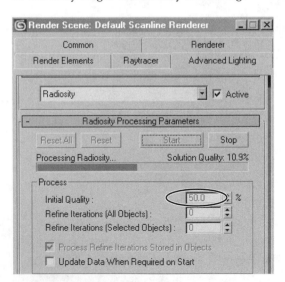

FIGURE 12.7 *Reduce the Initial Quality setting for
faster test renders.*

7. Right-click in the Camera01 viewport to make sure it is active, and click the
    Render button in the Render Scene dialog.

Even though the four lights in the scene have the same intensity as in the last exercise, the rendered scene is extremely dark in comparison. This is because the light distribution is focused into small spots on the floor and the attenuation significantly reduces the amount of light that can be bounced back into the scene by this geometry.

8. On the Modify panel, in the Intensity/Color/ Distribution rollout, in the Intensity area, enter 5000 in the numeric field on the left (**Figure 12.8**). In the Render Scene dialog, click the Reset button, and then click the Start button to process a new radiosity solution.

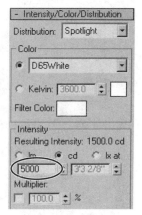

This light-intensity value is in candelas, a common measurement of light used by illumination engineers.

Increasing the intensity of the lights in the scene does not significantly improve the radiosity solution, primarily because of the geometry in the scene.

9. Close all windows and dialogs, and save the file. It should already be called Radiosity03.max.

Adjusting the lights is only one of the processes that must be done for a radiosity solution, but it is an important first step.

FIGURE 12.8 *Increase the intensity of the spotlights to add more light to the scene.*

Radiosity rendering requires you to systematically progress through all of the individual processes introduced in this chapter before attaining a convincing and efficient final rendering.

Radiosity Meshing Parameters

The radiosity lighting solution is stored in a special mesh object that has been created on the top of your existing geometry. At this point, the calculations are using the actual vertices in your geometry to store and distribute the light information across faces, and the vertices are too widely spread for an acceptable radiosity solution.

Calculating a radiosity solution and saving the file can result in significantly larger files on your hard drive, because of the lighting information that must be stored in the radiosity mesh.

The radiosity mesh is visible in the wireframe views after the radiosity solution has been calculated (**Figure 12.9**).

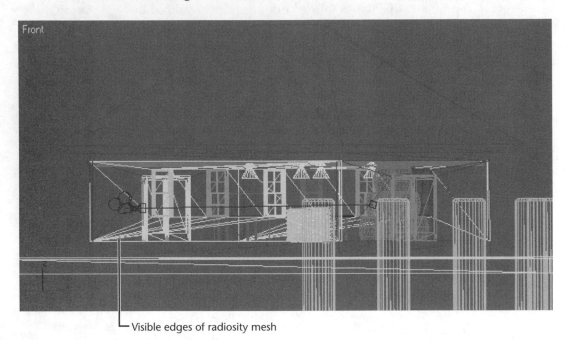

Visible edges of radiosity mesh

Figure 12.9 *The radiosity mesh is visible as extra edges in the wireframe viewports.*

An important step in preparing your model for radiosity lighting, then, is setting the proper meshing parameter. Adjusting the meshing parameter ensures a minimum distance between vertices on your objects' surfaces to facilitate the transfer of light and shadow information across faces.

In the next exercise, you'll learn how to adjust the density of the radiosity meshing parameters to provide more vertices for better light distribution. You'll also learn how to adjust refinement and filtering parameters to overcome less-than-optimal results when the radiosity solution is calculated.

It's important to analyze the scene carefully to determine which objects will contribute most to the radiosity solution—for example, the floor, the walls, the ceiling, and the barrels in this scene. While it is possible to mesh objects globally, the increased geometry will significantly slow processing and use computer resources unnecessarily.

Selectively meshing objects is much more efficient.

Exercise 12.3: Adjusting meshing parameters

1. Open the **Radiosity03.max** file from the CD-ROM or from the previous exercise, and save it to your project folder with the name *Radiosity04.max*.

2. Press the 9 key to open the Render Scene dialog, click the Reset button if necessary, and then click the Start button. When the calculations are complete, render the Camera01 viewport.

3. Open the RAM Player from the Rendering pull-down menu, and open the last rendered image in Channel A. Minimize the RAM Player.

4. Using the Select Objects dialog (you can access it by pressing the H key), select the following 25 objects: Barrel01 through Barrel19, Long_wall01 and Long _wall02, Short_wall01 and Short_wall02, shack_floor and shack_roof (**Figure 12.10**).

5. On the main toolbar, enter Large_mesh in the Named Selection Sets menu (**Figure 12.11**), and press Enter.

    Creating named selection sets is a good habit because you may have to try several iterations of meshing parameters before finding the optimum setting, and this will allow you to reselect them easily.

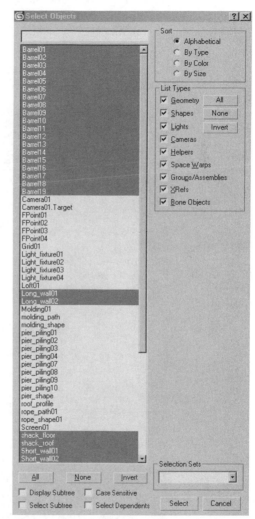

FIGURE 12.10 *Select only larger objects that contribute significantly to the radiosity solution.*

FIGURE 12.11 *When you select the 25 objects, create a named selection set to make it easier to reselect them, if necessary.*

6. Right-click in any viewport and, in the quad menu, click Properties. In the Object Properties dialog, click the Adv. Lighting tab. In the Geometric Object Radiosity Properties rollout, Object Subdivision Properties area, uncheck the Use Global Subdivision Settings box. Also clear the Use Adaptive Subdivision check box, and notice that Max Mesh Size is set to 3'0" (**Figure 12.12**). Click OK.

This meshes only the currently selected objects and maintains a maximum distance of 3'0" between any two vertices.

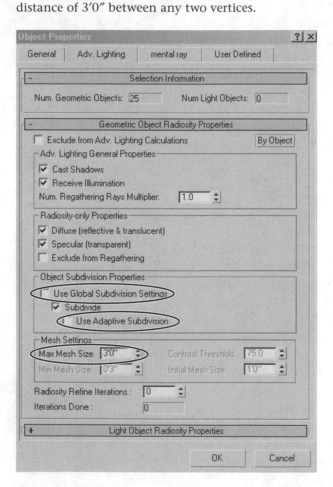

FIGURE 12.12 *For this example, set a constant meshing size over the entire selection set.*

7. In the Render Scene dialog, on the Advanced Lighting tab, Radiosity Processing Parameters rollout, click the Reset All button to discard both the lighting solution and the previously calculated radiosity mesh geometry. Then click the Start button, and when the calculations are finished, make sure the Camera01 viewport is active and click the Render button (**Figure 12.13**).

The wireframe viewports show a much denser mesh, and the walls and ceiling of the rendered image are now showing indications of bounced light and color bleeding.

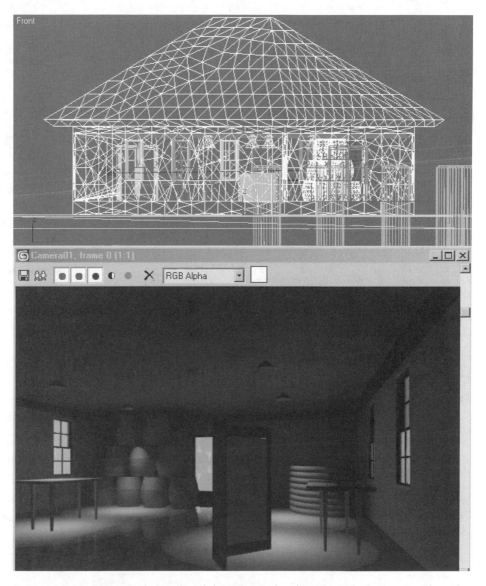

FIGURE 12.13 *Compare the results of the new rendered image with the increased mesh density in the wireframe viewports.*

8. Select the light in the scene called FPoint01 and, on the Modify panel, General Parameters rollout, Shadows area, check the On box to enable shadow casting. In the Spotlight Parameters rollout, enter 70.0 in the Hotspot/Beam field, and enter 120.0 in the Falloff/Field field (**Figure 12.14**). In the Render Scene dialog, in the Radiosity Processing Parameters rollout, click the Reset button and then click Start. Render the Camera01 viewport.

    Increasing the spread of the spotlight onto the walls to include more surface area that can bounce light adds significant amounts of light to the radiosity solution.

9. Close all windows and dialogs, and save the file, which should already be called Radiosity04.max. The radiosity process is beginning to take shape.

FIGURE 12.14 *Turn shadow casting on, and increase the size of the spotlight cone.*

Compared with the results you'd get from the same number of standard lights, you've accomplished a more convincing appearance with only four photometric lights and some basic meshing parameters. The trade-off, however, is longer calculation and rendering times against the faster initial lights setup.

Exposure Control

The last rendered image was a bit too bright, not because the light intensity was too high—assuming that we have lights set to the specifications of illumination engineers—but because of overexposure.

Much in the same way as compensation is used with film that has been overexposed because of too much light entering the camera lens, we must also compensate for out-of-range light levels in 3ds Max 8, by using exposure control.

When you loaded the radiosity renderer, you were prompted to enable Exposure Control and you chose to load it. In the next exercise, you'll adjust some of the settings in the Exposure Control dialog to compensate for the bright lights.

Exercise 12.4: Accessing and adjusting Exposure Control

1. Open the **Radiosity04.max** file from the CD-ROM or from the previous exercise, and save it to your project folder with the name *Radiosity05.max*.

2. Press the 9 key to open the Render Scene dialog, press Reset All, if necessary, to discard the current radiosity solution and geometry, and click the Start button to process the radiosity solution. Make sure the Camera01 viewport is active, and render it.

3. In the Radiosity Processing Parameters rollout, Interactive Tools area, click the Setup button to the right of Logarithmic Exposure Control (**Figure 12.15**). You can also press the 8 key for the keyboard shortcut.

   This is the exposure control that was added when you activated the radiosity renderer. The default Logarithmic Exposure Control adjusts brightness and contrast in a scene, based on an S-curve that affects midtone areas more than dark or light areas.

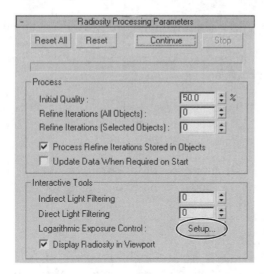

FIGURE 12.15 *Click the Setup button to access the exposure control parameters.*

4. In the Environment and Effects dialog, in the Logarithmic Exposure Control Parameters rollout, enter 60.0 in the Brightness field, press Enter, and render the Camera01 viewport. The overall scene is a bit darker. Enter 75.0 in the Contrast field and render the scene again. This darkens the dark areas slightly and brightens the lighter areas considerably more, for higher contrast. Enter 1.2 in the Mid Tones field and render the scene again. This brightens the midtone areas while having less impact on dark or light areas (see **Figure 12.16** on the next page).

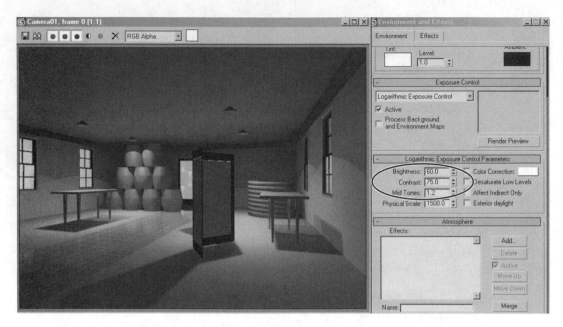

FIGURE 12.16 *Adjust the Brightness, Contrast, and Mid Tones adjustments, which are post-processing effects and do not require that the radiosity solution be recalculated.*

5. Close all windows and dialogs, and save the file. It should already be called Radiosity05.max.

    Exposure control is necessary to tweak the final image.

Adjusting exposure control is a subjective process that can be applied relatively quickly and is important to make the scene more convincing for your clients.

Radiosity Solution Refinement

For test rendering, you've been calculating the radiosity process to an Initial Quality setting of 50%, which is good enough to track the progress of radiosity in a timely fashion. For final rendering, you should set the Initial Quality back to the default 85% as a starting point. Increasing the Initial Quality settings will have diminishing returns the closer you get to 100%. If possible, try to keep Initial Quality below 90%.

In the next exercise, you'll learn about refine iterations, a process of analyzing the light distributed from vertex to vertex and refining the solution to balance bright and dark areas to smooth the light solution.

You'll then adjust the light filtering, which is a post-processing blurring effect that helps clean up any remaining problem areas. The ranges of filtering should remain between 0 and 3, because excessive blurring has a tendency to destroy small shadows.

Exercise 12.5: Increasing radiosity rendering quality

1. Open the **Radiosity05.max** file from the CD-ROM or from the last exercise, and save it to your project folder with the name *Radiosity06.max*.

2. Press the 9 key to open the Render Scene dialog, click Reset All, if necessary, and then click the Start button to process the radiosity solution again. Render the Camera01 viewport.

3. Open this last rendered image in Channel A of the RAM Player, and then minimize it.

4. In the Render Scene dialog, in the Radiosity Processing Parameters rollout, in the Process area, enter **85.0** in the Initial Quality field. Click the Reset All button and then the Start button, and render the scene again.

5. When the radiosity solution has been recalculated (finally) and the scene is rendered, open it in Channel B of the RAM Player.

   The 85% solution in Channel B is noticeably brighter because more bounced light was calculated. You'll also notice blotchy dark areas along the right-hand side where the wall meets the ceiling (**Figure 12.17**).

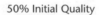
50% Initial Quality   85% Initial Quality

Blotchy areas ⌐

FIGURE 12.17 *Increase the Initial Quality setting for more accurate radiosity calculations.*

The blotchiness at the upper right is caused by the ceiling overlapping the top of the wall and the dark trim, leaving no corresponding vertices to transfer light smoothly. The current meshing parameters are set to 3'0", which is also too large for a clean solution.

6. Click the Named Selection Sets drop-down list on the main toolbar, and choose Large_mesh to select the objects previously set with meshing parameters.

7. In the Render Scene dialog, Radiosity Processing Parameters rollout, Process area, enter 10 in the Refine Iterations [Selected Objects.tif] field (**Figure 12.18**), and reset the radiosity solution with Reset All; then recalculate the solution and render the scene.

We have refined the initial calculations to attempt to balance light and dark areas between vertices. In the newly rendered image, the blotchiness is somewhat decreased, but it is still noticeable.

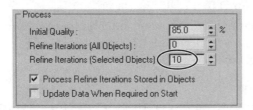

FIGURE 12.18 *The refine iterations need to be applied only to the geometry with meshing parameters set, so use the Refine Iterations (Selected Objects) numeric field.*

8. Instead of increasing refine iterations that would require a recalculation and longer render time, in the Indirect Light Filtering field of the Interactive Tools area enter 2, and render the Camera01 viewport (**Figure 12.19**).

Filtering does not require a recalculation of the radiosity solution, because it is a post-process. Also, the ceiling is lit only by indirect light, so the Direct Light Filtering would have no effect.

9. Close all windows and dialogs, and save the file. It should already be called Radiosity06.max.

Once you have reached an acceptable level of initial quality rendering, you can start experimenting with the refinements and filtering to balance quality and efficiency.

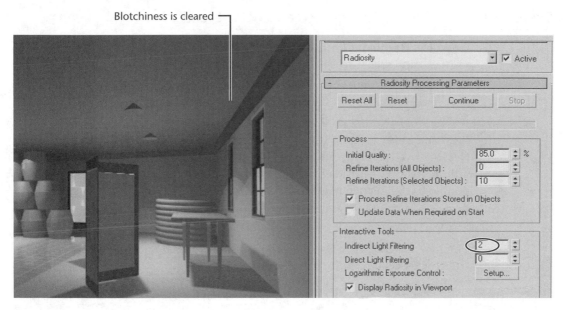

FIGURE 12.19 *Set the Indirect Light Filtering to 2 to slightly blur the image and smooth the blotchiness.*

Materials for Radiosity Rendering

You've learned the fundamental process and controls of radiosity rendering, but there are still two issues that need to be addressed in your rendered scene: reflectance and color bleeding.

Reflectance is the amount of light energy that is returned from striking a surface, and it is a product of the surface condition and color of the object it strikes. Also, the color of light bouncing from the surface is altered by the color of the material on the surface—for example, a red carpet will tint the white walls of a room so that they appear somewhat pink.

In 3ds Max 8, both reflectance and color bleed can be controlled in the material applied to the surface with a material type called Advanced Lighting Override. The old material is kept as a sub-material, and its properties are overridden by the new material.

In the next exercise, you'll use Advanced Lighting Override material to increase the amount of light energy and reduce the amount of the red bleeding from the bright red barrels at the end of the room.

Exercise 12.6: Adjusting reflectance and color bleed

1. Open the **Radiosity06.max** file from the CD-ROM or from the previous exercise, and save it to your project folder with the name *Radiosity07.max*.

2. Reset and recalculate the radiosity solution, and render the Camera01 viewport. Open the RAM Player and place this rendered image in Channel A; then minimize the RAM Player.

3. Press the M key to open the Material Editor, and activate the Barrel material in the top row. It's the green and red Multi/Sub-Object material. In the Material Editor, click the Multi/Sub-Object button, and, in the Material/Map Browser, double-click Advanced Lighting Override (**Figure 12.20**).

4. In the Replace Material dialog, make sure that the Keep Old Material as Sub-Material radio button is chosen, and click OK.

    The new material now overrides the existing material and provides new controls for reflectance and color bleeding.

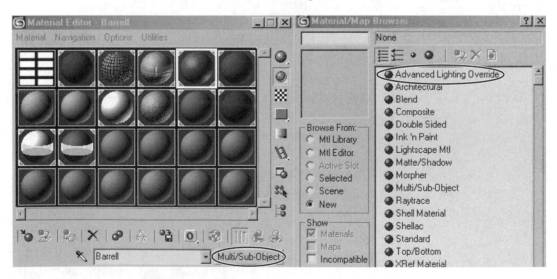

FIGURE 12.20 *Apply an Advanced Lighting Override material to the existing material.*

5. In the main menu, Customize pull-down menu, click Preferences. In the Preference Settings dialog, click the Radiosity tab. In the Material Editor area, check the Display Reflectance & Transmittance Information box (**Figure 12.21**).

note

You're overriding both the red and green sub-materials with this application of Advanced Lighting Override. It would also be possible to apply Advanced Lighting Override to only one of the sub-materials, or to both sub-materials and use different settings.

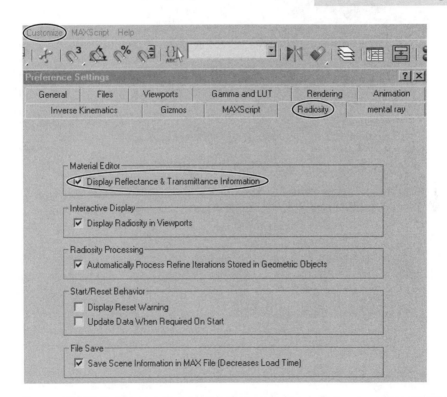

FIGURE 12.21 *You must customize the display to show reflectance and transmittance information in the Material Editor.*

This will cause the reflectance and transmittance information to be displayed below the sample windows in the Material Editor (**Figure 12.22**) after you close and reopen the Material Editor.

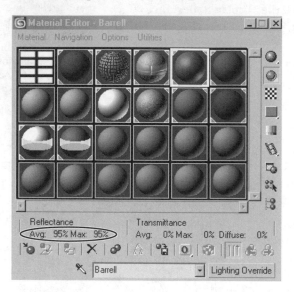

FIGURE 12.22 *The reflectance and transmittance values are displayed as an average and the maximum amount. A material must have less than 100 percent opacity before it can transmit light energy.*

6. In the Material Editor, in the Advanced Lighting Override Material rollout, enter 1.5 in the Reflectance Scale field. In the Color Bleed field, enter 0.25 (**Figure 12.23**).

The material now returns more light back into the scene, but less color. You can also see that the Reflectance value has changed from 95% to 84%. Changing the Color Bleed value also affects the Reflectance values.

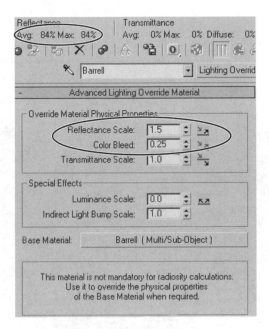

FIGURE 12.23 *Change the scale factors for Reflectance and Color Bleed.*

7. Close the Material Editor, and open the Rendered Scene dialog. Reset and recalculate the radiosity solution, and render the Camera01 viewport. Maximize the RAM Player and place this image in Channel B.

    The ceiling and wall near the barrel are decidedly less red and a bit brighter now (see **Figure 12.24** on the next page). Adjusting color bleeding and reflectance values can make the scene look more convincing.

No Advanced | With Advanced
Lighting Override | Lighting Override

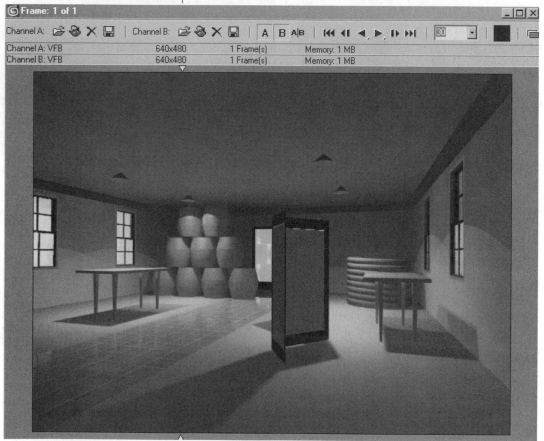

FIGURE 12.24 *Open the last rendered image in the RAM Player to compare it with the image rendered without Advanced Lighting Override.*

8. Close all windows and dialogs, and save the file. It should already be called Radiosity07.max. You've completed the essential steps of radiosity rendering.

Material adjustments can be an important part of a good radiosity rendering, and you can find guidelines on the typical reflectance values of commonly used architectural materials by entering reflectance in the 3ds Max 8 online Help search feature.

Summary

Don't be intimidated by the many steps involved in radiosity rendering. Once you've gone through the process a few times and can anticipate the results of your particular modeling techniques and materials, it can go relatively quickly and enhance your final rendered output.

Do remember that modeling techniques can have a significant impact on how much meshing and refining will be necessary for efficient radiosity rendering. Lighting is stored in vertices, and if the vertex positions on one object do not match the vertex positions on neighboring objects, much smaller meshing sizes must be applied to correct the issue, which will result in longer render times.

Once you have your meshing parameters established, you can start increasing the refine iterations to attempt to smooth out blotchy areas in the rendered image, and, finally, you can apply small amounts of filtering to clean up stubborn blotchy areas.

Advanced Lighting Override material will give you extra control over the amount of light returned from surfaces, as well as more control over the amount of color lifted from materials and transferred onto nearby surfaces.

CHAPTER 13

Basic Animation

In This Chapter

When setting up fundamental animation in 3ds Max 8, you'll find that a technique called *keyframe animation* can provide a fast and efficient recording of simple changes over time so that they become animations. In this chapter, you'll learn how to animate objects using a couple of keyframe-animation tools: the Set Key mode method of recording keyframes and the Track View–Dope Sheet method of timing keyframes.

Set Key mode lets you create a minimum number of keys at each keyframe that record only the object's change in position. This makes it much easier to locate and edit the keys when necessary.

Using the Track View–Dope Sheet editor, you'll learn how to edit animation keys in the context of the animated objects in the scene. Within the Dope Sheet editor, you'll also learn how to adjust range bars, which provide you a way to manipulate groups of animation keys as a single entity when adjusting the starting and ending frames or overall animation time for each animated object.

Key Terms

- **Keyframe**—A point in time that represents the end of an animated event.
- **Timeline**—A time "ruler," at the bottom of the display, where animation keys are recorded.
- **Track view**—An expanded representation of the timeline with more editing options.
- **Animation key**—An icon in the Track View–Dope Sheet or on the timeline at the bottom of the display that contains the animation data recorded at a specific time.

About Keyframe Animation

Keyframe animation has historical roots in traditional animation techniques. In early animation studios, work was distributed between master animators and junior animators. The master animators would draw the "key" frames of the action—for example, the main character standing on the left side of the view, and then another view of the character on the right side facing the opposite direction. The junior animators would then draw the character's intermediate positions on transparent acetate sheets to fill in the action from one position to the next. Then all of the sheets would be photographed and played back at 24 frames per second (fps) to appear as an animated sequence.

tip

Now might be a good time to go back to Chapter 1 and review the section on storyboarding. Very often a storyboard comprises primarily the keyframes sketched out to describe the intended story. While intended to serve as a planning tool before the project begins, the storyboard can also be used as a road map to help animators set up keyframes.

In 3ds Max 8, you're the master animator who records just the keyframes. Then you allow the software to act as the junior animator and create the intermediate motion.

Set Key Animation Mode

The exercises in this section focus on using Set Key animation techniques that let you control exactly what keys are created at any given point in time by using filters to eliminate creation of unwanted keys. Later in the chapter, you'll also learn to use Track View–Dope Sheet to edit the keys you create.

Using Set Key animation mode, you determine which category will have keys, such as only the position or rotation keys. You'll have to remember to click the Set Key button each time you want to record a key, but the reduced number of total keys is worth this extra step.

In the first exercise, you'll animate the position of the lobster boat in the outdoor scene so that the boat moves away from the side of the pier and then backs in against the front of the pier.

note

3ds Max 8 also has a somewhat simpler animation technique, called Auto Key mode. It automatically generates keys for any action whenever the Auto Key button is toggled on and you set the current time to any frame other than frame 0 in the timeline.

The main advantage to Set Key mode is that you can preview transforms without committing to them. Move plus or minus one frame, the transform is cancelled, and you won't automatically create a Key at frame 0.

Using Set Key mode filters, you could also change the rotation of the animated object without creating rotation keys, for example. In Auto Key mode all kinds animation keys are recorded.

Exercise 13.1: Animating a position using Set Key mode

1. Open the **Keyframe01.max** file from the CD-ROM, and save it to your project folder with the name *Keyframe02.max*.

2. On the main toolbar, click the Named Selection Sets drop-down list and choose Lobster_boat (**Figure 13.1**). Press the spacebar, which is a keyboard shortcut that locks the currently selected objects.

    This named selection set contains five objects, all parts of the boat, and by locking the selection set you make it impossible to accidentally select anything else in the scene while you're animating.

FIGURE 13.1 *Select the objects you will be animating, and lock the selection set.*

3. At the bottom of the display, turn on the Set Key toggle. The toggle, the time slider background, and the active viewport border all turn red to warn you that any action may create an animated sequence. Click the Key Filters button, and, in the Set Key Filters dialog, uncheck the boxes for Rotation, Scale, and IK Parameters, since you want to create keys only for Position changes (Figure 13.2). Close the Set Key Filter dialog.

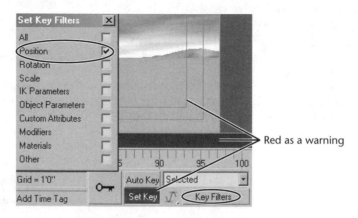

Red as a warning

FIGURE 13.2 *Toggle Set Key mode on, and then filter the categories of keys that will be recorded.*

4. Click the Select and Move button on the main toolbar to toggle it on, and make sure the time slider is set to frame 0 by dragging it all the way to the left of the timeline so that it reads 0/100. Click the large Set Keys button with the image of the key on it to record a position key at frame 0 (**Figure 13.3**).

Position key recorded at frame 0   Set Keys button

FIGURE 13.3 *Create a key at frame 0 to record the position of the boat and establish the starting point of the animation.*

5. Right-click in the Top viewport to activate it, and drag the time slider to frame 30. The slider button will read 30/100 to indicate that you are currently on frame 30, out of a total of 100 frames.

Animation in the United States is recorded at 30 fps, so this event will play back in 1 second when finally rendered.

6. In the Top viewport, move the boat forward, parallel to the pier, until it is about one boat length beyond the pier. Click the Set Keys button to create a new key on the timeline for the new position of the boat (**Figure 13.4**).

3ds Max 8 interpolates the boat's position in the frames between the two keyframes.

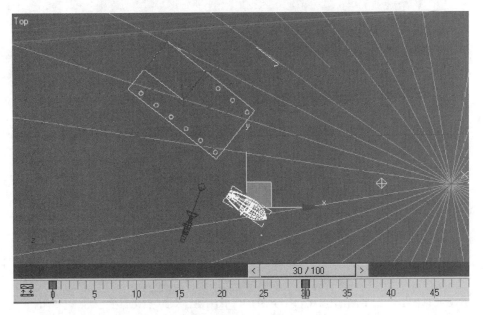

FIGURE 13.4 *Move the boat and create a new key to record the position.*

7. Scrub the time slider back and forth between frame 0 and frame 30, and you'll see that you've created an animation.

8. Drag the time slider to frame 60, and, in the Top viewport, move the boat to the center of the end of the pier, so that about one quarter of the rear of the boat overlaps the pier. Click the Set Keys button to create a key recording the new position (see **Figure 13.5** on the next page).

Three position keys are necessary for the boat to move away from and then back to the pier. Scrub the time slider, and you'll see how the boat moves.

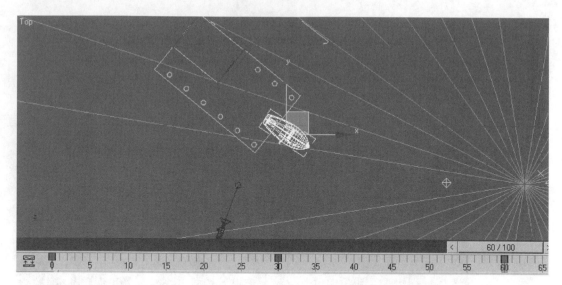

FIGURE 13.5 *Move the boat to the front of the pier, and create a new position key.*

9. Turn off the red Set Key toggle, and press the spacebar to unlock the selection set.

10. Save the file; it should already be called Keyframe02.max.

Using the Set Key mode of keyframe animation has allowed you to create only position keys on the timeline.

In the next exercise, you'll animate rotation keys in Set Key mode, to cause the boat to turn 90 degrees when it clears the pier, and then have the boat back into the front of the pier to create a more natural-looking motion.

Exercise 13.2: Animating rotation in Set Key mode

1. Open the **Keyframe02.max** file from the CD-ROM or from the previous exercise, and save it to your project folder with the name *Keyframe03.max*.

2. Right-click in the Camera01 viewport to activate it, and then click the Play Animation button at the lower right of the display (**Figure 13.6**). Click the Play Animation button again to stop the animation.

FIGURE 13.6 *Click the Play Animation button to view the animation in the active viewport.*

The boat moves quickly away from the pier and then slides back underneath it, all at approximately the same speed. It's a bit unconvincing, but you're learning first how to set the rotation, and then later you'll learn how to adjust the speed.

3. On the main toolbar, click the Named Selection Sets list and choose Lobster_boat, and then right-click in the Top viewport to activate it. Drag the time slider to frame 30 in the timeline. Click the Set Key toggle at the bottom of the display to toggle on Set Key mode.

    The display elements will turn red. You'll now set rotation keys.

4. Click the Key Filters button at the bottom of the display, and, in the Set Key Filters dialog, deselect the Position option and select Rotation (**Figure 13.7**). Close the Set Key Filters dialog.

    You only want to generate new rotation keys and not overwrite existing position keys at frame 30. The filters let you choose which keys will be recorded.

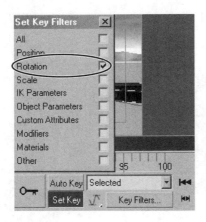

FIGURE 13.7 *In Set Key mode, you must remember to change filters before trying to animate rotation changes.*

5. Click the large Set Keys button, and notice in the timeline that frame 30 now shows a key that is half red and half green to indicate that there are both position and rotation keys at this frame (see **Figure 13.8** on the next page).

    This ensures that the rotation of the boat will stay constant until frame 30; otherwise, any new rotation would start from frame 0.

note

You can view all the graphics featured on the pages of this book in full color on the CD-ROM.

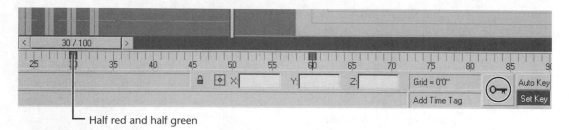

Half red and half green

FIGURE 13.8 *When there is more than one key on any given frame, the color coding can indicate which keys have been recorded with the Set Keys button.*

6. Drag the time slider to frame 60. Click the Select and Rotate button on the main toolbar, and, in the Top viewport, rotate the boat roughly 90 degrees clockwise so that the boat is pointing toward the viewer (**Figure 13.9**).

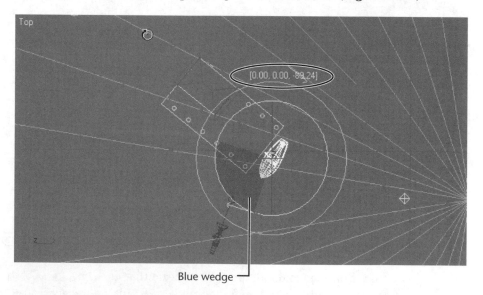

Blue wedge

FIGURE 13.9 *Rotate the boat 90 degrees clockwise at frame 60.*

7. Click the Set Keys button to record the new rotation at frame 60; the key will be half red and half green in the timeline. You can read the angle of XYZ rotation on the Transform gizmo and see a blue wedge appear, indicating the rotation amount, as you rotate the view in the active viewport.

8. Click in the timeline and drag a selection window around the two keys at frame 30. They will turn white. Click on the new white key and drag it left to frame 15 (**Figure 13.10**).

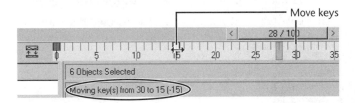

FIGURE 13.10 *Move the keys in the timeline by selecting and dragging them.*

9. Click the Set Key toggle to turn off Set Key mode. Right-click in the Camera01 viewport to activate it, and play the animation and then stop it.

    The boat now pulls away from the pier much more quickly, stops, and then turns and backs to the front of the pier much more slowly than previously. The spacing between the keys on the timeline affects the speed between animated events.

10. Close all windows and dialogs and save the file; it should already be called Keyframe03.max.

    Both the position and rotation keys have now been created and moved on the timeline to affect the speed of the animation. The closer together the keys are on the timeline, the faster the animation is from key to key.

You've learned how to create new keys for animating rotational changes in your scene, and then how to select and move keys in the timeline to change the timing of the animated events. Next we'll learn to use the Track View–Dope Sheet to edit the animation.

The Track View–Dope Sheet

Editing the timing of your animation by moving keys on the timeline is fine for simple animations, but when the animation gets more complex, it can be easier to use the Track View–Dope Sheet to edit timing. The Track View–Dope Sheet is a key-frame editor that gives you a better overview of the entire animation.

In the following exercise, you'll use the Dope Sheet to fine-tune timing changes for your animated boat so that the boat sits at the pier for a bit longer before moving forward and the whole animation takes place over a shorter time.

Exercise 13.3: Opening and setting up the Dope Sheet

1. Open the **Keyframe03.max** file from the CD-ROM or from the previous exercise, and save it to your project folder with the name *Keyframe04.max*.

2. Make sure that Lobster_boat is current in the Named Selection Sets list on the main toolbar. In the Graph Editors drop-down menu, choose Track View–Dope Sheet (**Figure 13.11**).

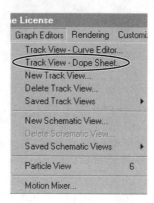

FIGURE 13.11 *Dope Sheet is one of the two Track View editor variants.*

The default Track View–Dope Sheet editor opens, displaying a hierarchical list of scene elements and objects on the left, and a gridded window with animation information on the right.

However, a hierarchical list of objects on the far left is a bit intimidating because it displays everything in the scene. You can reduce the clutter by filtering out unwanted information, which we'll do in the next step.

3. In the Track View–Dope Sheet dialog, click the Filters button in the toolbar. In the Filters dialog, in the Show Only area, uncheck the Visible Objects box and check the Selected Objects box (**Figure 13.12**). Click OK.

> **note**
>
> This chapter's Max Files folder on the CD-ROM includes a bitmap image. 3ds Max always looks for any necessary external files in the same folder as the main Max scene file. If you open a scene file from a location different from the original chapter folder, you may encounter a Missing External Files dialog. If you do, click Browse, and in the Configure External File Paths dialog, click Add. Use the Choose New External Files Path dialog to browse to the location of the CD versions of the Max scene files for this chapter, then click Use Path, and click OK. Click Continue to close the Missing External Files dialog.

Filters

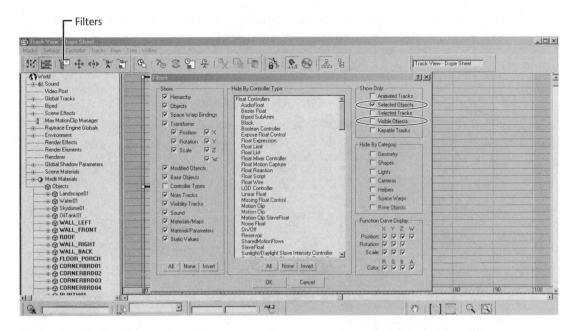

FIGURE 13.12 *The Filters option in Dope Sheet allows you to view only selected objects for a more uncluttered view.*

The Selected Objects filter makes it easier to locate objects in your scene because you can select them before opening the Dope Sheet, so that only selected objects will appear in the Objects list.

Right now the Dope Sheet is in Edit Ranges mode, which displays black lines, called range bars, with white boxes at each end that represent the start frame, the end frame, and the overall length of the animation. The top range bar represents all animation in the scene, while the lower range bars represent the animation of each object named in the left column. In the next step, you'll edit these range bars to adjust the animation timing.

tip

In the Dope Sheet hierarchical name column, selected objects appear with a yellow background behind the object icon. You can click these icons to select other objects in the scene so that you don't have to keep switching back and forth between the viewports and the Dope Sheet as much.

4. Click the plus button (+) to the left of HULL01 in the left column to expand it, if it isn't already expanded, and then expand Transform (**Figure 13.13**).

    The range bars let you globally change animation or alter individual elements of the animation.

Range of entire animation in the scene

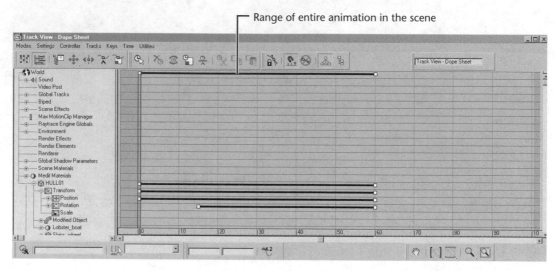

FIGURE 13.13 *Pick on the plus button to expand named objects in the hierarchical list and access sublevels of the animation control.*

5. Move your pointer over the range bar at the World level in the list at the top of the grid until it turns into a double-arrow cursor. Click the black bar and drag it until the end frame is at frame 80 (**Figure 13.14**).

    This slides the entire range of animation forward in time, so that now it starts at frame 20 and ends at frame 80. Next you'll change the overall length of the animation by changing the length of the range bar.

Double-arrow
cursor ⌐

End frame
at frame 80

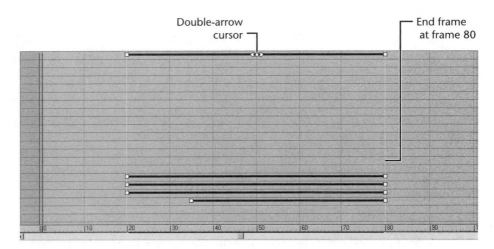

FIGURE 13.14 *Drag the entire range bar to move it in time without altering the length of the animation.*

6.   Move your pointer over the white box at the left end of the World range bar until you see a single left arrow pointer. Click and drag the start frame of the animation to frame 40 (**Figure 13.15**).

This scales the entire animation so that it starts at frame 40 and has a duration of 40 frames, but the relative distances for rotation and position keys remain constant.

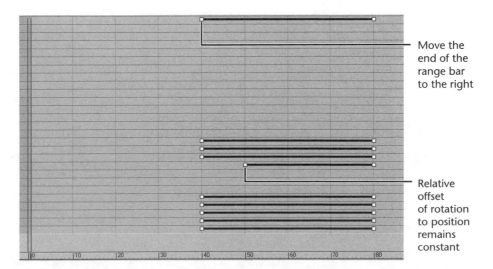

Move the
end of the
range bar
to the right

Relative
offset
of rotation
to position
remains
constant

FIGURE 13.15 *Reposition the left end of the range bar to scale the animation.*

7. Close all windows and dialogs, and save the file. It should already be called Keyframe04.max.

8. Play back the animation in the Camera01 viewport, and you'll see that the boat sits for a while, and then moves away and backs into the front of the pier very quickly. Stop the animation.

Editing animations in the Track View–Dope Sheet offers a better overview and more editing control of the elements of your animation.

> **note**
>
> The keys on the timeline have been moving as you've been editing the range bars to reflect the changes to the animation.

Summary

Set Key mode helps you to maintain a minimum number of keys to simplify editing. In the exercises in this chapter, you created keys only for position and rotation.

You can accomplish simple timing adjustments to your animation by moving keys in the timeline, but you get a more complete overview of the relationships of animated objects by using Track View–Dope Sheet and working with range bars.

CHAPTER 14

3D Animation

In This Chapter

In the last chapter, you learned how to use the Set Key method of animation, which is very effective for animation that requires only a few keyframes to describe some basic movement of the boat. However, there are times when you'll be creating more complex animations that require setting many keys and then editing them to fine-tune the final animation. In these cases, other techniques and tools that are available in 3ds Max 8, such as controllers and constraints, hierarchical linking, and ease curves, are very effective for animations that contain a lot of velocity changes.

This chapter shows you how to apply a path constraint to the position of an object so that you can use external information, in the form of a 2D shape, to control its position. You can think of animation controllers and constraints as "modifiers" that are applied to control the animation parameters of objects.

You'll also learn how to use *hierarchical linking*, or parent-child relationships between objects, to aid animation. You can use a parent object to control the animation of the children and provide secondary pivot points for complex rotations.

In Chapter 13, you learned how to change the velocity of animated objects by moving keys in the timeline or in the Dope Sheet, but when you need more control over the velocity of objects, you'll want to use *ease curves*. You'll learn a technique in this chapter for applying ease curves, which provide visual feedback about the velocity of an object in the form of a graph.

Key Term

- **Dummy helper**—A nonrenderable object that can be used in hierarchical linking to control objects or create alternate pivot points.

Animating Using Controllers and Constraints

In 3ds Max 8, all objects and animated parameters have either animation controllers or constraints assigned to them to describe their animatable behavior. Animation controllers and constraints are very similar. The main difference between them is that controllers directly affect the behavior of objects, while constraints require some sort of external information, such as shapes or other objects in the scene.

The goal of this chapter is to animate a truck moving along a road and control its animation velocity, getting it to stop for a specific amount of time and at a specific position before it moves on. You'll swap the default controller or constraint assigned to a dummy object for a constraint that makes more sense for the initial animation. Then you'll learn how to apply and adjust the ease curve for more specific velocity control.

Changing an Object's Controller Type

In the first exercise, you'll animate a dummy object to travel down the center of a road in a hilly landscape.

Using Set Key keyframe animation to accomplish this would require setting a lot of keys to describe this more complex motion, which would make it difficult to edit later. Instead, you'll change the default Position XYZ controller type on the dummy object to a path constraint, and then you'll choose a path along which the dummy will be animated.

The dummy helper object won't ever be seen in the rendered images, but it will be used to control the forward motion of the truck that you'll hierarchically link to it in another exercise later in this chapter. The reason for this extra step is to isolate the forward motion so that it may be easily edited as a discrete operation.

Exercise 14.1: Using the path constraint for animation

1. Reset 3ds Max 8 and open the **Constraint01.max** file from the CD-ROM. Save it to the project folder with the name *Constraint02.max*.

    The scene is a simple roadway up and over a hill, a truck and a crane, and a large wireframe dummy helper object in the middle of the road (**Figure 14.1**).

Dummy helper

FIGURE 14.1 *You'll animate the truck moving up the hill in this scene.*

2. In the Top viewport, select the green dummy object called Truck_Dummy01 by picking on one of its visible edges. On the main toolbar, click the Select and Move button, and move the object around a little bit.

    The dummy moves freely, because its default animation controller is a Position XYZ controller that is designed to allow free movement of objects. Next, you'll use the Motion panel to assign a different controller or constraint to the dummy object.

tip

When you have the time, you should select each object in the scene and check the Modify panel to see how the object was constructed. You can learn a lot from deconstructing objects this way.

3. Click the Motion panel button on the command panel, and then expand the Assign Controller rollout. Highlight Position: Position XYZ in the Assign Controller list. Click the Assign Controller button, just above the list. In the Assign Position Controller dialog, double-click Path Constraint in the list of available controllers (**Figure 14.2**).

Try to move the dummy object again, and you won't be able to, because it no longer has the Position XYZ controller type and needs to have an outside constraint.

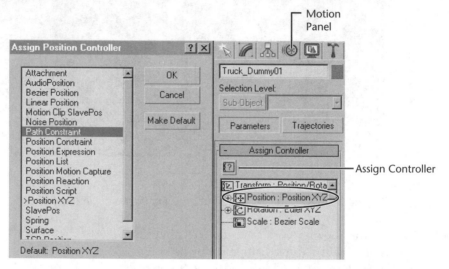

FIGURE **14.2** *Assign the path constraint to the dummy object on the Motion panel.*

4. In the Path Parameters rollout, click the Add Path button, and, in the Top viewport, click on the line, called animation_path, that runs down the center of the roadway to add it to the target list (**Figure 14.3**). Click the Add Path button again to toggle it off.

The dummy object jumps to the beginning of the animation path line, which now defines the dummy's position.

note

The line you've added to the path constraint as a path target serves a dual purpose: it has also been used as the loft path along which the roadway is lofted.

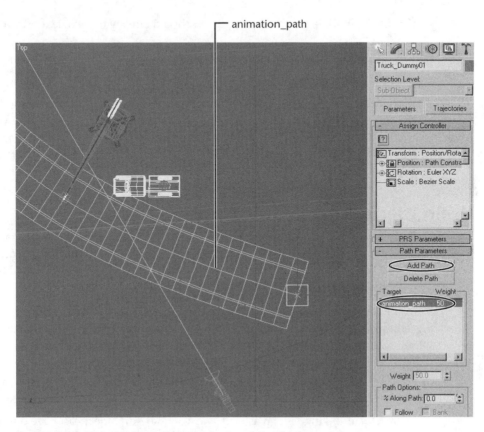

animation_path

FIGURE 14.3 *Pick the 2D path in the center of the roadway.*

5. Scrub the time slider at the bottom of the viewports and notice that the dummy object moves up the center of the road, holding its original orientation on the curves. On the Motion panel, in the Path Parameters rollout, in the Path Options area, select the Follow option, and scrub the time slider (**Figure 14.4**).

    The Follow option makes the dummy object stay perpendicular to the curvature of the path as it travels along the roadway.

FIGURE 14.4
Select the Follow option so that the dummy object remains perpendicular to the path.

6. Close all dialogs and save the file. It should already be called Constraint02.max.

   The path constraint has automatically created two keys in the timeline to position the dummy object at 0 percent of the way along the path at the start and 100 percent along the path at the end of the animation.

Rather than manually creating animation keys at strategic points along the center of the roadway, the path constraint has used a line to describe both the position and the rotation of the dummy, making it much easier to set up the initial animation. In the next section, you'll link the truck in the scene to the dummy so that the truck moves up the hill.

Using Hierarchical Linking for Extra Control

Simply moving the dummy object will not make an interesting animation, so you have to set up a relationship between the dummy object and the truck in the scene, so that it's the truck that travels down the road. This can be accomplished by hierarchically linking the child object, in this case the truck, to a parent object, the dummy.

You'll notice also that there is a cylindrical tank in the back of the truck that will remain in position as the truck is pulled down the road by the dummy. This is an oil tank that has previously been hierarchically linked to the truck, so the tank will remain in the back of the truck as the truck moves. You're animating an ancestry greater than just parent-child: the oil tank is a child, the truck is its parent, and the dummy is its grandparent.

Hierarchical linking can go as deeply as you like—an object can have only one parent, while a parent can have many children. For example, there could be several oil tanks in the back of the truck that are all children of the truck and grandchildren of the dummy.

Let's position the truck and link it.

Exercise 14.2: Aligning and linking the truck to the dummy

1. Open the **Constraint02.max** file from the CD-ROM or from the previous exercise, and save it to your project folder with the name *Constraint03.max*.

2. Select the truck in the Top viewport, and make sure the time slider is set to frame 0 so that everything is at the beginning of your animation.

3. On the main toolbar, click the Align button, and pick on the edge of the green dummy object at the end of the road in the Top viewport. In the Align Selection dialog, make sure that X Position, Y Position, and Z Position are all checked and that Pivot Point radio buttons are chosen in both the Current and

Target Object columns. In the Align Orientation [Local] area, check all three axes to align the truck to the dummy object (**Figure 14.5**). Click OK to accept the settings.

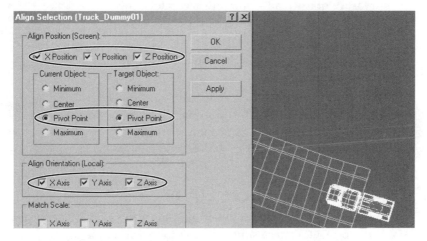

FIGURE 14.5 *The Align tool repositions and reorients the truck to the dummy object.*

4. In the Front viewport, zoom in so that the truck nearly fills the viewport. On the main toolbar, click the Select and Link button. In the Front viewport, pick on the truck and drag to the edge of the dummy object. Notice that as you drag from the truck to the dummy—a rubber-band-like line appears at the pointer (**Figure 14.6**). Release the mouse button when the pointer (which turns white) is paused over the dummy. The dummy will flash white briefly to indicate that the link has taken place. Click the Select Object tool on the main toolbar to cancel the Select and Link mode.

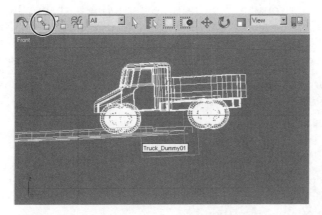

FIGURE 14.6 *Pick on the truck and drag to the dummy to establish a parent-child link.*

5. Scrub the time slider, and notice that the truck is now animated along the road with the dummy object and the lateral and vertical curvature of the road—or, more accurately, the animation path at the center of the road.

6. Close any windows and dialogs that may still be open, and save the file. It should already be called Constraint03.max.

    The child object, the truck, now mimics the animation of its parent, the dummy. However, the truck is free to have its own animation, as you'll discover in later exercises in this chapter.

tip

In the Select Objects dialog, you can check the Display Subtree option to see the names of child objects indented below their parent object names.

You can also use the page-up and page-down keys to step through and highlight the ancestry of linked objects.

Using the Track View–Curve Editor

In Chapter 13, you learned how to use the Track View–Dope Sheet to alter the timing of an animation, but it was a simple animation with minor adjustments to the timing that could easily be managed by adjusting range bars.

In the scene we're working with in this chapter, you'd need to set many keys to record the accurate lateral and vertical positioning of the dummy object as it travels along the road. The process of editing those keys to slow or stop the animation would also be difficult. This is a situation in which the Curve Editor is useful. The Curve Editor displays animations as function curves rather than just keys or range bars, making it easier to tell by the slope of the curve when objects are moving slowly or quickly, forward or backward.

You already have a basic animation in which the dummy object pulls the truck through the scene at a constant velocity. Instead of trying to change this base animation, you'll learn how to apply ease curves, which allow changes but leave the base animation intact. This is important because if you make mistakes when adjusting the velocity, you can easily delete the ease curve without affecting the base animation.

You'll also change the animation controller on the truck itself, so that the truck appears to be bouncing slightly as it travels along the road.

Applying Ease Curves for Velocity Control

Ease curves are superimposed on top of an existing animation to allow extra control that is entirely separate from the base animation. Applying the changes as a separate operation will allow you to easily delete the changes if something goes wrong, without affecting the original animation.

Exercise 14.3: Adding ease curves in the Curve Editor

1. Open the **Constraint03.max** file from the CD-ROM or from the previous exercise, and save it to your project folder with the name *Constraint04.max*.

2. Right-click in the Camera01 viewport to activate it, and then click the Play Animation button at the bottom right of the display.

   The dummy object pulls the truck along the road at a constant velocity. Let's access the Curve Editor.

3. From the Graph Editors pull-down menu, choose Track View–Curve Editor (**Figure 14.7**). Move and resize the Track View–Curve Editor dialog until it covers the bottom two viewports in the display (**Figure 14.8**).

   It will be easier to see the edits to the animation and the results, if you move the Curve Editor to the lower part of the display.

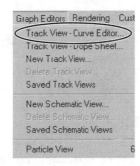

FIGURE 14.7
The Curve Editor is found in the Graph Editors pull-down menu.

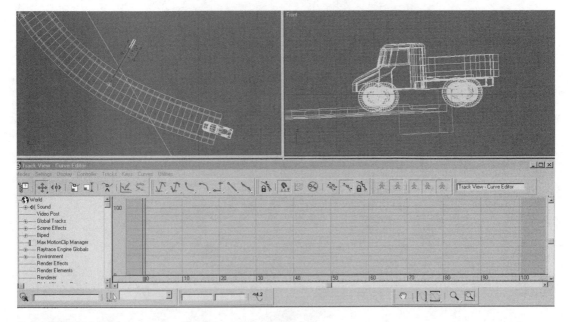

FIGURE 14.8 *Adjust the size and position of the Curve Editor.*

4. In the Front viewport, select the dummy object. The Curve Editor will find the dummy object in the left column and display its Percent function curve (**Figure 14.9**).

The graph displayed is the percentage of the dummy object along the path: 0 percent at the start and 100 percent at the end. It's a straight line representing constant velocity, and the ease curve should be superimposed over this base animation.

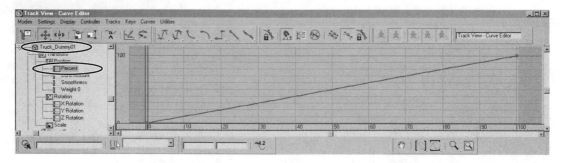

FIGURE 14.9 *The "curve" is a straight line because the dummy object is traveling at a constant velocity.*

5. Highlight Percent in the left column of the Track View–Curve Editor dialog, and then click the Curves drop-down menu and choose Apply–Ease Curve (**Figure 14.10**).

You may not notice that anything has changed, but if you look carefully, you'll see that a plus button (+) has appeared just to the left of Percent, indicating that something is now embedded below Percent in the hierarchy list.

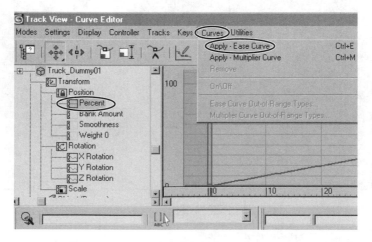

FIGURE 14.10 *Apply an ease curve to the Percent under Position.*

6. Click the plus button to the left of Percent to expand it, and highlight Ease Curve in the list (**Figure 14.11**).

The resulting curve looks the same except for a new key in the middle of the graph. The animation has not changed yet, but you can now edit this new curve to alter the object's velocity.

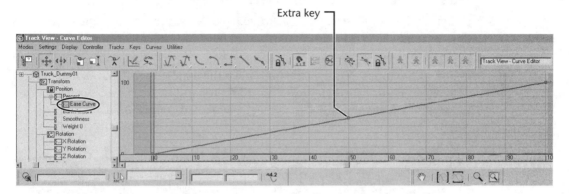

FIGURE 14.11 *The ease curve is superimposed over the percent curve.*

7. Close all windows and dialogs, and save the file. It should already be called Constraint04.max.

The ease curve has been applied, and you can now begin to adjust the object's velocity while getting visual feedback from the curve.

Ease curves can be applied to all forms of animation, not just changes in object positions. They can be applied to animated colors in a material, for example, or to the animated intensity of lights to alter the frequency of the changes.

Editing the Ease Curve to Affect Changes in Velocity

Once you've added ease curves, you can edit the Ease Curve graph by adding and moving keys along the line. Moving keys horizontally in the graph affects timing, while moving keys vertically affects the percentage along the path.

You can also change the incoming and outgoing tangency, or curvature, of the keys on the graph to fine-tune the action at that particular point in time. For example, you can change the tangency to cause an object to gradually slow into the position defined by the key, or you can adjust to stop abruptly from full speed.

Let's make some changes to the velocity of the truck in our scene.

Exercise 14.4: Adjusting the Ease Curve graph

1. Open the **Constraint04.max** file from the CD-ROM or from the previous exercise, and save it to your project folder with the name *Constraint05.max*.

2. From the Graph Editors pull-down menu, choose Track View–Curve Editor, and select the Truck_Dummy01 object in the Front viewport.

3. In the Track View–Curve Editor dialog, expand Percent in the left-hand column and highlight Ease Curve. Click on the square gray key in the middle of the curve; it will turn white.

    In the right numeric field at the bottom of the dialog, highlight 50.0000 and enter 25.0 (**Figure 14.12**). Press Enter. The key will move from 50 percent of the way to 25 percent of the way down the path at frame 50.

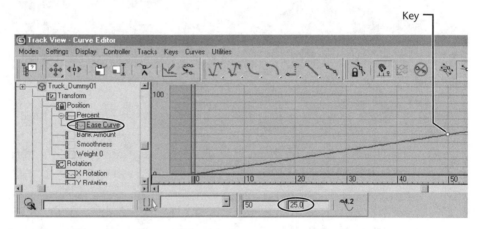

FIGURE 14.12 *Select the key on the graph, and change its percentage value numerically.*

4. Right-click in the Top viewport to activate it, and then click the Play Animation button at the lower right of the display. Stop the animation.

    Where the curve is flat, the truck is moving slowly. As the curve gets steeper, the truck is going faster. Next we'll insert a new key.

5. Click the Add Keys button in the dialog toolbar. Then click the green graph line near where it intersects the gray vertical line near frame 30. Enter 30 in both numeric fields and press Enter (**Figure 14.13**). Click the Move Keys button in the dialog to keep from adding more new keys.

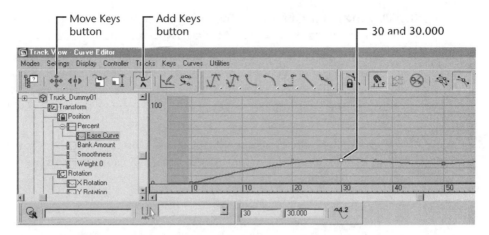

FIGURE 14.13 *Change the curve so that it slopes downward to make an object back up on the path.*

6. Play the animation in the Top viewport.

   The truck now speeds ahead, slows, backs up, and then builds speed toward the end. A curve that slopes downward to the right indicates backward motion.

7. Select the left key on the graph line at frame 30. Enter 15 in the left numeric field, and 17.000 in the right numeric field. Select the key to the right at frame 50 on the graph line, and enter 35 in the left numeric field and 17.000 in the right numeric field (**Figure 14.14**).

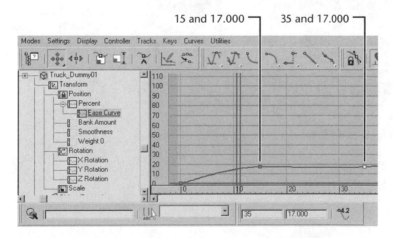

FIGURE 14.14 *Change both keys to have the same percent value.*

8. Play the animation. In the Top viewport, notice that the truck almost comes to a stop beneath the crane and then moves on.

   Even though both keys are at 17 percent along the path, the truck doesn't come to a full stop because there is Bézier tangency in the keys. The tangency curvature affects the velocity of the object before and after the key. Next we'll change the tangency in the keys to create a straight line, which will make the animated object remain still between the keys.

9. Right-click on the right key; in the Truck_Dummy01 dialog, click and hold the In tangency button, and choose the Linear tangency button from the flyout buttons (**Figure 14.15**).

   Next we'll change the outgoing tangency for key 2.

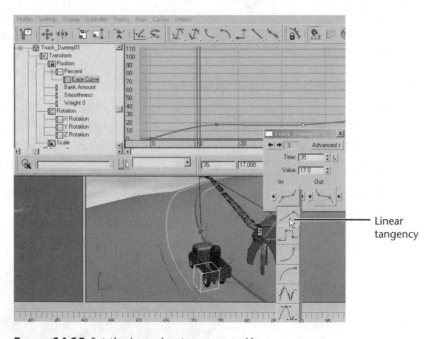

Linear
tangency

FIGURE 14.15 *Set the incoming tangency to Linear.*

10. In the Truck_Dummy01 dialog, click the left-pointing black arrow at the upper left of the dialog to select the next key to the left. Click and hold the Out tangency button, and change it to Linear (**Figure 14.16**). Play the animation.

When the keys are at the same percentage, and the incoming and outgoing tangencies are set to Linear, the object stops dead in its tracks.

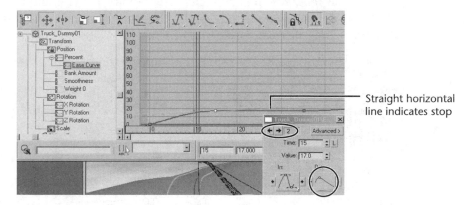

Straight horizontal line indicates stop

FIGURE 14.16 *Linear tangencies represent no curvature.*

11. Close all windows and dialogs, and save the file. It should already be called Constraint05.max.

A curve that slopes up to the right indicates forward motion and a horizontal curve indicates stop.

The ease curve lets you easily visualize and adjust the velocity of objects based on the steepness of the curve. Next, you'll make the truck bounce around a little bit as it travels up the road, to give it a comical appearance.

Changing the Controller to Apply Secondary Motion

You've changed the velocity of the truck as it travels along the path, and now you want to add a bit of character by making the truck bounce up and down as it travels.

The truck is a child of the dummy object, which is fully responsible for the forward motion. The truck can have its own animation, so you'll change its default controller TCB Position to Noise controller to apply random motion on the Z-axis.

Exercise 14.5: Adding a Noise controller to the truck for random movement

1. Open the **Constraint05.max** file from the CD-ROM or from the previous exercise, and save it to the project folder with the name *Constraint06.max*.

2. Select the truck in the Front viewport. On the Motion panel, expand the Assign Controller rollout, and highlight Position: TCB Position. Click the Assign Controller button, and double-click Noise Position in the Assign Position Controller dialog (**Figure 14.17**).

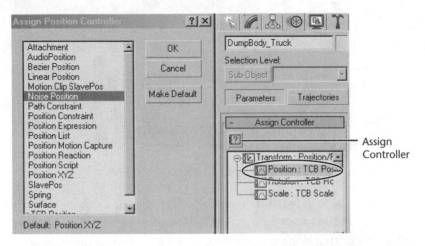

Figure 14.17 *Apply a Noise controller for random position changes based on a strength value.*

3. Right-click in the Camera01 viewport to activate it, and click the Play Animation button.

    The truck wobbles uncontrollably on all three axes as it travels along the path. However, you want the truck only to bounce up and down, which you can accomplish by adjusting the Noise controller.

4. In the Noise Controller dialog that has appeared, set the X Strength and Y Strength numeric fields to 0. You can accomplish that by right-clicking on the spinners or entering the number. Enter 20.0 in the Z Strength numeric field, and check the >0 box just to the right (**Figure 14.18**).

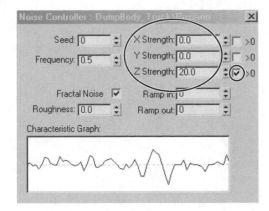

FIGURE 14.18 *The noise amount and direction can be controlled by adjusting the parameters.*

This restricts the noise to a maximum amount of 20 and will always generate positive numbers.

5. Play the animation. The truck now bounces less and only on the vertical Z axis. Stop the animation.

6. Close all windows and dialogs, and save the file. It should already be called Constraint06.max.

The truck's animation is totally independent of its parent, the dummy.

The Noise controller is a random number generator but has parameters that can be adjusted to make it useful.

Summary

By using controllers and constraints instead of creating animation keys by hand, you can create most basic animations much more easily and end up with more parameters that are easier to edit in the long run.

Hierarchical linking lets you create "layers" of animation that can be easily accessed and edited without affecting the rest of the animation.

CHAPTER 15

Effects

In This Chapter

Effects, or special effects, as they are sometimes known, can be thought of as a variety of processes you can add after you've finished the primary modeling, materials, lights, and animation of your scene. Used to enhance certain features or to draw the viewer's attention to certain elements in the scene, effects can range from fog on the horizon and clouds in the sky, to the glowing orb of the sun, to fireworks and objects colliding as they tumble through the air.

You'll return to the underwater scene from Chapter 5 to practice applying effects in this chapter. If you remember, all the objects in this scene are sharp and clear, regardless how near or far they are from the camera. To hide the edges of geometry and give the water in the scene the appearance of volume, you'll apply environment effects and particle systems. You'll also learn how to apply a type of fog to the sunlight source to simulate the streaking of sunlight as it passes through the cloudy water, making the scene more convincing. Then you'll apply a more generalized type of fog that is limited by the ranges you set for the camera in the scene, so that objects in the distance gradually fade from view. Finally, you'll learn how to use the Particle Flow feature of 3ds Max 8 to make it appear as though larger objects are suspended in the water and drifting slowly along in the currents. The combination of these effects is all-important in making viewers feel as though they are actually under water.

Always keep in mind that many effects in 3ds Max 8 can slow production significantly and should be used only to enhance or emphasize the story that you are trying to convey to your client.

Key Terms

- **Atmospheric effects**—Effects that create fog or a foglike appearance in lights.
- **Camera ranges**—By setting a near range and a far range on a camera, you can determine the starting point of the Fog effect and the point at which it becomes pure fog that obscures everything in view.
- **Particle Flow**—A feature that distributes a variety of particle types and modifies the behavior of the particles in the scene.

Atmospheric Effects

In a typical underwater scene, visibility is restricted by matter suspended in the water, such as sand, vegetation, and even tiny marine animals. You'll learn how to simulate some of this matter using atmospheric effects called Fog and Volume Light. The goal is to create the illusion that the viewer is peering into the depths of this particulate soup, which not only restricts vision, but also refracts the sunlight as it streams through the water.

In the first exercise, you'll apply a Volume Light effect to the direct light that is acting as the sunlight in your scene. This light has a map in the projector slot, which you learned about in Chapter 8, to project a mottled pattern of light on the ocean floor. The projector map will also interact with the Volume Light effect to make it appear as though the suspended matter varies in density.

Using the Volume Light Effect

It's not possible to see the beam of light emanating from a light source in 3ds Max 8 renderings; you can only see the effect of lights on objects in the scene.

However, sometimes you might want to make the lights in a scene more "tangible" by giving the light beams a presence that the viewer can relate to. The Volume Light atmospheric effect creates the illusion that a beam of light is striking fog or dust in the air, so the beam seems like it's visible. The visible beams change the mood of the scene and guide the viewer's gaze to important objects.

The Volume Light effect can be applied in one of two ways: from the Environmental dialog, found in the Rendering drop-down menu, or directly to the light itself. Both methods produce the same results. Let's apply the Volume Light effect to the beam of sunlight to make it look as though the light is being distorted by the water surface and is illuminating tiny particles suspended in the water.

Exercise 15.1: Using the Volume Light environment effect

1. Reset 3ds Max 8 and open **Effects01.max** from the CD-ROM. Save it to your project folder with the name *Effects02.max*.

2. Make sure the Camera01 viewport is active, and click the Quick Render button on the main toolbar (**Figure 15.1**).

Planes' edges

FIGURE 15.1 *Render the scene without any special effects.*

The rendered image has a map applied to the background to give it a blue-green "underwater" appearance, but objects in both the foreground and background are clear and sharp. It's also apparent that both the water surface and the ocean bottom are flat planes that show a distinct edge in the distance. You'll make it appear as though the water has some substance and depth.

note

The Raytrace reflection map in the water material has the Raytrace Atmospherics option disabled, so the rendering will not reflect any atmospheric effects and thereby blend in with the effects and become invisible. Disabling raytrace atmospherics will also increase rendering speed. The scene is rendered at 320 by 240 pixels for faster testing.

3. Make sure the Select Objects button on the main toolbar is toggled on, and, in the Front viewport, select the light at the upper right called Direct01. On the Modify panel, in the Atmospheres & Effects rollout, click the Add button. In the Add Atmosphere or Effect dialog that appears, double-click Volume Light (**Figure 15.2**).

A Volume Light entry appears in the box below the Add button. In the next step you'll highlight it and adjust its parameters.

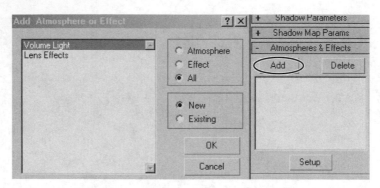

Figure 15.2 *Apply a Volume Light effect to the direct light acting as the sun in your scene.*

4. Highlight the Volume Light entry in the Atmospheres & Effects rollout, and click the Setup button to open the Environment and Effects dialog (**Figure 15.3**).

The default density for the Volume Light effect is much too high in the rendered scene and would be almost pure white. You'll lower the density and change the color of the fog to a light yellow to more closely simulate sunlight.

Figure 15.3 *Highlight Volume Light in the Modify panel box before clicking the Setup button.*

5. In the Environment and Effects dialog, Volume Light Parameters rollout, Volume area, enter 0.025 in the Density field. Click the white Fog Color swatch and, in the Color Selector, change it to a pale yellow (**Figure 15.4**).

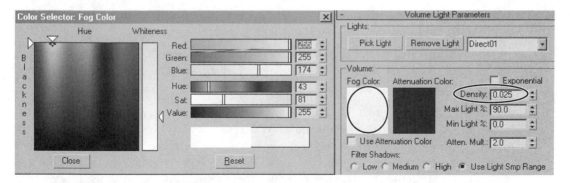

FIGURE 15.4 *Reduce the density and change the color of the Volume Light.*

6. Render the Camera01 viewport. The first thing you'll probably notice is that the rendering takes noticeably longer, but the light appears to be filtered through the water surface, providing a "volume" effect (**Figure 15.5**).

The Volume Light effect is fairly consistent and doesn't disguise the edges of the water and ocean-bottom planes. You'll learn how to do that with a different type of fog in the next exercise.

FIGURE 15.5 *The Volume Light effect makes the light visible as if refracted by the water surface and particles suspended in the water.*

7. Close all windows and dialogs, and save the file. It should already be called Effects02.max.

By transforming the crystal-clear atmosphere you started with, you've managed to change the mood of the scene. Viewers are now more likely to feel as though they are enveloped by a volume of water.

The Volume Light effect is applied directly to lights in the scene to make their beams visible. In this case, the light simulating the sun covers the whole viewing area, so the volume light fills the scene. If the coverage of a light is narrowed to a very small hotspot/falloff, a similar Volume Light can be used to simulate a laser beam. For example, applying the Volume Light to a spotlight could be used to simulate the headlights of a car on a foggy night or sunlight streaming through a window into a dusty room.

Let's continue working on the underwater scene by adding a fog into which distant objects will fade.

Adding Environment Fog

The next type of effect you'll apply to your scene is simply called Fog. It's an environment effect with parameters that are associated with the camera in the scene, rather than with a light, as the Volume Light effect was.

The only adjustment you'll need to make to the fog itself is to change its color. The fog's density will be determined by adjusting the camera ranges. No fog will appear between the camera and the near range, but then the density of the fog will increase between the near range and the far range. Beyond the far range setting, the Fog effect will obscure your view of all objects and any background maps in the scene.

Let's add environment fog to the scene and adjust the camera ranges so that the water appears even murkier, and, more important, the hard edges of the ocean bottom and the water are obscured to make the scene appear to have infinite depth.

Exercise 15.2: Applying Fog and Adjusting its Density

1. Open **Effects02.max** from the CD-ROM or from the previous exercise, and save it to your project folder with the name *Effects03.max*.

2. In the Rendering drop-down menu, choose Environment (**Figure 15.6**). This will open the Environment and Effects dialog.

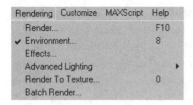

FIGURE 15.6 *Open the Environment and Effects dialog to apply the Fog effect to the scene.*

3. In the Environment and Effects dialog, in the Atmosphere rollout, click the Add button. In the Add Atmospheric Effect dialog, double-click Fog (**Figure 15.7**).

   The Fog entry now shows up in the Effects box. Next, you'll pan up in the dialog to access the Fog parameters.

> **tip**
>
> Notice in the Atmosphere rollout that the Volume Light effect you applied to the sunlight is listed in the Effects box. You could have applied the Volume Light effect from this dialog, and then you could have chosen which light you wanted the effect applied to. However, there's only one option for the Fog effect: You must apply it from this dialog.

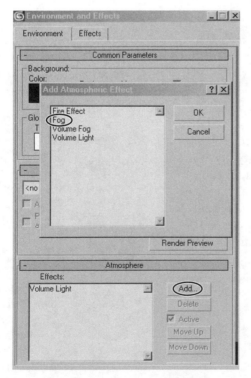

FIGURE 15.7 *Add a Fog environment effect to the scene.*

4. Click and drag on an empty area of the dialog, and, when you see the hand cursor, pan the dialog up to see the Fog Parameters rollout. Click on the large Color swatch and, in the Color Selector, change the color to a sea green. Perhaps settings of Red = 150, Green = 210, and Blue = 210 would be appropriate (**Figure 15.8**). Close the Color Selector and the Environment and Effects dialog.

The pure white fog would appear unconvincing in an underwater scene. If you rendered the scene now, the result would be a greenish image with no objects. In the next step, you'll learn how to adjust the camera ranges that determine where the fog begins and where it reaches maximum density.

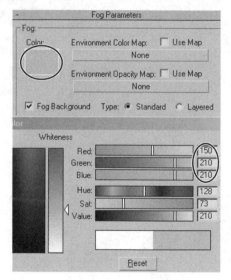

FIGURE 15.8 *Change the color of the fog to a greenish color for a more convincing underwater scene.*

5. In the Top viewport, select Camera01. On the Modify panel, in the Parameters rollout, in the Environment Ranges area, check the Show box (**Figure 15.9**). This enables you to see the camera ranges in the viewport but does not turn the ranges on or off.

By default, the near range is set to 0'0" and the far range is set to 10'0". This means that the fog begins at the camera and reaches full density 10 feet from the camera, obscuring all the objects in the scene.

FIGURE 15.9
Check the Show option of camera ranges so that you can see the ranges in the viewport.

6. Enter 100'0" in the Near Range field and 600'0" in the Far Range field. This means that there will be no fog from the camera out 100 feet, and then the fog will become gradually denser until it reaches full density at 600 feet from the camera.

In the Top viewport you'll see a light tan rectangle for the near range and a dark tan rectangle indicating the far range (**Figure 15.10**). These visible ranges on the camera help you to see the objects in the scene and their relationship to the fog ranges.

note

There's also a light blue rectangle in the camera pyramid that represents the camera's target position. In this example, it is very near the near range light tan rectangle.

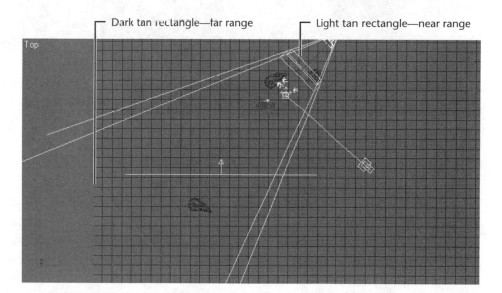

Dark tan rectangle—far range   Light tan rectangle—near range

FIGURE 15.10 *Set the Environment Ranges to start at the nearest rock in the scene and end before the corner of the ocean bottom.*

7. Right-click in the Camera01 viewport, and click the Quick Render button on the main toolbar. The scene will take noticeably longer to render because of the calculations for the fog.

However, the rocks in the foreground are relatively clear but become gradually foggier in the distance, and the ocean bottom and water surface no longer have the hard edge (see **Figure 15.11** on the next page).

FIGURE 15.11 *Render the camera viewport to see that the fog increases in density away from the camera.*

8. Close the rendered frame window and save the file. It should already be called Effects03.max.

You've added fog and adjusted camera ranges to make an underwater scene more convincing, but this same technique is useful as a distance cue in outdoor scenes to make distant landscape and objects appear farther away than they actually are. The effect could also be used, of course, to make a scene appear foggy. The key to making the fog appear convincing is to set the camera ranges appropriately for the type of fog you want.

Both of the fog techniques you've used so far give the illusion that there are fine suspended particles in the water, but most water actually has larger particles floating in it, too. You'll learn how to simulate these in the next section.

Adjusting Particle Flow Effects

You'll now learn about using the Particle Flow system in 3ds Max 8 to make it appear as though there are larger pieces of material drifting along with the tide or current. While the fog effects have been an illusion generated at render time, the particle systems actually emit 3D objects in the scene.

A particle emitter has already been placed in the scene. You'll learn how to adjust its parameters for the size, number, and speed of travel so that the particles appear to be drifting in the current.

Adjustments to the Particle Flow system are performed in a special dialog called Particle View, where series of events that affect the behavior of the particles are wired together in a series so that one event feeds into the next, providing visual feedback for easy editing. Let's go ahead and modify the Particle Flow system in the scene.

Exercise 15.3: Adjusting a Particle Flow System

1. Open **Effects03.max** from the CD-ROM or from the previous exercise, and save it to your project folder as *Effects04.max*.

2. In the Camera01 viewport, select the object called PF Source 01. It appears to be an orange icon of two rectangles with arrows and a circle (**Figure 15.12**).

   This icon is the particle emitter that has been disconnected from the event that describes its behavior. You'll open a dialog where the events are wired together and particle parameters are adjusted.

PF Source 01

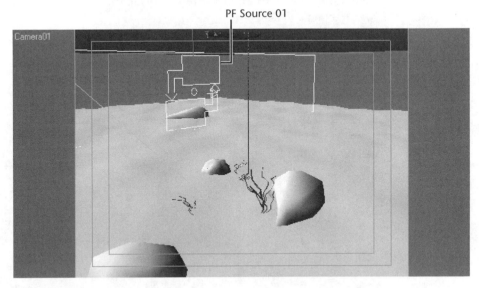

FIGURE 15.12 *Select the particle emitter that was previously placed in the scene.*

3. On the Modify panel, in the Setup rollout, click the Particle View button (**Figure 15.13**) to open the Particle View dialog. The Particle View dialog is where all aspects of the emitted particles are adjusted.

The upper left pane of the Particle View dialog is where the particle source and the events are laid out as discrete operations that act as containers for particle operators that modify particle behavior. Before the particles will actually appear in the scene, though, you'll have to wire the source to the event.

4. Click and drag from the small blue dot at the lower left of PF Source 01 to the circle at the upper left of Event 01 to wire the two together (**Figure 15.14**). Release the mouse button when you see the four-way arrow cursor make the connection.

The PF Source 01 is the emitter of the particles, and Event 01 contains the operators that modify the particles' behavior; the connection will display as a blue dotted line with an arrow representing the flow direction.

FIGURE 15.13 *Open the Particle View dialog to adjust the particles.*

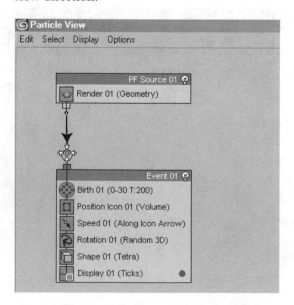

FIGURE 15.14 *Wire the source to the event by dragging the cursor from the blue dot to the circle.*

5. Right-click in the Camera01 viewport, and scrub the time slider to see the particles appear in the viewport as white ticks (**Figure 15.15**).

   You can also click the Play Animation button to see the particles appear in the first few frames and then drift slowly from left to right. In the next step, you'll learn how to adjust the particles so that there are a set number of particles visible at any time in the scene. The particles display as ticks rather than geometry, to make working in the viewports faster.

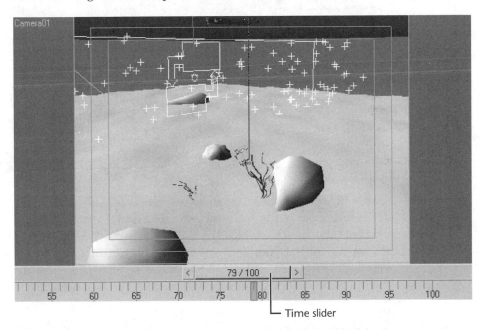

FIGURE 15.15 *Drag the time slider or play the animation to see the particles represented by ticks in the display.*

6. Stop the animation if it is playing. In the top of the Particle View dialog, in Event 01, highlight the first operator, called Birth 01. In the upper right pane, in the Birth 01 rollout, enter -100 in the Emit Start field and 100 in the Emit Stop field. Enter 100 in the Amount field (see **Figure 15.16** on the next page).

   This ensures that all particles are born 100 frames before your animation starts, to make sure that they are all visible at frame 0 and that they will all remain alive for the full 100 frames of the animation. The Amount setting means that there will always be 100 particles throughout the animation. Next you'll change the particles' speed.

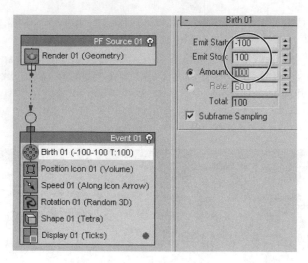

Figure 15.16 *Set the birth time, the birth life, and the total amount for continuous particles throughout the animation.*

7. In the Particle View dialog, in Event 01, highlight the Speed 01 operator. In the Speed 01 rollout, enter **50'0"** in the Speed field and **10'0"** in the Variation field (**Figure 15.17**).

    Increasing the particle speed to 50 feet per second not only makes the particles travel faster, but it also spreads them out, because the birth rate and particle amounts stay the same. This distributes the particles more evenly throughout the scene. The Variation setting will randomly cause the particles to travel between 40 feet per second and 60 feet per second, plus or minus 10 feet per second from the Speed setting of 50 feet. Let's reduce the size of the particles.

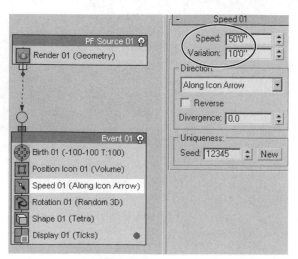

Figure 15.17 *Adjust the speed of the particles to distribute them more evenly through the scene.*

8. Highlight Shape 01 in Event 01; in the Shape 01 rollout in the upper right pane, enter 0'6" in the Size field (**Figure 15.18**).

The Shape 01 operator is now set to generate 6-inch tetra particles when rendered. What you see in the viewport are ticks generated in the viewport by that Display 01 operator at the bottom of Event 01. Again, this is to minimize the amount of geometry in the viewports for efficiency.

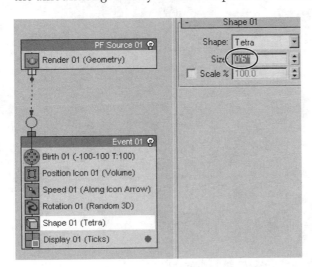

FIGURE 15.18 *Adjust the size of the tetra shapes that will show in the rendered image as particles.*

9. Close the Particle View dialog and render the Camera01 viewport. Upon close inspection, you'll see many particles in the camera view that are clearer closer to the viewer and fade back into the fog (see **Figure 15.19** on the next page).

You can also render the full 100-frame animation to a sequence of still images, as you learned in Chapter 9, or to an AVI file to view the animated particles in motion.

Particles

FIGURE 15.19 *Render the Camera01 viewport to see the particles suspended in the water.*

10. Save the file with its current name, Effects04.max.

You learned how to wire a particle event to a particle emitter and then adjust the particles' behavior in the Particle View dialog. While this was a simple example, it illustrates the important process of wiring events to determine the flow of particle control. Each discrete operator has parameters that allow you to set particles to represent small items floating in water.

Particle systems can also be used to create bubbles, to simulate a school of fish, or to show an underwater explosion. Particle systems are also used to create fireworks, billowing smoke, grass, or asteroids fields, just to name a few possibilities found above water.

Summary

Special effects and particle systems can be used judiciously to enhance many aspects of your scenes and still be cost-effective.

You've learned how to apply two types of fog: One type is a Volume Light effect that can be directly applied to lights in your scene to create the illusion that the light beam is visible as it passes through particles—in this case, very fine sand or vegetation suspended in water. The second type, called Fog effect, fills the view so that the ranges set in the camera determine where the fog starts and where it becomes full density from the viewer's position.

Finally, you learned how to add 3D particles to the scene that appeared to be floating along with the tide. By adjusting the speed, amount, and size of the particles, you were able to fine-tune their behavior.

CHAPTER 16

Simplified Animation Using Inverse Kinematics

In This Chapter

In Chapter 14, you used hierarchical linking to set up an ancestry of linked objects that included a dummy (the grandparent object), a truck (the parent object), and an oil tank (the child object), all of which were animated along the path. We return to hierarchical linking in this chapter, but this time, the hierarchy will include even more levels, so you'll use *inverse kinematics* to produce a complex animation in a minimum number of steps.

The combination of hierarchical linking and inverse kinematics lets you create systems of interconnected objects that are much easier to animate because the passing of information from one object to another means that far fewer keyframes have to be set manually.

This chapter introduces two forms of inverse kinematics. You'll use *interactive IK* to animate the tail of a lobster to flap as if it were swimming, and then you'll apply the *HI solver* to animate the lobster's claws. Using the HI Solver enables you to move only a goal object, which in turn moves the claws, and the knuckles connecting the claws to the body.

Key Terms

- **Inverse kinematics**—An animation technique in which the child object in a hierarchical relationship controls the motion of other objects in the chain.

- **Interactive IK**—A simple system of inverse kinematics animation with rotation controls for joints.

- **HI solver**—A history-independent animation keyframe calculation process in hierarchically linked objects that ignores previous keyframes in the timeline for efficiency in long animations.

- **Swivel angle**—The angle that defines a plane on which the HI solver articulates.

Understanding Inverse Kinematics

To understand inverse kinematics, you have to have a working knowledge of forward kinematics. If you wanted to use forward kinematics to, say, animate an arm reaching to pick up an object, you'd have to set the keyframes first for the upper arm, then for the forearm, and finally for the hand. Each new position would require you to repeat the steps, resulting in many keyframes that would be difficult to edit.

Inverse kinematics would simplify this task by letting you set keyframes for only the hand and have the other objects in that hierarchical linked chain keep their proper relationships to the hand while remaining connected to the body.

Using Interactive IK

For relatively simple, short animations in which interconnected objects must behave as a system, interactive IK offers flexibility and control by passing position and rotation information from the child object up through the ancestry.

A lobster swims backward through the water by rapidly contracting its tail, causing the tail to curl under the body. Lobster tails do not rotate side to side or upward.

In the next exercise, you'll learn how to hierarchically link the tail segments together and then set up restrictions to limit how each segment can rotate. Each tail segment will be able to rotate only a limited number of degrees clockwise, as seen in the Left viewport. Later you'll animate just the center tail fin to cause the tail to curl appropriately.

Exercise 16.1: Setting up interactive IK joints

1. Reset 3ds Max 8 and open the **LobsterIK01.max** file on the CD-ROM. Save it to your project folder as *LobsterIK02.max*.

   The scene contains the stylized lobster for which you created claws in Chapter 5. You'll now use the lobster to learn how to apply interactive IK by first hierarchically linking the tail segments to each other and to the lobster body.

2. In the Top viewport, select Tail_fin01, Tail_fin04, and Tail_fin05. On the main toolbar click the Select and Link button. Drag from one of the selected tail fin objects to Tail_segment04 (**Figure 16.1**). Release the mouse button when you see the cursor change; the end tail segment will flash white briefly to indicate that the link is successful.

   Because of the Symmetry modifier, all the tail segments are linked whether or not they are selected.

note

The pivot points of all the tail segments have already been positioned for correct rotation. Keep in mind that you used the Symmetry modifier on one half of the lobster, and that whatever other changes you will make to the right half of the lobster will automatically be transferred to the left half.

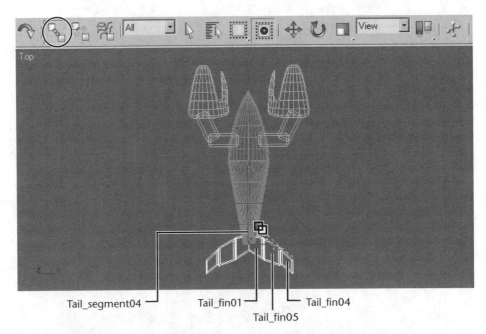

Tail_segment04   Tail_fin01   Tail_fin04

Tail_fin05

FIGURE 16.1 *Link the tail fin objects to the end tail segment.*

3. Maximize the Top viewport and use the Select and Link tool to link Tail_segment04 to Tail_segment03. Link Tail_segment03 to Tail_segment02, link Tail_segment02 to Tail_segment01, and finally link Tail_segment01 to Body01. Press the Page Up and Page Down keys to step through the hierarchy to ensure that the linking is correct. On the main toolbar, click the Select Object button to cancel the Select and Link tool.

This completes a hierarchy of the tail fins being made children of the end tail segment and each segment being made a child of the next. You'll now disable all rotation for the body and all of the tail segments and fins.

4. In the Top viewport, select Tail_fin01. On the Hierarchy panel, in the IK category, in the Rotational Joints rollout, clear the Active check boxes for all three axes (**Figure 16.2**). Repeat this step for each of the tail segments and the body.

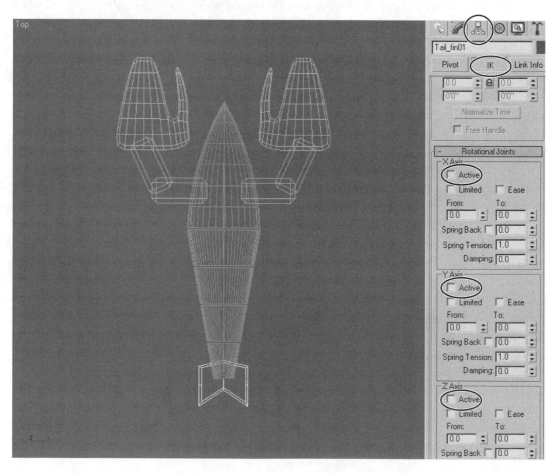

FIGURE 16.2 *Disable rotations of all three axes for all tail segments, the center tail fin, and the body.*

You must disable the active rotations for each object individually, but you can quickly navigate through the hierarchy with the Page Up key. It would now be impossible to rotate any of the body or tail objects using inverse kinematics, so you'll set up the appropriate axis and restrict the angle and direction to allow limited rotation appropriate for a lobster's tail. It is still possible to use the Select and Rotate tool to rotate, but the IK rotations are inactive.

5. In the Left viewport, select Tail_segment04, click the Select and Move button on the main toolbar, and then click the reference-coordinate-system drop-down menu and choose Parent. Notice that the rotation axis necessary to rotate the tail segment under the body is the X axis (**Figure 16.3**).

   The rotation axes for hierarchically linked objects are all based on the parent's coordinate system, so you'll now restrict rotation in the X axis.

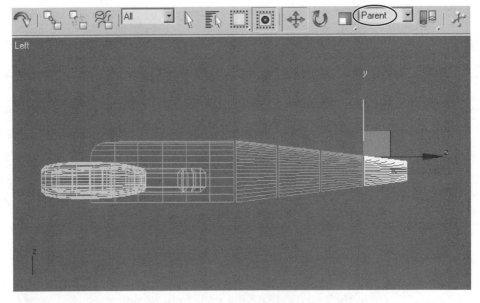

FIGURE 16.3 *Set the reference coordinate system to Parent to determine the correct axis for rotation restrictions.*

6. On the Hierarchy panel, in the Rotational Joints rollout, in the X Axis area, check the Active box to allow the joint to rotate on that axis. Then check the Limited box and enter 30 in the To field (**Figure 16.4**). Repeat this step for the other three tail segments (not the body).

The Active option allows the joint to rotate, the Limited option limits how much it can rotate, and the 30 entered in the To field restricts the rotation amount to 30 degrees clockwise. All tail segments have the same behavior.

7. Save the file. It should already be called LobsterIK02.max.

All the parts related to the tail have been hierarchically linked to the body, and restrictions on how much and in which direction each tail segment can rotate have been set. You're now ready to use interactive IK to animate the flipping tail by simply moving the center fin.

In this exercise, you've learned two very important lessons in using interactive IK: to avoid uncontrollable rotations, always disable all rotations before using interactive IK; and always set the reference coordinate system to Parent to determine which axes to activate and restrict.

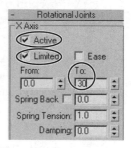

FIGURE 16.4 *Activate the X axis, and limit rotation to 30 degrees clockwise for each tail segment.*

Animating with Interactive IK

The joint restrictions have been set to control which axes the tail segments can rotate and to establish limits for the number of degrees and the direction in which they rotate.

Without interactive IK, you'd have to manually set keyframes for each tail segment in each new position, a tedious task at best. You'll now learn how to enable interactive IK and move only the center tail fin to create a few keyframes on each tail segment using the AutoKey feature. By moving just the parent tail fin, you'll animate in only a few simple steps the lobster snapping its tail. Otherwise, you'd have to animate each tail fin and segment individually.

Exercise 16.2: Setting the keyframes

1. Open the **LobsterIK02.max** file from the previous exercise or from the CD-ROM, and save it with the name *LobsterIK03.max*. In the Perspective viewport, select Tail_fin01.

If you were to try to move the selected object, it would move freely in any direction without affecting any of the other objects in the scene, because interactive IK has not yet been enabled. Let's enable it and see the results.

2. On the Hierarchy panel, in the IK category, in the Inverse Kinematics rollout, click the Interactive IK button to toggle it on (**Figure 16.5**).

This enables the joint restrictions so that the hierarchically linked objects behave appropriately when the tail fin is moved.

3. Click the Auto Key button at the bottom right of the display, and drag the time slider to frame 10. On the main toolbar, make sure that the Select and Move button is toggled on. In the Left viewport, click on the Transform gizmo yellow rectangle to restrict motion to the Y axis and Z axis, and move the tail fin down and under the lobster's body (**Figure 16.6**). Scrub the time slider, and you'll see the tail curl over the ten frames.

FIGURE 16.5 *You must enable interactive IK before any joint restrictions take effect.*

You may have to try moving the center tail fin several times to get it in the correct configuration because of the restrictions on the rotations of objects in the hierarchical chain. Also, you won't see keys on the timeline created for this object, as it's actually the tail segments with the rotation restrictions that are being recorded.

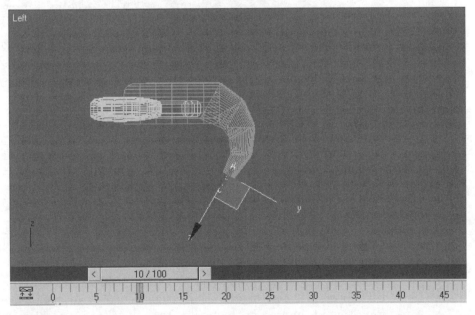

FIGURE 16.6 *With Auto Key toggled on, move the tail fin under the body at frame 10.*

4. Drag the time slider to frame 25 and, in the Left viewport, move the center tail fin back up so that the tail is straight (**Figure 16.7**). Scrub the time slider and notice that the tail makes a complete snapping action.

    Because of the rotational restrictions, you can't accidentally pull the tail beyond its original position. Next, you'll animate three additional tail snaps over the length of the animation.

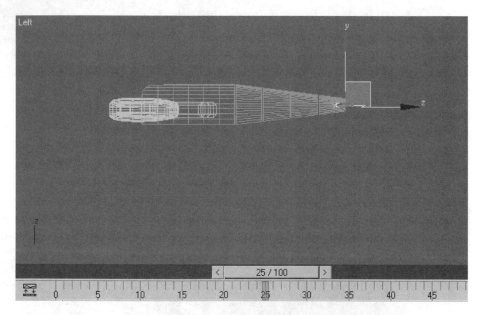

FIGURE 16.7 *At frame 25, create keys that position the tail straight again.*

5. Drag the time slider to frame 35 and curl the tail again, and then set the time slider to frame 50 and straighten the tail. Curl the tail at frame 60 and straighten it at frame 75, and curl again at frame 85 and straighten for the final time at frame 100. Toggle the Auto Key button off and click the Play Animation button. Stop the animation playback.

    The tail now repeats its snapping action over the full 100 frames, and you've had to animate the position of only one object to create the relatively complex animation.

6. On the Hierarchy panel, in the Inverse Kinematics rollout, toggle the Interactive IK button off. Drag the time slider to frame 0 and save the file. It should already be called LobsterIK03.max.

    Hierarchical linking, joint restrictions, and interactive IK have greatly simplified the process of animating the tail through control of animation axes and angles to restrict the motion of an object at the end of the hierarchical chain. You'll now animate the lobster's claws.

Animating with the HI Solver

You'll learn how to animate the lobster's claws and knuckles by linking the object hierarchically and then applying the HI solver. The history-independent solver will create a connection using the pivot points of the claws and knuckles to determine rotation joints. The solver will also have a goal at the end that you will animate to position the bones and objects. This goal is a tick mark that acts as a handle at the end of the hierarchical chain.

Applying the HI solver to the lobster claws from the previous exercise would cause problems because the Symmetry copy uses the original object's pivot points, resulting in strange rotations. Therefore, in the next exercise you'll use a similar file in which the Symmetry modifier has been removed from the claw and knuckles on the right side of the lobster. You'll then link the claw and knuckles to the body, apply the HI solver, and then clone the claws and knuckles as copies to the left side of the lobster.

The cloned claws and knuckles on the left side will be oriented in the wrong direction, and you'll learn how to use the Swivel Angle of the HI solver to correct the problem.

Exercise 16.3: Applying the HI solver

1. Reset 3ds Max 8. Open the **LobsterHI01.max** file from the CD-ROM, and save it to your project folder as *LobsterHI02.max*.

    This lobster has only one set of claws and knuckles, with no modifiers. The tail is still animated from the previous exercise, however. Let's link the claws and knuckles to the body.

2. On the main toolbar, click the Select and Link button, and drag from the claw to the first knuckle to link them. The knuckle will flash white briefly to indicate that the link was successful. Then link the first knuckle to the second knuckle, and finally link the second knuckle to the body.

3. On the main toolbar, click the Select Object button, and press H to open the Select Objects dialog. At the bottom of the dialog, check the Display Subtree box (see **Figure 16.8** on the next page). Double-click Claw02 in the list to select it.

    The objects appear as an indented hierarchical list. The left-most objects are parents to the indented objects. Now you'll apply the HI solver to the hierarchical chain.

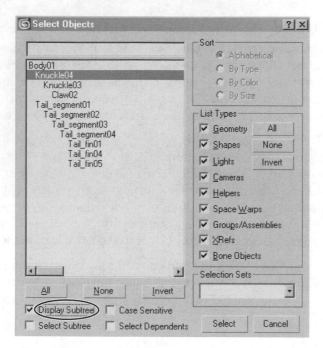

FIGURE 16.8 *Link the claw, knuckles, and body, and then check that the link was successful in the Select Objects dialog.*

4. In the Animation pull-down menu, choose IK Solvers > HI Solver (**Figure 16.9**).

   The HI solver is especially useful in long animations because it calculates new transformations relative to any previous key, rather than recalculating all the way back to frame 0 the way interactive IK does. Let's apply the solver.

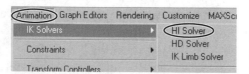

FIGURE 16.9 *The solver is found in the Animation menu on the main menu bar.*

5. In the Top viewport, click on Knuckle04, next to the body (**Figure 16.10**).

    A large white goal will appear at the pivot point of the claw, and a white tri-angle will connect the pivot points of the three objects. Move the goal in the Top viewport, and you will see that the objects' positions are controlled by the lengths of the objects themselves, and that the rotation is restricted by the goal's position.

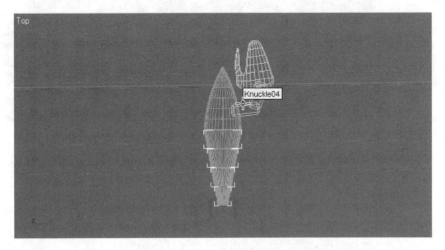

FIGURE 16.10 *Apply the HI solver from the claw to the knuckle next to the body.*

6. In the Top viewport, select the solver goal, the claw, and the two knuckles. Make sure the Select and Move button on the main toolbar is toggled on. Press the Shift key, and move the objects until the end of Knuckle04 is in the correct position on the left side of the body. In the Clone Options dialog, click OK to accept the default copy options (see **Figure 16.11** on the next page).

    The whole system of the linked objects and the solver is cloned to create the left claw. You'll now learn about using Swivel Angle to rotate the claw and knuckles into the proper orientation.

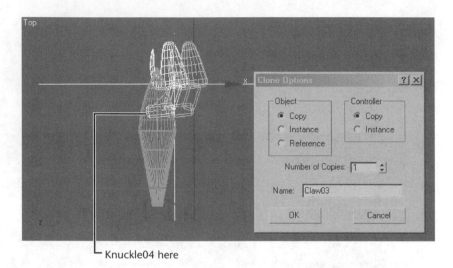

Knuckle04 here

FIGURE 16.11 *Create a copy clone of the animated system to the left side.*

7. In the Perspective viewport, select the new goal called IK Chain02. On the Motion panel, in the IK Solver Properties rollout, enter 180.0 in the Swivel Angle field, and press Enter to flip the claw and knuckles. Move the goal to position the claw more appropriately (**Figure 16.12**).

By rotating the swivel angle 180 degrees, you flip the solver plane upside down so that it is oriented in a mirror image of the original. The claw and knuckles can now be animated at various frames by moving each goal with the Auto Key on.

FIGURE 16.12 *Rotate the Swivel Angle 180 degrees to the animation system.*

8. Save the file. It should already be called LobsterHI02.max.

You now have an alternate method of animating a hierarchical chain with control over both position and rotation of objects while animating only one element of the chain.

For a simple animation like this, it's not so important which animation method you choose, but the HI solver method certainly is more efficient in animations more than several hundred frames long, with many keyframes positioning the control object.

Summary

Hierarchical linking is important for creating chains of objects that can pass transformations up and down the chain. Things become even simpler when you apply inverse kinematics to the hierarchical chain so that the end child object can control all the objects up to the base parent object.

By restricting rotation axes and rotation angles and then using interactive IK, you can freely animate objects without fear of getting yourself into physically impossible situations. This would be an appropriate method of animating mechanical systems such as power shovels or cranes.

History-independent animation solvers can also be applied to hierarchically linked chains for more control and efficiencies in long animations. Humanoid characters' arms and legs are a typical application for HI solver.

CHAPTER 17

Dynamics and Scripting

In This Chapter

Using keyframe animation to manually cause objects to collide is a daunting and tedious task. The randomness of the movement and rotation of even a simple object, such as a sphere bouncing on a floor, would require a lot of trial and error to produce acceptable results. However, by applying collision-dynamics calculations using a component of 3ds Max 8 called *reactor*, you can simulate many different types of collisions, such as rigid body, soft body, cloth, or water dynamics, without having to perform many modifications and set many animation keys necessary for convincing action.

In this chapter, you'll learn how to set up and apply two types of collisions: rigid body and cloth dynamics simulations. The setup process for each is different. While both rigid body and cloth objects must be assigned to a collection, which defines the basic behavior of the object, the cloth must have a reactor Cloth modifier applied before it can be assigned to the cloth collection. The modifier contains parameters that describe the specific behavior of the cloth.

You'll also learn how to preview the dynamics simulations before committing to them, and how to use the Snapshot tool in 3ds Max 8 to create a fixed copy of a falling tablecloth. Finally, you'll learn how to run MAXScript code in 3ds Max 8. MAXScript is a programming language included with Max that can be used to extend the software's capabilities.

Key Terms

- **Dynamics**—The complex mathematical calculations of colliding objects or distorting surfaces reacting to gravity, air resistance, or wind.

- **Collection**—A group of objects with similar behavior, such as rigid, soft, or rope.

- **Snapshot**—A tool that can be used to "freeze" a deforming animated object.

Using Reactor to Simulate Collision Dynamics

To absorb the fundamentals of reactor dynamics, you'll perform two exercises in this section: setting up a rigid body collision simulation and setting up a cloth collision simulation. You will animate an object tumbling and colliding as it falls through space, and you will simulate a tablecloth falling and draping itself over a table. The uses of reactor dynamics are wide-ranging—you could also use reactor dynamics to simulate flexible ropes and cables attached to objects at either or both ends of objects bobbing in a pool of water.

You must first assign behavioral properties to objects by adding the objects to a collection that describes the general type of object they are, such as rigid body or cloth, and then you must assign more-specific properties of the objects, such as weight and friction.

Because there are so many steps that are calculated by the reactor simulation, it is often difficult or impossible to undo the calculations, so you'll learn how to use a preview window to make sure the action is what you expect before finally committing to it.

Rigid Body Dynamics

As you can probably tell from the name of this type of dynamics, you'll calculate the collision of hard objects tumbling through space, in this case a barrel falling onto a table and then onto the floor.

While this may sound like a simple example, it's anything but. As the falling barrel strikes objects, it must rotate about that contact point. To make things more complicated, each object has only one non-animatable pivot point. You could simulate multiple pivot points using dummy objects, but the process would soon become extremely complex, and the resulting animation would lack the randomness needed to make it seem convincing.

In this exercise, the barrel is already suspended in space above the edge of the table, so all you have to do is add the necessary objects to a rigid body collection, set the objects' properties, and process the dynamics calculations. Let's drop the barrel!

Exercise 17.1: Colliding rigid bodies

1. Reset 3ds Max 8, and open the **Reactor01.max** file from the CD-ROM. Save it to the project folder with the name *Reactor02.max*.

2. On the main toolbar, click the Named Selection Sets drop-down list and choose the selection set called Rigid Body (**Figure 17.1**).

    This selection set contains the barrel, a table and legs, the walls, and the floor—all objects with which the barrel will potentially collide.

FIGURE 17.1 *Select all the objects that will become members of the rigid body collection with a named selection set called Rigid Body.*

3. On the reactor toolbar, which runs vertically along the left side of the display, click the Create Rigid Body Collection button (**Figure 17.2**).

FIGURE 17.2 *Click the Create Rigid Body Collection button on the reactor toolbar.*

The Modify panel, RB Collection Properties rollout, now shows a list of all the selected objects that have been added to the rigid body collection, and the rigid body icon appears in the scene (**Figure 17.3**).

You now have to tell the object how to behave.

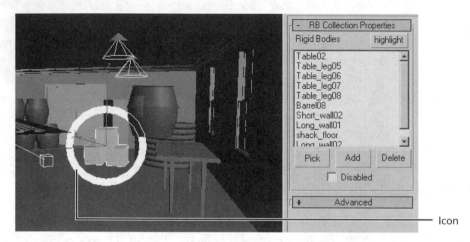

FIGURE 17.3 *The selected objects are placed in the rigid body collection.*

4. The rigid body icon is now the selected object; use Named Selection Sets to select the Table02 and WallsFloor selection sets so that you can set their properties. You can use the Ctrl key to add to selection sets in the Named Selection Sets drop-down list. Scroll the reactor toolbar, if necessary, and click the Open Property Editor button (**Figure 17.4**). The reactor properties will affect the object's behavior in collisions.

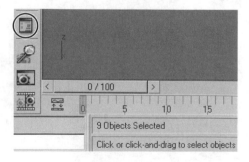

FIGURE 17.4 *Click the Open Property Editor button at the bottom of the reactor toolbar.*

5. In the Rigid Body Properties dialog, Physical Properties rollout, check the Unyielding box (**Figure 17.5**).

Setting objects to Unyielding causes them to be unaffected by gravity or collision with other objects in the reactor calculations. Next you will set the barrel's properties.

6. In the Camera01 viewport, select Barrel08, the one hovering just over the table at the right side of the viewport. In the Rigid Body Properties dialog, in the Physical Properties rollout, enter **10.0** in the Mass field. In the Simulation Geometry rollout, you'll see that the Mesh Convex Hull radio button is selected (**Figure 17.6**).

This assigns a weight of 10 kg to the barrel so that it will interact with gravity when the reactor solution is calculated. The Mesh Convex Hull setting means, for example, that the actual shape of the barrel is considered during the calculations, not just the barrel's bounding box, which would be more efficient but inaccurate. Let's preview the animation.

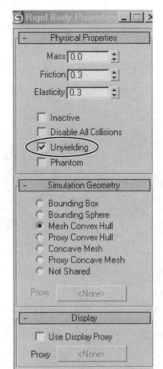

FIGURE 17.5
Set all the objects with which the barrel will collide to Unyielding in the Rigid Body Properties dialog.

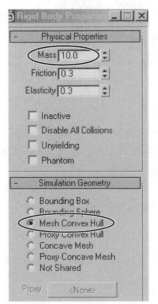

FIGURE 17.6
Set the barrel's weight to 10 kg, and make sure the barrel's mesh is being used in the calculations.

7. Click the Preview Animation button, which is the second icon from bottom of the reactor toolbar to open the reactor Real-Time Preview window. It shows only the objects included in this rigid body collection simulation (**Figure 17.7**).

    The ability to preview the animation allows you to change the object's properties if necessary before committing to the final calculations.

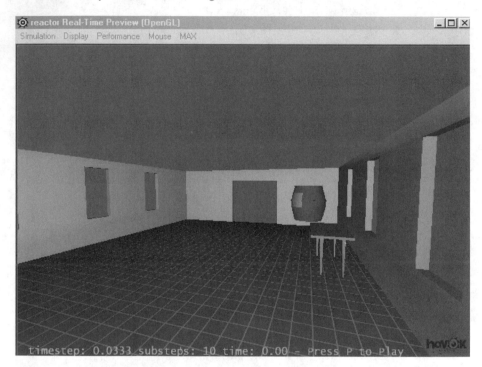

FIGURE 17.7 *Click the Preview Animation button in the reactor toolbar, and the reactor Real-Time Preview window appears.*

8. Press the P key to play the simulation preview in the window. You can press R to reset the preview and then play it again. Close the reactor Real-Time Preview window.

    The barrel drops because of gravity, hits the edge of the table, and falls to the floor. But the barrel appears very heavy and not particularly lively; you want your barrel to react more like an empty plastic barrel.

9. In the Rigid Body Properties dialog, in the Physical Properties rollout, enter 1.0 in the Elasticity field (**Figure 17.8**). Click the Preview Animation button, and press the P and R keys a few times to see the difference in the barrel's behavior. Close all windows and dialogs.

    This makes the barrel appear more flexible and a bit livelier when it strikes the table and floor. Let's create the actual animation.

10. From the Edit pull-down menu, choose Hold (**Figure 17.9**). This stores the entire scene in a buffer file on the hard drive so that if something is wrong with the animation you create, you can easily return to this point in your editing with the Fetch command. Click the Create Animation button at the bottom of the reactor toolbar. Click OK in the dialog that opens, warning that this action cannot be undone.

    The collision solution is calculated, and rotation and position keys are placed on every frame to record the barrel's action. Click the Play Animation button at the lower right of the display to see the barrel fall onto the table and then onto the floor in the Camera01 viewport.

11. Save the file. It should already be called Reactor02.max

    Get into the habit of using the Hold command in 3ds Max 8 just prior to performing final calculations, because it can be very difficult to undo the animation once it has been calculated and recorded with keys on every frame.

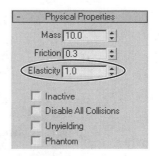

FIGURE 17.8 *Increase the Elasticity of the barrel to 1.0.*

FIGURE 17.9 *From the Edit menu, choose the Hold command to save the current scene to the hard drive before calculating the final animation.*

Rigid body dynamics calculations require that all objects to be included in the simulation belong to a rigid body collection. They also require that the properties be edited so that they are unyielding in the scene, or be given parameters, such as mass and elasticity, to simulate the type of collision you want.

Now let's animate a tablecloth draping over a table.

Simulating Cloth

Creating cloth simulations with reactor dynamics requires the extra step of applying the reactor Cloth modifier to the cloth object before adding it to a Cloth collection. You then adjust the properties for the cloth object in the Cloth modifier.

In the next exercise, you'll use cloth simulation as a modeling tool. You'll animate the tablecloth dropping onto the table and legs, which are rigid body objects. The tablecloth will drape and fold as it approaches the table. However, it's not a flapping tablecloth that you need in your scene, but one that just drapes statically, so you'll use the Snapshot tool to freeze the tablecloth at one of the animation frames. You'll then delete the animated tablecloth and use the snapshot copy in your scene.

Exercise 17.2: Simulating cloth using reactor dynamics

1. Open the **Reactor02.max** file from the previous exercise or from the CD-ROM. Save it to the project folder with the name *Reactor03.max*.

2. Choose the named selection set called Table from the drop-down list on the main toolbar.

    This selects the table and four table legs under the cloth on the left side of the camera viewport that you will turn into unyielding rigid body objects.

3. On the reactor toolbar, click the Create Rigid Body Collection button. This adds the selected objects to the collection. Use the named selection sets to select Table again. On the reactor toolbar, click the Open Properties Editor button, which is the fourth button from the bottom, and in the Physical Properties rollout, select Unyielding.

    The table should not be affected by geometry but should be included in the collision simulation. So far, the steps are the same as in the previous exercise for creating rigid body collisions, but now you'll learn how the cloth setup requires an additional step of applying a modifier.

4. In the Camera01 viewport, select the tablecloth positioned just above the table. Near the bottom of the reactor toolbar, click the Apply Cloth Modifier button, which looks like a T-shirt with a letter *M* (**Figure 17.10**).

    The Cloth modifier must be applied to the object before it can be included in a cloth collection.

5. On the reactor toolbar, click the Create Cloth Collection button near the top; it looks like a T-shirt with a letter *C* (**Figure 17.11**).

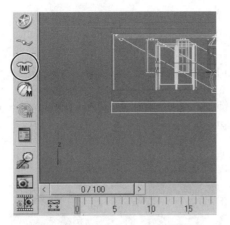

FIGURE 17.10 *Apply the Cloth modifier to the tablecloth before adding it to a cloth collection.*

FIGURE 17.11 *Add the tablecloth to the cloth collection.*

The properties for cloth objects are set on the Modify panel, not in the Rigid Body Properties dialog that you've been using. Let's change some of the cloth properties.

6. In the Camera01 viewport, select the tablecloth, and, on the Modify panel, in the Properties rollout, enter 0.5 in the Mass field and check the Avoid Self-Intersections box (**Figure 17.12**).

Reducing the mass makes the tablecloth lighter, and the Avoid Self-Intersections option keeps the tablecloth from passing through itself as it falls and folds.

FIGURE 17.12 *Make the cloth lighter in weight, and set it to collide with itself when necessary.*

7. On the reactor toolbar, click the Preview Animation button. When the reactor Real-Time Preview window opens, press the P key to start the preview. Be patient; it may take a second or two for the preview to start.

Notice that as the tablecloth begins to fold around the table, it looks as if it's still hovering above the table (**Figure 17.13**). That's because the simulation geometry that's being used to create the collisions is somewhat larger than the objects themselves. You'll learn how to adjust that offset distance between the object and the simulation geometry in the next step.

Cloth is above table

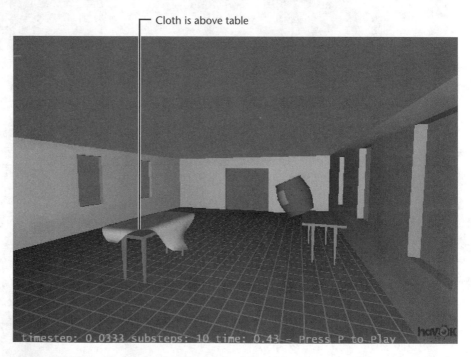

timestep: 0.0333 substeps: 10 time: 0.43 – Press P to Play

FIGURE 17.13 *Preview the animation of the falling cloth.*

8. Close the preview window. On the Utilities panel, in the Utilities rollout, click the reactor button (**Figure 17.14**). On the reactor panel, World rollout, enter 0'1" in the Col. Tolerance field and press Enter (**Figure 17.15**).

This sizes the simulation geometry 1 inch larger than the actual geometry for the collision calculations.

tip

The collision tolerance setting should never be smaller than 1/40 of the World Scale figure, which is just a bit more than 39 inches by default. The World Scale setting ensures that real-world units for weight and gravity, for example, are used in the calculations. For closer tolerances, you must reduce the World Scale size, but then the calculations will no longer be physically accurate.

FIGURE 17.14 *Open the Utilities panel, and click the reactor button.*

9. Preview the animation action, and you'll see that the cloth comes much closer to the table before it begins folding. Close the preview window and, in the Edit pull-down menu, click Hold. On the reactor toolbar, click the Create Animation button. The calculations may take a while.

The create-animation step cannot be undone, but because you saved the scene in the Hold buffer, you can use the Fetch command to return to that point, if necessary. However, you don't need an animated tablecloth in the scene, so now you'll learn how to use Snapshot to create a static copy.

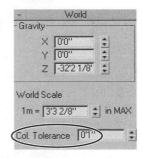

FIGURE 17.15 *Reduce the collision tolerance setting to 0'1".*

10. Right-click in the Camera01 viewport to activate it and scrub the time slider to see the tablecloth drop around the table. Then drag the time slider to frame 50. The tablecloth has a fairly natural drape to it at this point. Make sure the tablecloth is selected, and, from the Tools pull-down menu, choose Snapshot. In the Snapshot dialog, click OK (**Figure 17.16**).

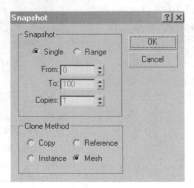

FIGURE 17.16 *Access the Snapshot tool from the Tools pull-down menu, and click OK to accept the defaults.*

The Snapshot tool, by default, creates a single mesh copy of the tablecloth at the current frame and increments the name of the new object.

11. Scrub the time slider and notice that there are now two tablecloths, one animated and one static. In the next step, you'll delete the animated tablecloth.

12. Drag the time slider to frame 0, and make sure you have the original tablecloth selected. Then press Delete to delete it. Select the deformed static tablecloth called TableCloth02, and use the Select and Move tool on the main toolbar to move the tablecloth closer to the table in the Camera01 viewport (**Figure 17.17**).

The tablecloth now appears as though it were simply draped over the table.

FIGURE 17.17 *Delete the animated tablecloth, and move the static tablecloth closer to the table.*

13. Save the file. It should already be called Reactor03.max.

You've learned how to use reactor dynamics as a modeling tool.

Reactor cloth simulation differs from rigid body collision simulation in that the cloth needs a modifier before it can be added to a cloth collection. In this exercise, you've used the reactor simulation with Snapshot to create a static model of a table-cloth that would normally be fairly difficult to model manually. This process is very useful for creating flags, drapes, or other fabric objects.

MAXScript Routines

MAXScripts are written in a high-level computer language that you have access to in 3ds Max 8 to create routines that will simplify multiple repetitive steps, or to perform operations for which 3ds Max 8 doesn't have a special tool.

It's beyond the scope of this book to teach you how to write scripts, but this section provides a preview of the power of MAXScripts by showing you how to run a typical script to create an array of lights in your scene.

The script you'll use in the next exercise was written by Ronnie Olsthoorn and was posted on ScriptSpot (www.scriptspot.com), a Web site where you can download many MAXScripts for free.

Exercise 17.3: Running a MAXScript

1. Reset 3ds Max 8, and open the **Scripting01.max** file from the CD-ROM. Save it to your project folder with the name *Scripting02.max*.

This is the same outdoor scene you used in Chapter 7.

2. From the MAXScript pull-down menu, choose Run Script (**Figure 17.18**).

FIGURE 17.18 *Run the script from the MAXScript pull-down menu.*

3. In the Choose Editor File dialog that appears, navigate to the folder with your Max files for this chapter, and double click E-Light_MAX5.ms (**Figure 17.19**).

This opens the E-Light dialog that was created as part of the MAXScript to allow you to change parameters for the routine.

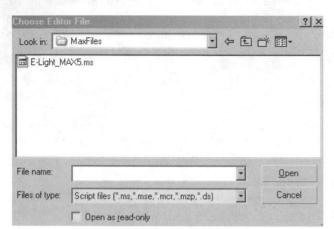

FIGURE 17.19
Double-click E-Light_MAX5.ms in the folder that contains the Max files for this chapter.

4. In the E-Light dialog, in the Dome Settings rollout, enter 24000 in the Radius field. This will set the radius of a dome of lights that will be created. In the Light Settings rollout, enter 3.0 in the Multiplier field. You can see at the bottom of this rollout that there will be 91 lights created. Expand the Create Environment Light rollout, and click the Create Environment Light button (**Figure 17.20**).

This creates a dome array of spotlights all pointing at the center of the scene and all casting shadows.

5. Activate the Camera01 viewport, and click the Quick Render button on the main toolbar to see the rendered image (**Figure 17.21**).

The rendered image shows very soft shadows under the pier from the many overlapping lights that you can see in the Front viewport.

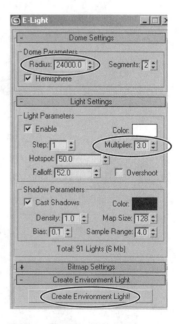

FIGURE 17.20 *Change the parameters for the radius of the lights and the multiplier value, and then create the light array.*

FIGURE 17.21 *Render the camera viewport, and compare the image with the light dome of shadow-casting spotlights that create the effect of some very soft shadows.*

5. Close all windows and dialogs, and save the file. It should already be called Scripting02.max.

    By using this simple script, you've accomplished something that would be rather difficult to create manually.

I encourage you to learn all you can about 3ds Max 8 before relying on scripts and shortcuts. In any case, you must know 3ds Max 8 extremely well before you can write your own scripts.

Summary

You've learned two important methods of speeding up your workflow: first, by using reactor dynamics to animate objects in ways that would be very difficult to accomplish by hand; and second, by learning how to run MAXScripts.

Even though reactor dynamics was created for animation purposes, it can still be used as a modeling tool in conjunction with the Snapshot tool, which creates copies of the animated mesh frozen at a certain point in time. You used this with a cloth example, but you could also use it with rigid body collisions to create a rock pile instead of manually placing each rock. Just let a collection of rocks tumble down another surface, select all the rocks when they come to rest, and then use Snapshot to create a static copy.

CHAPTER 18

Scene Assembly

In This Chapter

In 3ds Max 8, scene assembly is a workflow, rather than a tool or a technique. It's the process of putting together all the elements that make up a complete project, from models or scenes, maps, and materials, to previously rendered images and sequences.

If you work alone, your scene-assembly requirements may be simple, but as project size and collaboration between other team members or production companies increase, the importance of a comprehensive scene-assembly plan is magnified. Let's say, for example, that your in-house production comprises a modeling team, a lighting team, a materials team, and a video editing team. A project manager or technical director must be able to efficiently direct the content between the various groups to get the job done.

To help you develop an understanding of how scene assembly must be implemented to gain an efficient workflow, this chapter shows you a few of the individual tools and processes for managing content and compositing scenes. You'll use the Asset Browser to locate files on your hard drive from which you can merge files or objects into your current scene. You'll also learn how to use the Replace command to replace low-polygon placeholder objects in your scene with the high-poly versions that will be used at render time. Finally, you'll use the Video Post module of 3ds Max 8 to composite, or overlay, two previously rendered sequences of images with alpha channels. This will facilitate background and foreground rendering to occur at the same time to increase production.

Key Term

■ **Compositing**—The layering of images with transparency information.

The Asset Browser

Let's suppose you are the technical director for a project, and one of your teams has created an interior scene and another team has created an animated lobster. Your job is to combine the two scenes into a single Max file.

The Asset Browser utility in 3ds Max 8 lets you preview thumbnail images of Max scenes and bitmaps in the browser window and then drag them into your current Max scene. This increases productivity by giving you the option of identifying scenes and images visually rather than by name.

In the first exercise in this chapter, you'll use the Asset Browser to open the scene in a new Max session, and then to merge the animated lobster into the scene.

When you're searching through very large folders, the Asset Browser window can become rather confusing, so you'll also learn how to use the Asset Browser's filtering capabilities to show only the file types you need.

Exercise 18.1: Accessing files using the Asset Browser

1. Reset 3ds Max 8 to make sure you have an empty scene. On the Utilities panel, in the Utilities rollout, click the Asset Browser button (**Figure 18.1**). Click OK to dismiss the Asset Browser warning message.

    The Asset Browser will open in a new window with two panes, an Explorer-type navigator pane on the left and a thumbnail pane on the right.

2. In the left pane, navigate to the Max Files/ Ch18_maxfiles folder on the CD-ROM (**Figure 18.2**). The thumbnails appear in the right pane to show the folder's contents.

    Your folder structure will look different from the one in the figure, but the thumbnails will be the same. In the next step, you'll filter out only the files you want to work with currently.

FIGURE 18.1 *The Asset Browser is accessed from the Utilities panel.*

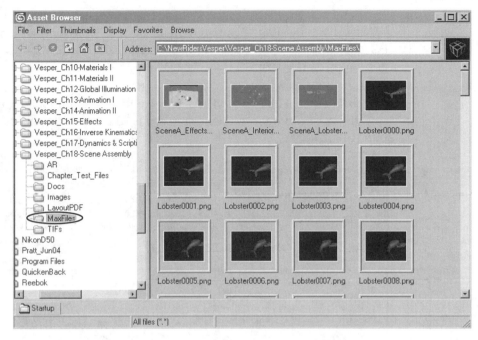

FIGURE 18.2 *Navigate to the folder containing Max files for Chapter 18.*

3. In the Asset Browser window, from the Filter drop-down menu choose the 3ds Max Files option to filter out all the image files in the folder and show only the five Max files (**Figure 18.3**).

    Filtering the thumbnails makes finding files easier, but it can also be more efficient because fewer files have to be cached by the browser. Next we'll open a scene from the browser.

FIGURE 18.3 *Filter the browser to show only Max files in the thumbnail pane.*

4. Highlight the thumbnail called SceneA_Interior01.max. The thumbnail border turns red to indicate that the thumbnail is active. Drag the thumbnail into the Perspective viewport of the current Max scene, and choose Open File from the pop-up menu (**Figure 18.4**).

Opening a file using the Asset Browser is the same as opening the file from the File pull-down menu in 3ds Max 8, but you have the thumbnail image to identify the scene you want to open. Now you need to bring the animated lobster into this scene.

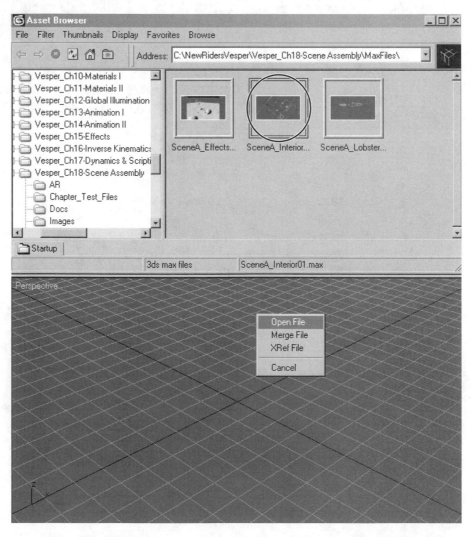

FIGURE 18.4 *Drag and drop the thumbnail of the scene that you want to open in the current Max session.*

5. Highlight and drag the SceneA_LobsterIK01.max thumbnail from the browser pane into the Camera01 viewport, and choose Merge File from the pop-up menu. Click near the bottom center of the Camera01 viewport to place the merged objects. The objects being merged are automatically selected after the merge. On the main toolbar, enter Lobster in the Named Selection Sets field, and press Enter (**Figure 18.5**). (Opening the lobster scene would replace the current scene.)

The lobster scene contains several objects, so creating a named selection set immediately on merging will make it much easier to select them later.

Let's move the lobster into the camera view, because it is merged using its original coordinates, which are away from the current scene.

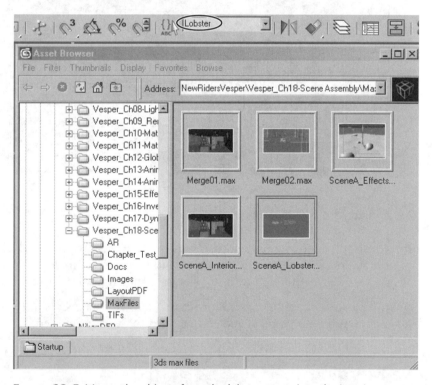

FIGURE 18.5 *Merge the objects from the lobster scene into the interior scene, and immediately name a selection set of those objects.*

6. On the main toolbar, click the Select and Move button, and then zoom out in the Top and Left viewports so that you can see the lobster and the Transform gizmo. Move the lobster selection set in front of, and just below, the camera (**Figure 18.6**).

Scrub the time slider, and you'll see that the lobster's animated tail was merged along with the 3D objects.

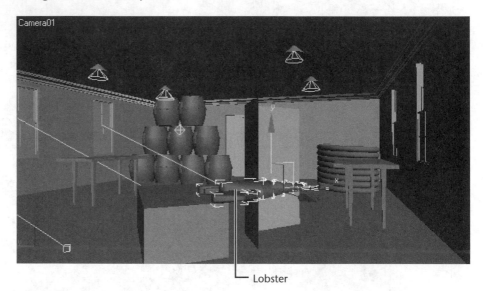

Lobster

FIGURE 18.6 *Move the lobster into place in front of the camera.*

7. Close all windows and dialogs. On the main toolbar, from the File pull-down menu choose Save As and save the file to your project folder with the name *Merge01.max*. You don't want to overwrite the original interior-scene file.

Opening a scene from the Asset Browser will replace whatever is in the current Max session; merging a scene will add the contents to the current scene.

Selective Merging

There is another, slightly different, method of merging objects from one file into the current scene. In the next exercise, you'll learn how to use merging to bring only selected objects of a file into the current scene. This is convenient when you know there are individual objects, created by other team members, stored in a file, but you don't want the whole file.

You'll also learn how to use the Replace command to merge complex objects from another file to replace simple objects used as stand-ins in your current scene. For example, you need to animate a camera moving through your scene around a lobster trap that another team is in the process of building, so you create a simple object in your scene and position it so that you'll know how to move your camera around it. Using this simple object in your current scene is also much more efficient when navigating through your display, because the more complex object would bog down the display.

Exercise 18.2: Merging and replacing objects

1. Open **Merge01.max** from the previous exercise or from the CD-ROM, and save it to your project folder with the name *Merge02.max*.

   There's a large rock in the underwater scene that you'd like to have in the current interior scene, but you don't want to add the entire underwater scene. Let's merge files from the pull-down menus.

2. From the File pull-down menu, choose Merge and, in the Merge File dialog that appears, navigate to the CD-ROM and double-click SceneA_Effects01.max (**Figure 18.7**). This is the underwater scene that contains the object you want to merge; you now have to choose the object.

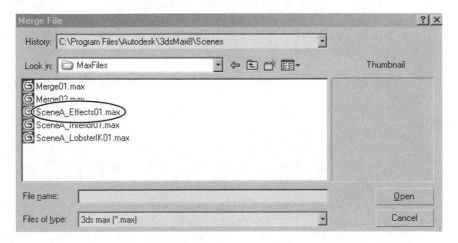

FIGURE 18.7 *Access the underwater scene on the CD-ROM from the Merge File dialog.*

3. In the Merge dialog that appears, double-click Rock05 in the list of objects (**Figure 18.8**). Move the rock in the viewports until it sits on the floor somewhere in front of the folding screen. You could also highlight several objects in the list to merge multiple objects at the same time.

By merging from the File pull-down menu, you're able to choose each object you want to merge into the current scene. Let's replace the box in front of the camera with a lobster trap.

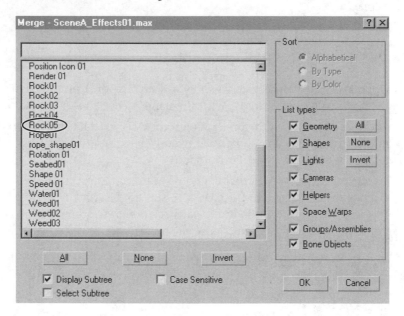

FIGURE 18.8 *In the Merge dialog, choose the object(s) you want to merge into your scene.*

4. From the File pull-down menu, choose Replace (**Figure 18.9**), and, in the Replace File dialog that appears, open SceneA_Effects01.max. In the Replace dialog that appears, double-click Lobster_trap01 (**Figure 18.10**). Click Yes in the 3ds Max dialog that opens to also replace the materials. This is the same scene you got the rock from previously.

The box in your current scene becomes an open mesh lobster trap with its pivot point in exactly the same location as the box's pivot point. It's important to note that the box in the current scene is also called Lobster_trap01. You can replace objects only with objects of exactly the same name.

5. Close all windows and dialogs, and save the file. It should already be called Merge02.max.

You've merged new individual objects into your scene and replaced a simple stand-in object with a more complex object you want in your renderings.

FIGURE 18.9
Open the underwater scene with the Replace command.

FIGURE 18.10
Double-click Lobster_trap01 in the Replace dialog to replace the box in your scene that has exactly the same name.

The ability to merge individual objects instead of entire scenes offers more flexibility in using content that has already been created. Replacing objects allows you to use very efficient stand-in objects and then substitute them with the complex geometry before the final rendering. Productivity will be increased because the graphics card doesn't have to keep track of the dense meshes in the viewports. Other teams can also be working on the final models while you have placeholders in your scenes.

Compositing Rendered Scenes

Another time-saving scene-assembly technique is the process of compositing rendered images as layers. A particular scene consisting of all the objects you want in your final rendering might take a long time to render, or you may have two teams working on individual parts—the background and foreground.

Rendering the foreground or background scene by itself might go relatively quickly, but rendering the combination is slow, so you'll learn how to combine two prerendered sequences in a very short time. Even though the compositing is an extra step, the combined time is much shorter than the time it takes to render the scene as a whole.

Compositing requires that all layers of images, except the base layer, are rendered with alpha channel transparency information. In the next exercise, you'll use 3ds Max 8's Video Post module. This works fine for simple compositing, but in a production situation you'd want to use special programs such as Autodesk's Combustion or Adobe's Premiere or After Effects.

Exercise 18.3: Compositing images in Video Post

Note: To set up this exercise, you will need to copy all of the .png image files from the Max Files/Ch18_maxfiles folder on the CD-ROM to the project folder on your hard drive.

1. Reset 3ds Max 8. In the Rendering pull-down menu, choose Video Post (**Figure 18.11**).

    This module lets you stack image events in a queue, highlight them in the queue, and then apply a Composite operator that will combine them. First you have to queue up the two layers of image events.

2. In the Video Post dialog, click the Add Image Input Event button. In the Add Image Input Event dialog that appears, click the Files button. In the Select Image File for Video Post Input dialog that appears, navigate to the project folder on your hard drive. Highlight Underwater0000.png in the list of files, and check the Sequence option at the bottom of the dialog (**Figure 18.12**). Click the open button on the right.

FIGURE 18.11 *Open Video Post from the Rendering pull-down menu.*

These steps will place the sequence of images in the Video Post queue to become the background. You'll now have to tell Video Post which of those images to use.

Add Image Input Event

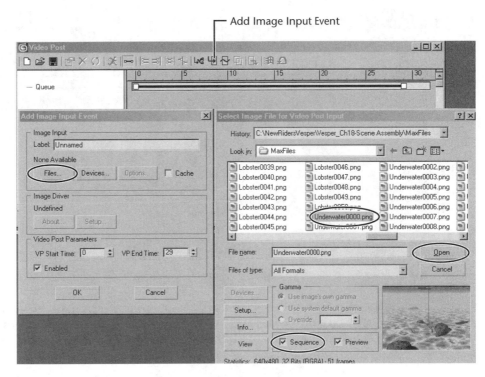

FIGURE 18.12 *Add the sequence of underwater images as the first event in the Video Post queue.*

3. In the Image File List Control dialog that appears, click OK (**Figure 18.13**) to accept all 51 frames in the sequence. Click OK in the Add Image Input Event dialog to enter the sequence in the queue in the form of an IFL (image file list) file type in the Video Post dialog (see **Figure 18.14** on the next page).

The file entered in the queue is an ASCII file containing a list of all the image names for Video Post to process.

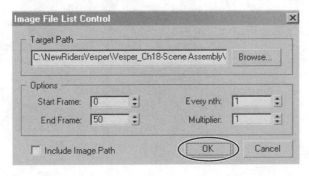

FIGURE 18.13 *Click OK to designate all 51 frames in the sequence as the background.*

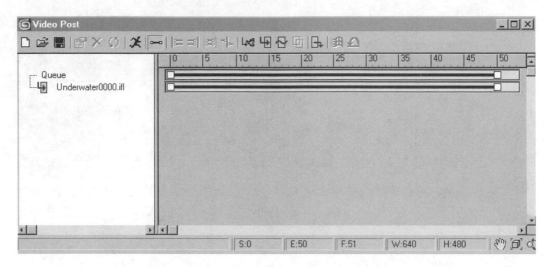

FIGURE 18.14 *The entry in the Video Post queue is an IFL file listing the sequence of underwater images.*

4. Make sure that no entries are highlighted in the Video Post queue, and repeat Steps 2 and 3 to create an IFL file containing the names of all the Lobster images, which consist of an animated lobster against a black background (**Figure 18.15**). The black background will become the alpha channel transparency.

    The queue will be evaluated from top to bottom, and the alpha channel will allow the background to show through. But first you have to queue up an output image to save the composite.

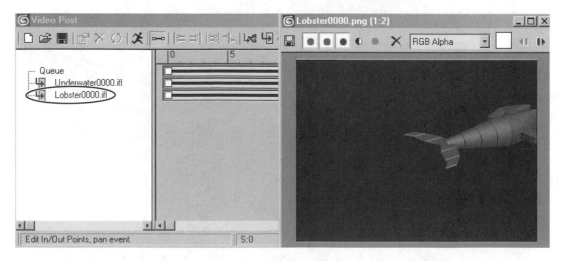

FIGURE 18.15 *Add a second Image Input Event with images of an animated lobster.*

5. In the Video Post dialog, click the Add Image Output Event button. In the Add Image Output Event dialog, click the Files button, and in the Select Image File for Video Post Output dialog, enter Composite.png in the File Name field. Click Save, and click OK in the PNG Configuration dialog that opens. Click OK in the Add Image Output Event dialog (**Figure 18.16**).

These actions will create a new entry in the queue that will save the composited images into a new file sequence. You now have to tell the two input events to be composited using the alpha channel.

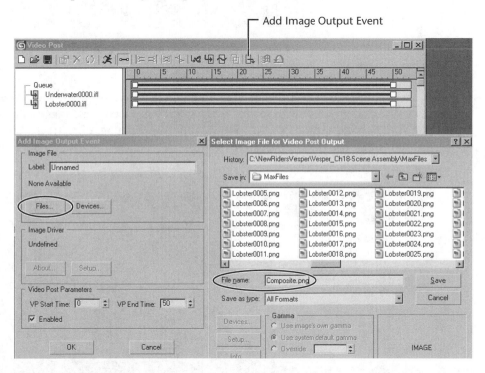

FIGURE 18.16 *Add an Image Output Event to the end of the queue that will save the images to a new file sequence.*

6. In the Video Post dialog, highlight the two .ifl file events in the queue using Ctrl + click, and then click the Add Image Layer Event button. In the Add Image Layer Event dialog, choose Alpha Compositor from the drop-down list (see **Figure 18.17** on the next page). Click OK. The two input events become indented under the Alpha Compositor event in the queue. You'll now execute the queue sequence.

The queue input entries must be indented at the same level beneath the Alpha Compositor for the events to be properly calculated.

Add Image Layer Event

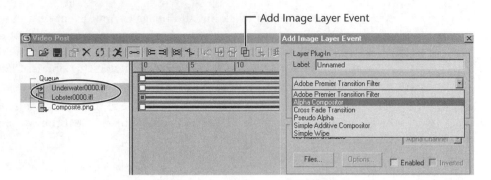

FIGURE 18.17 *Highlight the input events in the queue, and add a Alpha Compositor layer event.*

7. In the Video Post dialog, click in an empty space in the queue pane to un-highlight all entries so that everything will be evaluated, and click the Execute Sequence button. In the Execute Video Post dialog, click the Render button to accept the defaults (**Figure 18.18**).

Execute Sequence

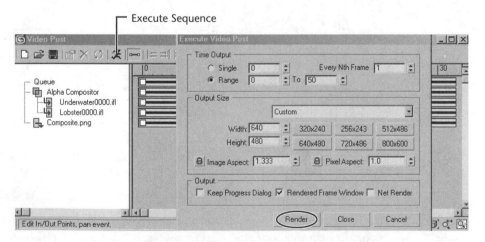

FIGURE 18.18 *Click the Execute Sequence button in the Video Post dialog to evaluate the queue and save the new animated sequence.*

The sequence is executed, and you can see the progress in the Video Post Queue window: the animated lobster in the foreground is composited over the animated background scene, and the files are saved to your hard drive (**Figure 18.19**). You can use RAM Player from the Rendering pull-down menu to view the new animated sequence, starting with Composite0000.png.

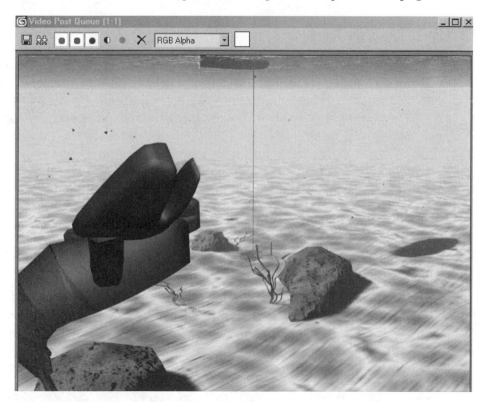

FIGURE 18.19 *As the Video Post queue is executed you'll see the lobster being composited over the underwater scene, one frame at a time.*

8. In the Video Post dialog, click the Save Sequence button, which looks like a diskette (at the upper left of Figure 18.19); in the Save Sequence dialog, enter Lobster in the File Name field and click Save.

    This saves the Video Post queue in case you need to open it and edit it later.

9. Close all windows and dialogs. You don't need to save this file, as there's nothing in the scene.

The Video Post module is useful for performing simple compositing operations, and it also can be used to stitch a series of the rendered images end to end, for example. The point is, two teams can create renderings that can then be combined into the final rendered scene, saving time on a project overall.

Summary

You've learned a few examples of scene-assembly techniques that can help speed production by allowing different teams to perform different operations simultaneously and then a technical director can assemble the into a comprehensive project. You can merge whole scenes or just selected objects from scenes, and you can replace like-named objects to allow the use of simple stand-in geometry for efficiency.

Index

S